DATE		
	~~REFERENCE~~	

LANDSCAPE IN THE WORKS
OF MARCEL PROUST

AMS PRESS
NEW YORK

THE CATHOLIC UNIVERSITY OF AMERICA
STUDIES IN ROMANCE LANGUAGES AND LITERATURES
VOL. XXXV

LANDSCAPE IN THE WORKS OF MARCEL PROUST

BY

FRANCES VIRGINIA FARDWELL, A. B., M. A.

A Dissertation

SUBMITTED TO THE FACULTY OF THE GRADUATE SCHOOL OF ARTS AND
SCIENCES OF THE CATHOLIC UNIVERSITY OF AMERICA IN PARTIAL
FULFILLMENT OF THE REQUIREMENTS FOR THE DEGREE OF
DOCTOR OF PHILOSOPHY

THE CATHOLIC UNIVERSITY OF AMERICA PRESS
WASHINGTON, D. C.

1948

Library of Congress Cataloging in Publication Data

Fardwell, Frances Virginia, 1917–
    Landscape in the works of Marcel Proust.

    Reprint of the 1948 ed., which was issued as v. 35 of
Studies in Romance languages and literatures of the
Catholic University of America.
    Thesis—Catholic University, 1948.
    Bibliography: p.
    1. Proust, Marcel, 1871-1922. 2. Nature in
literature. I. Title. II. Series: Catholic Univer-
sity of America. Studies in Romance languages and
literature, v. 35.
PQ2631.R63Z585 1972   843'.9'12   76-168004
ISBN 0-404-50335-7

From the edition of 1948, Washington
First AMS edition published in 1972
Manufactured in the United States of America

AMS PRESS INC.
NEW YORK, N. Y.   10003

To

MY MOTHER AND FATHER

TABLE OF CONTENTS

PREFACE

The main object of this study is to give an understanding and appreciation of landscape and its role in the works of Marcel Proust. We have chosen to study Proust's landscape as it is one aspect of his tremendous novel which he himself considered of primary importance and which has not yet been satisfactorily treated. This writer's investigation was prompted, among other considerations, by a letter which Proust wrote to Robert Flers in 1913 asking him to announce the immediate publication of the first volume of his novel which he estimated to be " un roman à la fois plein de passion et de méditations et de paysages." [1]

In addition to an analysis of the vital function of landscape in Proust's work as a whole, we will attempt to bring out the originality of his literary method of presenting individual impressions of natural scenery. By traversing the Proustian universe through his landscapes we will try to point out how he has drawn the wealth of his entire novel from the soil, people, and language of France which he considered biological elements of the French landscape. We will try further to determine why and how certain landscapes provided him simply with the inspiration to write while others served as a medium for the exhibition of his literary methods. Then we will endeavor to penetrate the essence of his purely " ideological " scenes and the connection of such " dream " landscapes with his love, travel and general culture interests.

A full analysis of Proust's art lavished on these scenes, if successful, would be tantamount to explaining his literary achievements and personality from a particularly fertile angle. At the same time it would reveal how Proust, in a typically French manner, carries forth the ancient idea of a humanistic civilization into the modern world by means of painting " landscape " through the medium of tradition and cultural elements.

Proust's work has in recent years engaged the thought of many

---

[1] *CG. IV.*, p. 99, also quoted by André Ferré in his *Géographie de Marcel Proust* (Paris: Editions du Sagittaire, 1939), p. 50.

distinguished scholars. Much has been written about the psychology, aesthetics, social preoccupations, medical and physiological aspects, music, and painting of his novel, and although many have referred to his landscape in connection with these various aspects of his art it is surprising that none have attempted a decisive study of it as a salient feature in the works of a man whose entire life was a series of enchanted " souvenirs " of country lanes, cathedral towns and seaside resorts. Several studies which have devoted considerable space to the geographic and aesthetic aspect of his landscape in general have been of value in furnishing ideas which led to the inception of this investigation.[2] These works will be discussed at length in the introduction.

It is the hope of this writer that his additional findings may (1) clarify the still wavering picture of Proust as gained hitherto from other aspects of his literature and life, (2) make more visible the landscapes studied for their own sake as artistic entities, and (3) illustrate the various aspects of Proust's psychology of nature and art.

I wish to express my appreciation to Dr. Helmut Hatzfeld for suggesting and guiding this dissertation and to Reverend Dr. David Rubio, O. S. A., and Dr. Alessandro S. Crisafulli for their careful reading and valuable criticism of the manuscript. I am particularly indebted to my mother and father for making this study possible.

[2] Ferré, *op. cit.*, and M. Chernowitz, *Proust and Painting* (New York: International University Press, 1945).

ABBREVIATIONS

S. I.	Du Côté de chez Swann, 1er volume.
S. II.	Du Côté de chez Swann, 2e volume.
JF. I.	A l'Ombre des jeunes filles en fleurs, 1er volume.
JF. II.	A l'Ombre des jeunes filles en fleurs, 2e volume.
JF. III.	A l'Ombre des jeunes filles en fleurs, 3e volume.
G. I.	Le Côté de Guermantes, I.
G. II.	Le Côté de Guermantes, II.
SG. I.	Sodome et Gomorrhe, I.
SG. II.(1).	Sodome et Gomorrhe, II, 1er volume.
SG. II.(2).	Sodome et Gomorrhe, II, 2e volume.
SG. II.(3).	Sodome et Gomorrhe, II, 3e volume.
P. I.	La Prisonnière, 1er volume.
P. II.	La Prisonnière, 2e volume.
AD. I.	Albertine disparue, 1er volume.
AD. II.	Albertine disparue, 2e volume.
TR. I.	Le Temps retrouvé, 1er volume.
TR. II.	Le Temps retrouvé, 2e volume.
PM.	Pastiches et mélanges.
CG.	Correspondance générale de Marcel Proust, 6 volumes.

CHAPTER I

INTRODUCTION

The artist's view of nature is not entirely spontaneous or independent. It is primarily influenced by the cultural heritage of his nation. For this reason an investigation of the treatment of landscape by any French author must consider that author's approach as the final link of a whole chain of attempts at landscape representation in French literature. Though Marcel Proust is so unique in this line that he would not need an explanation based on the historical evolution of landscape patterns, a rigorous historical method advises the usual procedure anyway.

Representation of landscape in literature as well as painting, throughout civilization, has been man's method of expressing the relation of the human spirit and psyche to nature and the exterior world. Just because such a representation must be preceded by a spiritual or intellectual experience, it has been something more than a mere medium for the exhibition of man's ability in artistic creation and composition. The French concept of civilization is closely connected wth the relation of the French people to the soil of France. The feeling of the Frenchman for his land is rooted in the cultivation of the soil and the humanizing of nature; consequently, in France the relations between man and the earth are more archaic and more lasting than in other Western European countries. A popular mysticism of the soil of France actually exists.[1] One has only to think of Maurice Barrès or Charles Péguy in recent days. Such personalism of the national and cultural consciousness of the French people as it has been nourished through the ages by French soil exhibits itself most clearly through the medium of the literary landscape.[2]

An outline of landscape representation in French literature was

---

[1] R. E. Curtius, *The Civilization of France* (London: Allen, 1932), pp. 43-48.
[2] *Ibid.*, p. 69.

1

presented for the first time in 1935 by Eduard von Jan in his book *Die Landschaft des französischen Menschen.*[3] Unfortunately, his study does not include the nineteenth and twentieth centuries, a period in which great writers from Chateaubriand to Proust made of literary landscaping a most interesting and unique art.

At the beginning of the twentieth century when European civilization seemed at its peak the literary landscape reached its apotheosis in Marcel Proust's impressive novel *A la recherche du temps perdu.*[4] In this gigantic work which not only reflects the life of Proust but that of his entire time, his landscape pictures include also, by way of retrospection, all the culture of distant epochs.

A glimpse into the history of literary landscape painting in France will reveal interesting stepping stones which in their genuine form throughout earlier centuries seem responsible for Proust's intellectual and spiritualized representations. The salient characteristic of each literary epoch as far back as the Middle Ages is echoed in some aspect of his landscape art.

There is very little to be said of landscape painting during the Middle Ages. Nature descriptions were usually of a symbolic character. Landscapes in the court poetry of the age were pictures of cultivated gardens which were represented as places of edification. In medieval literature when representation of the actual was avoided, details of nature were brought out only to offer an opportunity for pious contemplation.[5] In *Du Côté de chez Swann* we will find the cultivated park at Tansonville a place of intellectual inspiration and discovery, and we will often note the narrator deeply contemplating the details of nature, though the mental attitude is intellectual rather than pious—the secularized " contemplation " well known since Petrarch.

Landscape pictures of the Renaissance are given by von Jan the expression " Kulturlandschaften " because the falsification of nature by civilization was the aesthetic standard of the time. Both poetry and painting of the period show a return to the " architektonisch

---

[3] Eduard von Jan, *Die Landschaft des französischen Menschen* (Weimar: H. Böhlau, 1935), p. 3.

[4] Marcel Proust, *A la recherche du temps perdu* en 16 volumes (Paris: Gallimard, 1919-1927).

[5] von Jan, *op. cit.*, pp. 4-8.

Monumentalen," i. e. a grandiose reconstructed pseudo-realistic
nature. Neither Rabelais nor Montaigne had any interest in landscape as a unity in itself, i. e. without people. They always looked
for some indication of humanity or cultivation of the land. In
Montaigne's diary it is the people who give charm to his glowing
description of an Alpine landscape.[6] The same is true of many of
Proust's landscape pictures.

The lyrics of Ronsard indicate an advance in landscape description in that they parallel the amorous sentiments of the poet with
the nature around him. For instance, note the following lines:

> Le plus touffu d'un solitaire bois,
> Le plus aigu d'une roche sauvage,
> Le plus desert d'un separé rivage,
> Et la frayeur des autres les plus cois,
> Soulagent tant les souspirs et ma vois,
> Qu'au seul escart d'un plus secret ombrage,
> Je sens guarir ceste amoureuse rage,
> Qui me r'afole ou plus verd de mes mois.[7]

The experience of Marcel Proust with Mme de Stermaria in the
Bois de Boulogne will not be different in kind. Preference for the
anti-realistic landscape appears in single features of the poetry of
the Pléiade. Du Bellay in his *Antiquitez de Rome* was the first
Frenchman to view the ruins of Rome with the poet's eye, but he
isolated them as though they were in a museum and not a part of
the landscape. On the other hand he saw in them not their present
form but the spirit which long ago caused the monuments to rise.[8]
This is precisely one of Proust's twentieth century methods of seeing
all the history and life of another age in Gothic churches, feudal
chateaux and the remains of medieval towns. In the sixteenth century there was still no possibility of an attempt to combine in one
picture the many isolated features. The landscape *as a whole* never
evoked in the poet a sense of relation between the scene and his
own emotional experience.[9]

Travel descriptions of the seventeenth century expressed themselves fully on architectural and cultural documents whereas actual

[6] *Ibid.*, pp. 17-18. [8] *Ibid.*, pp. 23-24.
[7] *Ibid.*, p. 22. [9] *Ibid.*, p. 26.

landscape elements were only superficially mentioned. Similar arbitrary juxtaposition of impressions according to the author's taste one may observe highly developed in Proust's ideological pictures of "Balbec" and Venice. During this same period there existed a preference for river scenery. There is, for instance, the Lignon landscape of *Astrée* and Mlle de Scudéry's *Carte de Tendre* with its *Inclination Fleuve*. As early as D'Urfé and Racan river scenery was looked at with imagination.[10]

But in the seventeenth century there was still an almost exclusive dependence of landscape on the civilization of man. Malherbe and Boileau give pictures of landscape adorned with architectonic elements and the baroque poet Saint-Amant discovers a new sensation in the enchantment of ruins. Since Saint-Amant's *Solitude* and La Fontaine's *Adonis*, solitude in connection with landscape seems to have been a favorite theme, preparing the way for romanticism.[11]

Finally in the seventeenth century Nicholas Poussin and Claude Lorrain, inspired by the Italian poets, introduced real landscape painting into French culture,[12] and an occasional remark by Madame de Sévigné revealed a new sensibility of landscape in literature. Then the literary influence of James Thomson was strongly felt in Eighteenth-Century France. In 1730 with his *Seasons* he made the landscape picture characterized by the changes of nature during the year [13]—a device which the Frères de Limbourg had already discovered at the end of the Middle Ages. We will find that nearly all of Proust's landscapes are characterized by season. For instance, he pictures Combray in the spring, summer at Balbec, the Bois de Boulogne in the autumn, and the military town Doncières in the winter.

There was in France during the eighteenth century a mighty revolution in the relation of man to nature. The individual no longer sought in nature the traces of human activity but something completely free from reason and experience, something new which he could not as yet determine but which appeared to him as something unheard of, far surpassing the treasures of wisdom. Rousseau was the man who first approached nature with this kind of spiritual

[10] *Ibid.*, p. 31.
[11] *Ibid.*, pp. 36-39.
[12] *Ibid.*, p. 46.
[13] *Ibid.*, p. 53.

attitude. He came to recognize the beauty in the harmony of the separate nature elements. This was the true literary discovery of landscape. As a youth he experienced nature as something dreamily voluptuous and later as something which gradually arranged itself, assumed form and could become visible. In the *Nouvelle Héloïse* are found what one can for the first time refer to as landscape representations, i. e. representation of a locality known to the author personally and associated with him.[14] This was the pattern for the Romantic landscape known to everyone from Lamartine's *Le Lac* or Victor Hugo's *Tristesse d'Olympio*. Stylistically Rousseau's landscapes offer as novel, innumerable variations of epithets and metaphors grasping the ephemerality of nature impressions. His decisive service lies nevertheless in the fact that it was he who first recognized the deepest and most direct relation between man and landscape and made it a primary subject of artistic expression.[15] The " Promeneur solitaire " is the Columbus of the literary landscape. In principle, Proust's spiritual attitude toward nature stems from Rousseau who unlocked to European literary art a new trend. This in the future ruled over literature in a quite pronounced degree and included very definitely the literary landscape as an outcut of nature.

From Rousseau there emerge two lines of development; one leads through Bernardin de Saint-Pierre into the exotic landscape, the other through Chateaubriand into the romantic which has first an exotic, then a historic and finally a contemporary atmosphere. The significant advance of landscape description in Bernardin de Saint-Pierre is its turn in a strongly marked degree to the senses. Rousseau's impressions are almost exclusively optical, whereas, with Bernardin de Saint-Pierre, it is all the senses which react to an impression. Sensitivity to color and odor determines the individuality of landscape representation in the *Etudes* and *Harmonies* as well as in *Paul et Virginie*. In the presentation of definite sense impressions Bernardin shows himself master. Through careful observation of the effects of light he was the first in French litera-

[14] *Ibid.*, pp. 54-55.
[15] *Ibid.*, p. 62. Cf. also Eva Maria Neumeyer, " The Landscape Garden as a Symbol in Rousseau, Goethe and Flaubert " *Journal of the History of Ideas*, VIII (1942), pp. 187-217.

ture to paint the nuance of exact color which gave to his landscape description its distinctive quality and value, a technique which in Proust's landscapes becomes a highly refined art surpassing both Bernardin de Saint-Pierre and Chateaubriand due to the fact that it has been schooled also in the discoveries of the much later impressionist painters. Bernardin, however, was especially interested in the color of the sky and as a painter of cloud formations he foreshadowed the very literary impressionism of the nineteenth century.[16]

Until the appearance of Rousseau, landscape representation in French literature can hardly be assigned any intrinsic value. Even in Rousseau the scenery is more strongly limited by civilization elements than it may appear at first glance. But his disciple Bernardin de Saint-Pierre has definitely created landscape representation directly related to nature and the universe. It must be repeated that the first " integral " landscape representations in French literature have an exotic land for their subject. For hundreds of years the individual in France had seen landscape only through his own work of cultivation without noticing its intrinsic beauties, the way even today most peasants still regard nature. When this medium was banned and landscape was shown him free of all the embellishments of man, then it was a tropical island. Thus it came about that landscape description in the eigtheenth century first remained bound to the exotic world. Chateaubriand's *Atala* had a success similar to Bernardin de Saint-Pierre's *Paul et Virginie*. It will be shown that, unlike Bernardin de Saint-Pierre and Chateaubriand, Proust did not need impressions coming from a foreign land to set free the powers of his soul. The exotic vogue endured only until the Frenchman found the way to the landscape of his immediate surrounding world through analogy and the expansion of his mental attitudes. When this occurred, the landscape poetry of France was immediately led to a climax through Lamartine, Victor Hugo, de Musset and Michelet.[17]

But the literary landscape reaches an even higher peak during the late nineteenth and twentieth centuries. Through Gautier's " transposition d'art," the Goncourts' impressionism, Flaubert's

---

[16] von Jan, *op. cit.*, pp. 72-75.   [17] *Ibid.*, pp. 81-82.

nature-realism, Verlaine's "Indécis," Loti's sensuous seascapes, Baudelaire's correspondence of the senses in close contact with the painter's approach to nature, even Zola's naturalism and Verhaeren's "naturism" we are led to Proust's conception of landscape which culminates this rich literary heritage in the light of modern trends. Like the Goncourts he constantly checked his landscapes with those of the painters and he is unthinkable as a mere continuation of this line of literary figures without an analogy to Monet, Manet, Renoir, Degas, Seurat, Gauguin, Turner and others.

Furthermore, one must consider a few details of the life of Marcel Proust (1871-1922) to determine the source of his interest in the beauties of natural scenery. As a mere boy, asthmatic since the age of nine, he felt the enchantments of nature and it was the double tragedy of his life that the open country air, the aroma of trees and the perfume of flowers which he adored nearly suffocated him. He was forced to enjoy nature only from a distance.[18] Every year he spent the summer months with his parents at an uncle's estate in Illiers, a village between Nogent-le-Rotrou and Chartres, and it was during that time that the young Proust discovered the flowers that he loved so much during the rest of his life. Later, when his health no longer permitted him to go to the country he spent his summers at Cabourg, or Trouville where he sought the more invigorating air of the seaside.[19] In this connection Robert Dreyfus in his *Souvenirs sur Marcel Proust* writes:

Marcel Proust adorait la campagne, la mer, et il ne pouvait subir les émanations de la nature ni ses forces violentes. Elles lui faisaient mal. Au point qu'un jour (bien plus tard) il dut se décider à quitter Paris en voiture fermée pour aller se promener en Normandie, parce qu'il ne pouvait plus se passer de voir les pommiers en fleurs et se résignait à ne les voir qu'à travers les vitres.[20]

In spite of his delicate health Proust attended the Lycée Condorcet and it is significant that during his school days there he excelled in natural history which left a lasting impression upon

[18] Léon Pierre-Quint, *Marcel Proust, sa vie, son oeuvre* (Paris: Simon Kra, 1925), p. 23.

[19] *Ibid.*, pp. 25-26.

[20] Robert Dreyfus, *Souvenirs sur Marcel Proust* (Paris: Grasset, 1926), p. 15.

him. His landscapes contain numerous parallels between man and rare species of plants and thus displayed his taste for botanical things.[21]

Proust longed to travel but again because of his health he had to give up all hope of it. His only journey abroad was a short visit to Venice with his mother and Reynaldo Hahn. We shall examine the dreams inspired in him by this city where so many writers have loved and suffered. After 1900 except for the summers spent at seaside resorts he no longer left Paris. For a few years he was able to visit the cathedrals and historic places which interested him so much and he got as far as Senlis and Amiens but his biographers tell us that these were very difficult changes of scene. When he was afraid of being too late in the morning to witness certain aspects of a landscape, he stayed up all the night before. These last journeys were undertaken for study rather than pleasure. The suffering which they inevitably caused him he imposed upon himself for the sake of knowing better the churches and scenes he wished to describe.[22]

There is abundant evidence in everything that Proust wrote of an unusual sensitiveness to landscape phenomena. By means of his earlier and less significant works we can follow his interest through his adolescent years and contemplate the blossoms which we will later find in full bloom. At the age of fifteen he had written of the powerful impression left upon him by the sight of the three steeples of Caen which was so characteristic of his future style and which was reproduced without any touching up in *Pastiches et mélanges*[23] and as " les clochers de Martinville " in *Du Côté de chez Swann*.[24]

Robert Dreyfus, a schoolmate of Proust's, has happily preserved for us sketches which Proust composed in 1888 for the small literary review, *Revue de Lilas*, drawn up at the Lycée. These fragments are an interesting contribution to the landscape problem for the surprising parallels that they reveal to his landscape descriptions in the first fifty pages of *Du Côté de chez Swann*.[25] For instance, Proust wrote at the age of seventeen the following passage :

[21] Pierre-Quint, *op. cit.*, pp. 27-28.   [22] *Ibid.*, pp. 42-43.   [23] *PM.*, pp. 92-94.
[24] *S. I.*, pp. 258-261, noted by Pierre-Quint *op. cit.*, p. 30.
[25] Dreyfus, *op. cit.*, p. 57.

Tout le monde est couché dans le grand appartement silencieux. J'entr'ouvre
la fenêtre pour revoir une dernière fois la douce face fauve bien ronde, de
la lune amie. J'entends comme l'haleine très fraîche, froide, de toutes les
choses qui dorment,—l'arbre d'où suinte de la lumière bleue—de la belle
lumière bleue transfigurant au loin par une échappée de rues, comme un
paysage polaire électriquement illuminé, les pavés bleus et pâles. Par-dessus
s'étendent les infinis champs bleus où fleurissent de frêles étoiles . . .[26]

Here is the supersensitive Proust in front of all the possible charms
of a landscape dipped in moonlight. Again in the beginning of *Du
Côté de chez Swann* he writes:

J'ouvris la fenêtre sans bruit et m'assis au pied de mon lit; je ne faisais
presque aucun mouvement afin qu'on ne m'entendît pas d'en bas. Dehors, les
choses semblaient, elles aussi, figées en une muette attention à ne pas
troubler le clair de lune, qui doublant et reculant chaque chose par l'ex-
tension devant elle de son reflet, plus dense et concret qu'elle-même, avait à
la fois aminci et agrandi le paysage comme un plan replié jusque-là, qu'on
développe. Ce qui avait besoin de bouger, quelque feuillage de marronnier,
bougeait. Mais son frissonnement minutieux, total, exécuté jusque dans
ses moindres nuances et ses dernières délicatesses, ne bavait pas sur le
reste, ne se fondait pas avec lui, restait circonscrit. Exposés sur ce silence
qui n'en absorbait rien, les bruits les plus éloignés, ceux qui devaient venir
de jardins situés à l'autre bout de la ville, se percevaient détaillés avec un
tel " fini " qu'ils semblaient ne devoir cet effet de lointain qu'à leur pianissimo, comme ces motifs en sourdine si bien exécutés par l'orchestre du
Conservatoire que, quoiqu'on n'en perde pas une note, on croit les entendre
cependant loin de la salle du concert et que tous les vieux abonnés,—les
soeurs de ma grand'mère aussi quand Swann leur avait donné ses places,—
tendaient l'oreille comme s'ils avaient écouté les progrès lointains d'une
armée en marche qui n'aurait pas encore tourné la rue de Trévis.[27]

We see here the later Proust of digressions and metaphorical grasping of landscape. The fact that all of these images drawn by Proust
at the age of seventeen—the silence of nocturnal solitude, open
window, moonlight, sleeping things, glittering trees—came to life
again in him, similar and in the same order of succession, after a
quarter of a century when he dreams of his childhood, is evidence of
the permanence of his nature impressions. Proust did not work
from these old notes as Dreyfus assures us that they had always
remained in his possession.[82] These and other sketches published by

[26] *Ibid.*, p. 58.   [27] *S. I.*, p. 53.   [28] Dreyfus, *op. cit.*, p. 64.

Dreyfus reveal Proust's early adolescent sensitivity to the elements of landscape prior to his readings and his art studies.

An interest in natural scenery is foreshadowed in Proust's early publication of *Les Plaisirs et les jours* [29] which contains much nature description. In the chapter which he calls "Les Regrets, Rêveries Couleur du Temps" there are, for instance, sketches of the Tuileries, Versailles, the Bois, the shores of the lake, moonlit scenes, and other landscape pictures.[30]

In *Pastiches et mélanges* published the same year as *Du Côté de chez Swann* there are interesting descriptions of Proust's journeys through Normandy and accounts of his expeditions to the Gothic cathedrals that he loved so much.[31] Especially interesting is his description of the cathedral of Lisieux illuminated by the lights of his car.[32] Also there is an elaborate description of river scenery and its surrounding fields which has been reproduced with a few alterations in the first volume of *Du Côté de chez Swann*.[33]

Robert Proust and Gallimard in 1927 published a volume under the title *Chroniques*,[34] a collection of articles by Proust, written between 1892 and 1924, most of which had been published in *Le Figaro*. In one group of these articles which is classified as "Paysages et Réflexions" we find the original sketch of three striking landscape descriptions—"Epines blanches, Epines roses," "L'église de Village," and "Vacances de Pâques"—as they were written for *Le Figaro* in 1912 and 1913 and which he later reproduced in *Du Côté de chez Swann* in their entirety.

In view of this wealth of evidence of Proust's attention to landscape it is surprising—as mentioned in the preface—that scholars have not yet made a complete study of it as an outstanding feature of his novel. André Ferré in *Géographie de Marcel Proust* has it is true devoted a few pages to the study of "les paysages proustiens." [35] He has made general remarks on the place they occupy

[29] Marcel Proust, *Les Plaisirs et les jours* (Paris: Calmann-Lévy, 1896, new edition, Gallimard, 1924).
[30] *Ibid.*, new edition, pp. 173-239.
[31] *PM.*, pp. 92-96 and 101-170.
[32] *Ibid.*, pp. 94-96.
[33] *Ibid.*, pp. 236-237.
[34] Robert Proust, *Chroniques* (Paris: Gallimard, 1927).
[35] André Ferré, *op. cit.*, pp. 50-68.

in the novel, the role they play, the action they frame, and the inspiration they excite, but his comments though usually sound are abstract and he makes no attempt at an extensive or profound study of individual landscape representation. He is not concerned with the artistic unity of landscape as subject of an " interprétation de texte."

In his recent publication *Proust and Painting* [36] Maurice Chernowitz has presented an excellent treatment of the art of painting in the work of Proust. With unusual sensitivity and an extensive knowledge of painting Chernowitz has analyzed some of Proust's most striking landscape pictures—especially his seascapes—from an artistic point of view and only in connection with their relation to painting. This writer is indebted to Mr. Chernowitz for his " clear and clever " presentation of Proust's aesthetics and pictorial technique, and his deep remarks on elements of Proustian style as far as certain landscapes are concerned.

Anton Polanscak in *La Peinture du décor et de la nature chez Proust* [37] has given an interpretation of Proust as a painter from an angle which differs from Chernowitz's point of view. He presents a study of the " image " as Proust's principal literary means of attaining perfection in the recreation of the exterior world. He investigates the organic liaison between Proust and his nature impressions. His study stresses the importance of sensation in Proust's pictorial art. This rather superficial dissertation is not comparable to Chernowitz's scholarly interpretation of Proust's art.

P. L. Larcher has published a charming pamphlet of Proustiana which he calls *Le Parfum de Combray*.[38] It is a sort of guide book to the early Proustian landscape, the Eure-et-Loire Department, where his country relatives lived in the village of Illiers (later called Combray) and where he placed *Du Côté de chez Swann*. Larcher makes a Proustian pilgrimage to Illiers and identifies what he finds there with the landscapes described in *Du Côté de chez Swann*.

This writer believes that an understanding and an analytically

---

[36] Chernowitz, *op. cit.*

[37] A. Polanscak, *La Peinture du décor et de la nature chez Proust* (Paris: Etudes et Editions, 1941).

[38] P. L. Larcher, *Le Parfum de Combray* (Paris: Mercure de France, 1945).

buttressed appreciation of Proust's organic "landscape"—not merely his geographic or nature "images"—will bring one closer to the heart of his impressions of the exterior world than other attempts made previous to this study. Enjoying nature from a distance, in closed carriages, behind glass windows, in remembrance, Proust has given representations of strange landscapes, seascapes, skyscapes and townscapes, which will only reveal their secret to the anatomist who cuts out their elements without destroying their most delicate organism.

CHAPTER II

THE PSYCHOLOGICAL LANDSCAPE

There are certain landscapes in *A la recherche du temps perdu* which play a part so profoundly significant that they are decisive in the very genesis of the book.[1] The thoroughly psychological function of these landscapes demands their distinction from others in which are manifested interesting psychological nuances only. As previously mentioned many have referred to these scenes and have even attempted analyses in interpreting other elements of Proust's art, but it appears that the depth of his impressions has not been thoroughly penetrated. As far as can be determined by this writer the organization of landscape in the mind and work of Proust from psychological experiences has not yet been considered. In order to understand these landscapes, it is necessary to review as we proceed the profound experience which accompanies their revelation. Much has already been said about the psychology of Proust and those who know him may find all the following remarks a superfluous repetition of things already known; those, however, who do not know him, could not understand the makeup of his landscape pictures without them.

Under the influence of visual, olfactory, gustative, and auditory sensations a series of delightful landscapes are recalled by Proust like the dreams of an opium smoker. These landscapes are intimately related to the cycle of his inspiration and thus form the background upon which his story unfolds. The revelation of Combray from the taste of a madeleine dipped in tea is that which first reveals the mysterious force of his poetic soul while other landscapes recalled from the past in a similar fashion (such as Venice and Balbec) disclose the exalted moments which animate his entire work. It is significant that in addition to these inspirited recollections of past scenes all other gusts of exaltation are experienced by Proust at the sight of certain landscapes which inspire the literary expression of their objects and thus become the source

---

[1] Ferré, *op. cit.*, p. 57.

and subject of his great book.[2] The mechanism of these evocations
supposing a material base—tea, tree, flower, odor, sound, etc.—
indicates the interpenetration of " cozy " elements.[3]

Subjective Recollections

" Combray "

The first example of this type of landscape comes from the taste
of " une petite madeleine " dipped in tea—a landscape from which
is revealed to Marcel all the details of his life at Combray. It is
in a state of " découragement," weary and cold after a dull wintry
day, and with the prospect of a depressing morrow, that he sips the
tea in which he had soaked a piece of cake. The taste of this
concoction causes " un plaisir délicieux " to invade his senses. This
emotional state becomes a sort of natural " extase " in which the
narrator becomes indifferent to the vicissitudes of life and ceases to
feel mortal.[4] At first he cannot seize or define this fleeting sensation but his mind follows and tries to recapture it. So that nothing
may interrupt it, he obliterates from his thoughts every extraneous
idea and during a moment of repose, when he makes no effort to
think, i. e. to establish relation between sensation and memory,
" revelation " produces itself. He realizes that that which is palpi-
tating in the depths of his being is a visual memory linked to the
taste of the madeleine and it is only after further intellectual effort
that this memory finally reaches a clear surface of his consciousness.[5] This communication with the past reviewed, Dandieu says,
has a special emotional " état " which the mystics experience also.[6]

It is after this rigorous process of analyzing the ephemeral
nature of his emotion that suddenly the memory returns and he
finds that the sensation recalls the taste of the little madeleine which
on Sunday mornings his aunt Léonie used to give him, after dipping
it in her own cup of lime flower tea. The sight of the madeleine had
recalled nothing to his mind before he tasted it perhaps because in
the interval he had so often seen such things without tasting them.

---

[2] *Ibid.*, pp. 57-60.

[3] Arnaud Dandieu, *Marcel Proust; sa révélation psychologique* (Paris:
Firmin-Didot, 1930), p. 141.

[4] *S. I.*, p. 70.   [5] *Ibid.*, pp. 71-72.   [6] Dandieu, *op. cit.*, p. 65.

But he tells us that when from a long distant past nothing subsists, the odor and taste of things remain poised a long time, like souls, and bear unfaltering, in the tiny and almost impalpable drop of their essence the vast structure of recollection: [7]

Et dès que j'eus reconnu le goût du morceau de madeleine trempé dans le tilleul que me donnait ma tante (quoique je ne susse pas encore et dusse remettre à bien plus tard de découvrir pourquoi ce souvenir me rendait si heureux), aussitôt la vieille maison grise sur la rue, où était sa chambre, vint comme un décor de théâtre s'appliquer au petit pavillon, donnant sur le jardin, qu'on avait construit pour mes parents sur ses derrières (ce pan tronqué que seul j'avais revu jusque-là) ; et avec la maison, la ville, la Place où on m'envoyait avant déjeuner, les rues où j'allais faire des courses depuis le matin jusqu'au soir et par tous les temps, les chemins qu'on prenait si le temps était beau. Et comme dans ce jeu où les Japonais s'amusent à tremper dans un bol de porcelaine rempli d'eau, de petits morceaux de papier jusque-là indistincts qui, à peine y sont-ils plongés s'étirent, se contournent, se colorent, se différencient, deviennent des fleurs, des maisons, des personnages consistants et reconnaissables, de même maintenant toutes les fleurs de notre jardin et celles du parc de M. Swann, et les nymphéas de la Vivonne, et les bonnes gens du village et leurs petits logis et l'église et tout Combray et ses environs, tout cela qui prend forme et solidité, est sorti, ville et jardins, de ma tasse de thé.[8]

It is interesting to note that as soon as the " rapport affectif " is identified between the present sensation and the visual memory the landscape of Combray comes to life in all its glory.

Proust stresses that it is only through comparison that reality is expressed [9] and so to illuminate this past evoking reverie, i. e. to give further verbal expression to a sense impression, he compares, in a unique simile, the emotional experience to a game in which the Japanese amuse themselves by soaking in a bowl of water small pieces of paper which take on color and shape, the moment they become wet, and become permanent and recognizable flowers, houses, or people.[10] In like manner the moment he recognizes the taste of the madeleine soaked in lime he sees the past complete in its detailed reality. The sensation creates an emotion

[7] *S. I.*, p. 72. This Proustian revelation comes through the unconscious mind and is imposed from without unforewarned, although apparently subjective and born of memories. Cf. Dandieu, *op. cit.*, p. 139.
[8] *S. I.*, p. 73.   [9] *TR. II*, p. 40.   [10] *S. I.*, p. 72.

from which the whole of Combray takes shape and springs into being, houses, town and gardens alike, from his cup of tea.[11]   In addition to its value in content this comparison reveals the picturesque unusualness of Proust's style and the interfusion of artistic culture in his work.

Such total revelation of a past scene produces itself for Proust only when, as in this event, the mind discovers an identity between the past and the present.[12]   Now the faculty of the mind which links the past and the present is the memory.   Furthermore, it is the involuntary memory (souvenir) which withdraws a scene from the past and the voluntary memory (mémoire) which transmits it to us by language,[13] usually in a work of art.   This recalls the method of Bergson who teaches that pure intellectualism cannot learn the secret of life.[14]

This resurrection of Combray is so total for Proust that he actually sees in deep contemplation the objects which formerly surrounded him, and which his involuntary memory presents to him.[15]   The ecstasy which ensues from the totality of the revelation is something like a mystical experience in the natural realm which gives him the impression of ceasing to live in the present—thus he plunges profoundly into the past.[16]

Consequently, the recollection of a landscape from which the details of his childhood detach themselves becomes the source and inspiration of much of his work.   In fact, a large part of his entire novel is the purely mental reconstitution of its evocation.

" Venise "

In *Le Temps Retrouvé* a series of landscapes is evoked by similar psychological experiences.   For instance, the sensation of standing on two uneven flagstones awakens a dazzling, elusive vision of Venice which is accompanied by a happiness analogous to that which he experienced while eating the madeleine.   There is only a material difference in the landscape evoked:

[11] *Ibid.*, p. 72.

[12] *TR. II*, p. 14.

[13] Emeric Fiser, *L'Esthétique de Marcel Proust* (Paris: A. Rieder, 1933), p. 196.

[14] *Ibid.*, p. 213.   [15] *Ibid.*, p. 200.   [16] *TR. II*, pp. 19-20.

Un azur profond enivrait mes yeux, des impressions de fraîcheur, d'éblouissante lumière tournoyaient près de moi et dans mon désir de les saisir,
sans oser plus bouger que quand je goûtais la saveur de la madeleine en
tâchant de faire parvenir jusqu'à moi ce qu'elle me rappelait, je restais,
quitte à faire rire la foule innombrable des wattmen, à tituber comme
j'avais fait tout à l'heure, un pied sur le pavé plus élevé, l'autre pied sur
le pavé le plus bas. Chaque fois que je refaisais rien que matériellement
ce même pas, il me restait inutile; mais si je réussissais, oubliant la
matinée Guermantes, à retrouver ce que j'avais senti en posant ainsi mes
pieds, de nouveau la vision éblouissante et indistincte me frôlait comme si
elle m'avait dit: " Saisis-moi au passage si tu en as la force et tâche à
résoudre l'énigme du bonheur que je te propose." Et presque tout de suite,
je le reconnus, c'était Venise dont mes efforts pour la décrire et les pré-
tendus instantanés pris par ma mémoire ne m'avaient jamais rien dit et
que la sensation que j'avais ressentie jadis sur deux dalles inégales du
baptistère de Saint-Marc, m'avait rendue avec toutes les autres sensations
jointes ce jour-là à cette sensation-là, et qui étaient restées dans l'attente,
à leur rang, d'où un brusque hasard les avait impérieusement fait sortir,
dans la série des jours oubliés. De même le goût de la petite madeleine
m'avait rappelé Combray.[17]

The uneven flagstones remind his senses of the uneven steps in the
baptistry of Sain Mark's, the sensation of which brings back to his
mind, momentarily, dazzling Venetian lights and azure blue waters.
The vision extends in every direction and all dimensions the bare
and barren impressions he had had of Venice, and likewise all the
sensations he had experienced there.[18] But the narrator still questions why these images of Combray and Venice, at the moment
evoked give him a happiness sufficient to render him indifferent to
death.[19]

" La rangée d'arbres "

Shortly after the revelation of Venice the sound of a spoon
against a plate evokes a scene viewed from a railway carriage:

. . . les sensations étaient de grande chaleur encore mais toutes différentes,
mêlée d'une odeur de fumée apaisée par la fraîche odeur d'un cadre fores-
tier; et je reconnus que ce qui me paraissait si agréable était la même
rangée d'arbres que j'avais trouvée ennuyeuse à observer et à décrire, et
devant laquelle, débouchant la canette de bière que j'avais dans le wagon, je
venais de croire un instant, dans une sorte d'étourdissement, que je me

---

[17] *Ibid.*, pp. 8-9.   [18] *Ibid.*, p. 21.   [19] *Ibid.*, p. 9.

trouvais, tant le bruit identique de la cuiller contre l'assiette m'avait donné, avant que j'eusse eu le temps de me ressaisir l'illusion du bruit du marteau d'un employé qui avait arrangé quelque chose à une roue de train pendant que nous étions arrêtés devant ce petit bois.[20]

During a railway journey to Paris, not long before this experience, the spectacle of the setting sun on the trees that lined the railway track caused him to lament his inability to sing the praises of nature:

Arbres, pensai-je, vous n'avez plus rien à me dire, mon coeur refroidi ne vous entend plus. Je suis pourtant ici en pleine nature, eh bien, c'est avec froideur, avec ennui que mes yeux constatent la ligne qui sépare votre front lumineux de votre tronc d'ombre. Si jamais j'ai pu me croire poète, je sais maintenant que je ne le suis pas.[21]

Not to lose our thread, let us repeat here that the subject matter of Proust's dreams as far as his past experiences are concerned is not less important than these dreams themselves which always embrace a landscape.

" Balbec "

Still another time the napkin with which he wipes his mouth, because it has the same sort of stiffness as the towel with which he dried himself before his window the first day of his stay at Balbec, spreads out in its various folds and creases, like a peacock's tail, the plumage of a green and blue ocean. He draws enjoyment, not only from the colors of this vision, but from a whole moment of his life which had brought them into being, but which perhaps some feeling of fatigue or sadness had prevented him from enjoying at Balbec and which now freed from all the imperfections of objective perception fills him with joy.[22] This stiffness of the napkin calling up Balbec before him caresses his imagination not only with a mental picture of the sea as it was that morning long ago, but also with the odor of the room, the force of the wind and all that was attached to the sensation of the open sea.[23]

The bewildered narrator remarks that these landscapes have no relation to what he used to endeavor to call to mind about Venice, Balbec or Combray. In this connection he reasons that the dif-

[20] *Ibid.*, pp. 9-10.
[21] *TR. I.*, p. 221.

[22] *TR. III.*, pp. 10-11.
[23] *Ibid.*, p. 21.

ference between each of these real impressions and the corresponding artificial one is due to the fact that the slightest word we have spoken at a certain time in our life is surrounded and illumined by things that logically have no relation to it and are separated from it by our intelligence, which has no need of them for reasoning purposes.[24]

Since these landscapes are so intimately connected with Proust's literary inspiration, it is essential that we understand the profound experience which excites them. It is not until after this last series of revelations that Proust can explain the real significance of his inspired moments. When comparing his various happy impressions of Combray, Venice and Balbec, he discovers that he had felt them as if they were occurring simultaneously in the present moment and in some distant past, leaving him uncertain as to which period he was in.[25] Actually, at the moment of these revelations he was enjoying scenes common to both an earlier day and the present moment—scenes independent of all considerations of time. In this process of identifying the past with the present, he found himself in the only environment in which he could live and enjoy the essence of things, i. e. entirely outside of time. This explains why his apprehension of death vanished the moment he instinctively recognized the taste of the little madeleine, because at that moment he became a timeless person and, consequently, unconcerned with the vicissitudes of the future. This timeless person alone has the power of recapturing " le Temps Perdu." [26] It is only when the miracle of a resemblance with past scenes enables him to escape out of the present that he can recapture time lost for he believes that by this identification of the past and present he has created an eternity—a bliss excluding death.

Many times in the course of his life Proust was disappointed by the sight of a landscape because at the time he was observing it his imagination, the only organ with which he could enjoy beauty, was not able to function, by virtue of the law which decrees that only that which is absent can be imagined. Now, the operation of this harsh law was neutralized by a miraculous expedient of nature by which a sensation was reflected both in the past (which made it

[24] *Ibid.*, p. 12.   [25] *Ibid.*, p. 14.   [26] *Ibid.*

possible for his imagination to take pleasure in it) and in the present, the physical stimulus adding to the dreams of the imagination that which they usually lack, the idea of existence—and this subterfuge made it possible for the being within him to seize, isolate, immobilize for the duration of a lightning flash what it never apprehends, namely a fragment of time in its pure state.[27]   A single minute released from the chronological order of time recreates in him the human being similarly released, in order that he may sense that minute.   One may readily comprehend how such a being can be confident in his joy.   Situated thus outside the scope of time what could he fear from the future? [28]

At the very heart of the place where Proust happened to be when these souvenirs were revealed to him, whether it was his room in Paris or the library of the Prince de Guermantes, there was within him, radiating outward around him from a small zone, a sensation which was common both to the place where he was and to some other place—the bedroom of Aunt Léonie, a railway carriage, the baptistry of Saint Mark's.[29]   Moreover, it was not merely an echo or a duplication of a past sensation which he experienced but that sensation itself.   In each case the sensation common to both occasions sought to recreate about itself the former setting, while the present setting, which was occupying its space, opposed with all the resistance of its mass this invasion of a Paris residence by a Normandy beach, a railway embankment, etc.[30]   Always in these resurrections of the past, the distant place evoked about the common sensation grappled for a moment, like a wrestler, with the actual scene.   The latter always was the victor but the vanquished seemed to him the more beautiful, so that he was in a state of ecstasy seeking to penetrate as soon as they appeared, that Combray, that Balbec, that Venice which rose out of the past and invaded the very heart of these places in the present, only to be forced to retreat again.

[27] *Ibid.*, p. 15.

[28] *Ibid.*, p. 16.

[29] *Ibid.*, p. 17.

[30] *Ibid.*, p. 18, cf. also Dandieu, *op. cit.*, pp. 123-124, for an explanation of the primitive notion of the " participation " of two sensations, one in the present and the other in the past, as is experienced in the Proustian revelation.

But during the instant that they lasted, these scenes of the past were so complete that his entire being believed itself surrounded by them, bewildered by an uncertainty similar to that which one experiences before an ineffable vision at the moment of losing consciousness in sleep.[31] Thus the contemplation of these fragments of landscape removed outside the realm of time, although part of " eternity," was transitory. Yet he felt that the pleasure it had given him at rare intervals in his life was the only one that was fecund and real.[32] The unreality of other pleasures was sufficiently evident in their inability to satisfy or in the despair that followed whatever satisfaction they gave. On the other hand as he analyzed more deeply the sound of the spoon against the plate or the taste of the herb tea, he became more and more exalted with an ever increasing joy which transported into his room the bedroom, of his Aunt Léonie and in its wake all of Combray and its surrounding countryside.[33]

Proust's emotional experience of the resurrection of the past corresponds to the modern secularized and pseudo-spiritual notion of immortality, and the landscapes which are the contents of his souvenirs are like the massive pillars of a cathedral from which all the ribs of the naves detach themselves.[34]

Objective Impressions

In another way obscure impressions of landscape sometimes occupied Proust's thoughts after the manner of these subjective recollections, but these others concealed in themselves not a sensation of bygone days, but a new truth, a priceless image, which he sought to discover by efforts like those one makes to recall something forgotten, and which he would make an effort to seize and transcribe.[35] During his walks around Combray when a child, he used to hold attentively before his mind some object that had forced

---

[31] *TR. II.*, p. 19.
[32] *Ibid.*, p. 20.
[33] *Ibid.*, pp. 20-21.
[34] Dandieu, *op. cit.*, p. 73.
[35] *TR. II.*, p. 23. This idea of a " vérité nouvelle " is psychologically the same as " beauté "—they both imply a revelation, cf. Dandieu, *op. cit.*, p. 103.

3

itself upon his attention—a cloud, a triangle, a steeple, a flower—
because he felt that there might be underneath it something quite
different which he ought to try to discover, a thought which it
transcribed after the manner of those hieroglyphics which one might
think represented only material objects: [36]

Sans doute, ce déchiffrage était difficile, mais seul il donnait quelque
vérité à lire. Car les vérités que l'intelligence saisit directement à claire-
voie dans le monde de la pleine lumière ont quelque chose de moins profond,
de moins nécessaire que celles que la vie nous a malgré nous communiquées
en une impression, matérielle parce qu'elle est entrée par nos sens, mais
dont nous pouvons dégager l'esprit.[37]

" Les Clochers de Martinville "

One of the most interesting of these impressions is his representation of the steeples of Martinville in which one may observe how
the apparition of a landscape produces for Proust the shock of a
creative emotion. Once his ecstatic enthusiasm achieves itself, he
expresses in a page of style the object which was born of it—that
which pre-imagined in a sketch the general design of the whole
work. Both Fiser and Ferré evaluate this landscape along with
that of Combray as the essential base of Proust's entire novel. " He
listens to the mysterious call of ' les clochers ' and his work con-
stitutes one of the most beautiful answers that man has ever made in
the world of art and of creation." [38]

The psychological process by which Proust achieves artistic expression of his impression of the steeples of Martinville is that
which is termed by most Proustian scholars " spiritualization of
exterior reality." [39] As the object of this spiritualization is almost
exclusively landscape, it is necessary to consider briefly what the
process involves. An examination of the various passages which
reveal these creative emotions will show that a certain " découragement," the apparition of a landscape which gives a singularly pro-

[36] *TR. II.*, p. 24.

[37] *Ibid.*, p. 24.

[38] Fiser, *op. cit.*, p. 161; cf. also Ferré *op. cit.*, p. 57. Cf. *P. II.*, for
Proust's explanation of " l'étrange appel."

[39] Fiser, *op. cit.*, p. 28-31; cf. also *Ibid.*, p. 35.

found joy, the contemplation of the scene and its reconstitution purely mental are the principal elements of the experience.[40]

Proust's vision of landscape is never separate from the " état d'âme " which accompanies it because " toute impression est double, à demi engainée dans l'objet, prolongée en nous-même par une autre moitié que seuls nous pourrions connaître . . ." [41] Therefore, an exterior perception never appears alone. It is intimately welded to its interior echo.[42] It is from this precept that he proceeds to the recreation of the exterior, i. e. physical aspects of the scene, by his thought, in the outline of the interior world.[43] Thus Proust materializes in literature what all the post-impressionist painters from Cézanne to Picasso attempted with much less success. But this interior vision must be investigated thoroughly. Furthermore, he insists that it is only by this procedure that one renders a vision of the world of objects true:

Seule l'impression si chétive qu'en semble la matière, si invraisemblable la trace, est un critérium de vérité et à cause de cela mérite seule d'être appréhendée par l'esprit ; car elle est seule capable, s'il sait en dégager cette vérité, de l'amener à une plus grande perfection et de lui donner une pure joie.[44]

Reality visible only to the mind is the most original—it is something absolutely new. Therefore, Proust subordinates the exterior aspects of a landscape to his own profound impression.[45]

Spiritualization of the exterior accomplishes itself totally only in moments of clairvoyance and according to the effort spent by the mind.[46] It is only during these exceptional moments, when the object and the profound " moi " are united by absolute interpenetration, that he can possess the reality of a scene. All his interior self adds itself to the contemplated scene to give it vitality and spiritual reality.[47]

Let us observe this psychological process in the " déroulement " of Proust's impression of the landscape of the steeples of Martinville. Riding home one evening about dusk he receives an impression which he immediately subjects to a thorough examination:

[40] *Ibid.*, p. 38.
[41] *TR. II.*, p. 43.
[42] Fiser, *op. cit.*, p. 23.
[43] *Ibid.*, p. 26; cf. also *TR. II.*, p. 26.
[44] *Ibid.*, p. 26.
[45] *Ibid.*, p. 26-28.
[46] Fiser, *op. cit.*, p. 31.
[47] *Ibid.*, p. 34.

Au tournant d'un chemin j'éprouvai tout à coup ce plaisir spécial qui ne ressemblait à aucun autre, à apercevoir les deux clochers de Martinville, sur lesquels donnait le soleil couchant et que le mouvement de notre voiture et les lacets du chemin avaient l'air de faire changer de place, puis celui de Vieuxvicq qui, séparé d'eux par une colline et une vallée, et situé sur un plateau plus élevé dans le lointain, semblait pourtant tout voisin d'eux.[48]

As soon as the mind is alarmed the spiritualization process begins. The "plaisir spécial" caused by the apparition of "les deux clochers" immediately links the exterior vision with an "état d'âme." Thus the landscape at once acquires an extraordinary importance. Next he attempts to perceive in what direction the mind must seek to interpret the emotional complex of this unity of subject and object. It is necessary to pose the problem, and in order that the mind can usefully continue its researches he shows it the unknown: [49]

En constatant, en notant la forme de leur flèche, le déplacement de leurs lignes, l'ensoleillement de leur surface, je sentais que je n'allais pas au bout de mon impression, que quelque chose était derrière ce mouvement, derrière cette clarté, quelque chose qu'ils semblaient contenir et dérober à la fois.[50]

He feels that the reality of the scene veils something from him and that he is not penetrating the depth of his impression. The steeples have the air of concealing something beyond that which he sees and something which they invite him to approach and seize from them— an interior existence differing from his own vision. Now that the direction is found the mind advances to the search of the truth, " ce dont elles n'étaient qu'en couvercle." [51]

He next endeavors to penetrate with his mind beyond the thing seen. Spiritualization is now only in its first phase. As already mentioned its solution calls for a vigorous effort of the mind. So urgent was the task imposed on his conscience by these impressions that to strive for a perception of what lay hidden beneath them was a strenuous effort and a moral obligation: " Je ne savais pas la raison du plaisir que j'avais eu à les apercevoir à l'horizon et

[48] *S. I.*, p. 258.
[49] Fiser, *op. cit.*, p. 40.
[50] *S. I.*, pp. 258-259.
[51] *Ibid.*, p. 257.

l'obligation de chercher à découvrir cette raison me semblait bien pénible." [52]

Spiritualization in its first phase appears often but loses its real value when not investigated thoroughly. Proust comments that many people are content to leave an impression as something that cannot be expressed and confine their attention to those phases which allow us to experience the pleasure without analyzing the sensations thoroughly. Those who stop at this point extract nothing from the impression.[53]

Fiser remarks that the great originality of Proust appears where he forsakes the exterior scene and the work of spiritualization continues exclusively on the " modèle interne." [54] For instance, Proust says: " j'avais envie de garder en réserve dans ma tête ces lignes remuantes au soleil." [55] He reconstructs the physical aspects of the landscape in his memory as perfectly as if he had an immediate sensation of them. Therefore, the creative work of spiritualization has as its guide not the exterior object of perception but the " modèle interne " of the memory: [56] " force me fut, faute d'autre compagnie, de me rabattre sur celle de moi-même et d'essayer de me rappeler mes clochers." [57]

The intellectual effort directed upon this landscape is that alone which can give the spectator a notion of its intimate essence. It obliterates the barrier which separates nature from its spectator, extracts truth, leads the mind to a greater perfection and thereby imparts to it a pure joy: [58]

Bientôt leurs lignes et leurs surfaces ensoleillées, comme si elles avaient été une sorte d'écorce, se déchirèrent, un peu de ce qui m'était caché en elles m'apparut, j'eus une pensée qui n'existait pas pour moi l'instant avant, qui se formula en mots dans ma tête, et le plaisir qui m'avait fait tout à l'heure éprouver leur vue s'en trouva tellement accru que, pris d'une sort d'ivresse, je ne pus plus penser à autre chose. A ce moment, et comme nous étions déjà loin de Martinville, en tournant la tête je les aperçus de

---

[52] *Ibid.*, p. 259.

[53] *TR. II.*, p. 43.

[54] Fiser, *op. cit.*, p. 38. Cf. Dandieu, *op. cit.*, p. 54 for explanation of " modèle interne."

[55] *S. I.*, p. 259.

[56] Fiser, *op. cit.*, p. 38.

[57] *S. I.*, p. 259.

[58] *TR. II.*, p. 26.

nouveau, tout noirs cette fois, car le soleil était déjà couché. Par moments les tournants du chemin me les dérobaient, puis ils se montrèrent une dernière fois et enfin je ne les vis plus.[59]

Proust has projected himself and his imagination into the heart of the scene and through this immanence he attains a kind of spiritual strength in the midst of materialism. The scene thus becomes part of his interior life and displays, like a sort of rind stripped apart, its hidden essence which remains unknown to the ordinary perception. Furthermore, he renders his emotion of joy by analyzing it into its personal elements. For Proust the joy of penetrating the unknown " se formule en mots." " This concept suggests Leonardo da Vinci's doctrine, with which Proust was familiar, regarding painting as ' cosa mentale.' Claude Monet, who invented a new art of looking at nature, likewise said: ' On n'est pas artiste si l'on ne porte son tableau dans la tête avant de l'exécuter . . .' " [60] It is in a sort of intuitive intoxication that this intimate fusion with the contemplated scene produces itself. The spectator records the sensation: " le plaisir que m'avait fait tout à l'heure éprouver leur vue s'en trouva tellement accru que, pris d'une sorte d'ivresse, je ne pus plus penser à autre chose." The thought of penetrating the veil of nature, of discovering a new truth is that which gives this " ivresse " to the writer.

But this essence of things hidden is not a mysterious entity. It is analogous to a " jolie phrase; " it is the poetic vision of the scene:

Sans me dire ce qui était caché derrière les clochers de Martinville devait être quelque chose d'analogue à une jolie phrase, puisque c'était sous la forme de mots qui me faisaient plaisir . . .[61]

Proust writes that as soon as the intellect has interpreted the obscure sense of pleasure it must convert the scene which inspired the emotion into a mental equivalent, which means for him the creation of a work of art. And so in a series of unique visual and kinetic images he gives an impressionistic transcription of the steeples of Martinville as they remained in his memory: [62]

---

[59] *S. I.*, p. 259.

[60] Chernowitz, *op. cit.*, pp. 137-138.

[61] *S. I.*, p. 260.

[62] Chernowitz, *op. cit.*, p. 166. This description of the steeples of Martin-

Seuls, s'élevant du niveau de la plaine et comme perdus en rase campagne, montaient vers le ciel les deux clochers de Martinville. Bientôt nous en vîmes trois: venant se placer en face d'eux par une volte hardie, un clocher retardataire, celui de Vieuxvicq, les avait rejoints. Les minutes passaient, nous allions vite et pourtant les trois clochers étaient toujours au loin devant nous, comme trois oiseaux posés sur la plaine, immobiles et qu'on distingue au soleil. Puis le clocher de Vieuxvicq s'écarta, prit ses distances, et les clochers de Martinville restèrent seuls, éclairés par la lumière du couchant que même à cette distance, sur leurs pentes, je voyais jouer et sourire. Nous avions été si longs à nous rapprocher d'eux, que je pensais au temps qu'il faudrait encore pour les atteindre quand, tout d'un coup, la voiture ayant tourné, elle nous déposa à leurs pieds; et ils s'étaient jetés si rudement au-devant d'elle, qu'on n'eut que le temps d'arrêter pour ne pas se heurter au porche. Nous poursuivîmes notre route; nous avions déjà quitté Martinville depuis un peu de temps et le village après nous avoir accompagnés quelques secondes avait disparu, que restés seuls à l'horizon, à nous regarder fuir, ses clochers et celui de Vieuxvicq agitaient encore en signe d'adieu leurs cimes ensoleillées. Parfois l'un s'effaçait pour que les deux autres pussent nous apercevoir un instant encore; mais la route changea de direction, ils virèrent dans la lumière comme trois pivots d'or et disparurent à mes yeux. Mais, un peu plus tard, comme nous étions déjà près de Combray, le soleil étant maintenant couché, je les aperçus une dernière fois de très loin qui n'étaient plus que comme trois fleurs peintes sur le ciel au-dessus de la ligne basse des champs. Ils me faisaient penser aussi aux trois jeunes filles d'une légende, abandonnées dans une solitude où tombait déjà l'obscurité, et tandis que nous nous éloignions au galop, je les vis timidement chercher leur chemin et après quelques gauches trébuchements de leurs nobles silhouettes, se serrer les uns contre les autres, glisser l'un derrière l'autre, ne plus faire sur le ciel encore rose qu'une seul forme noire, charmante et résignée, et s'effacer dans la nuit.[63]

Though this landscape is of psychological origin, it is also a work of art. Proust reproduces these steeples sharply outlined against the setting sun, according to the optical illusion of which his first glance at them is composed.[64] His likening the spires to three birds perched upon the plain, immediately makes us feel the distance in his impression; likewise, it is this effect of remoteness which gives to the spires the appearance of three birds.

Furthermore, he seems to experience a deception of form, move-

ville is actually Proust's impression of the steeples of Caen and the original sketch may be found in *PM.*, pp. 92-94.

[63] *S. I.*, p. 260.

[64] Cf. *JF. III.*, p. 103.

ment and space and not only space in distance but in time as well.
The deceptive effects are due to the odd angles of perspective from
which he views the scene.[65]   Interest in spatial sensations is
betrayed here by the fact that each spatial distance seems to correspond to a similar distance in time; hence, the double deception
and surprise of the spectator when, after having estimated the time
that it would take to reach the spires by the apparent distance from
them, he is suddenly set down at their feet.[66]

Tone and distance are relative as the perspective is not separate
from the play of light. Even at a distance he perceives the setting
sun playing and smiling upon the spires. His adjectival clause
" je voyais jouer et sourire " contains both visual and kinetic impressions and it carries a tone of friendliness which indicates the
writer's attitude toward the scene. His representation of the
steeples, as alone on the horizon and waving their sunbathed pinnacles which veered in the light like three golden pivots, takes the
reader into something like the " pointillism " of Seurat blended
with the irony of Giraudoux.

These steeples are real by the fact that they enter into intimate
relation with the narrator. The immovable spires which he ap-
proaches do not exist but the spires which reply to him (inspire a
sense of pleasure), which are not mute to his desires (reveal
essence) and do not deceive his expectation (enhance pleasure), are
living. They are no longer inanimate but magnificent beings—
they " montaient vers le ciel . . . venant se placer . . ." and the
one " s'écarta, prit ses distances," etc. They are no longer strangers
but live a life which he understands and which is also his. They
place themselves in the picture and then " à nous regarder . . .
agitaient encore en signe d'adieu . . . pussent nous apercevoir . . .
et disparurent." [67]

Proust's personifications contain a large portion of narration
which unfolds as a moving picture upon a screen. But suddenly the
movement is arrested and painted upon a canvas. As is evident in

[65] Chernowitz, *op. cit.*, p. 166.

[66] J. Murray, " Le Symbolisme spatial dans l'oeuvre de Marcel Proust,"
French Quarterly, XI (1929), pp. 96-108.

[67] Fiser, *op. cit.*, p. 46.

his elaboration of the scene viewed from a greater distance, the laws of perspective increase his illusions. It is the after-glow of the setting sun on the vanishing horizon that gives to the steeples the appearance of three flowers painted upon the sky above the low line of fields.

The steeples are most striking delineated against the rose glow of an evening sky. Having already endowed them with human features he next invents for them a fairy tale in which they are transfigured into young girls:

Ils me faisaient penser aussi aux trois jeunes filles d'une légende, aban-données dans une solitude où tombait déjà l'obscurité . . . je les vis timide-ment chercher leur chemin et après quelques gauches trébuchements de leurs nobles silhouettes, se serrer les uns contre les autres, glisser l'un derrière l'autre, ne plus faire sur le ciel encore rose qu'une seule forme noire, charmante et résignée, et s'effacer dans la nuit.[68]

Proust's aesthetics emphasizes that the task of the artist is not only to extract the contents of things but to give to these contents a character of stability. For him this equals creative individuality.[69] Here there is at issue something like a personal classicism which judges and symbolizes the impression. The allegory may seem to be handled too mechanically but the poet weaves an atmosphere of twilight tenderness which makes the vision acceptable. In the last sentence it is interesting to note the aspect of timidity so characteristic of Proust's analogical representations of young girls. By a subtle combination of sentiment, fancy and insight he gives to the landscape a touch of poetry and depth wherein illusion and truth (knowledge of physical facts) are so blended that it seems as if one could not be without the other.

It is noteworthy in this representation of a landscape that though Proust's " starting point is the primitive impression, his conception extends to a large part of the world within, directing his Impressionism . . . toward an intellectualized form." [70] Furthermore, he holds that only an artist is capable of converting this vision into an intellectual equivalent. Proust thus writes:

[68] *S. I.*, p. 261.
[69] Chernowitz, *op. cit.*, p. 138.
[70] *Ibid.*, p. 165.

L'impression est pour l'écrivain ce qu'est l'expérimentation pour le savant avec cette différence que chez le savant, le travail de l'intelligence précède et chez l'écrivain vient après. Ce que nous n'avons pas eu à déchiffrer, à éclaircir par notre effort personnel, ce qui était clair avant nous, n'est pas à nous.[71]

Chernowitz points out that these "illusions which make space, distance and form deceptive (in landscape) are extended not only to all the senses but even to the psychological realm, to the disguised, equivocal manner of presenting characters."[72]

This spiritual recreation of a scene, which for Proust is synonymous with artistic expression, makes of his impression great art:

Et comme l'art recompose exactement la vie, autour des vérités qu'on a atteintes en soi-même flottera toujours une atmosphère de poésie, la douceur d'un mystère qui n'est que le vestige de la pénombre que nous avons dû traverser, l'indication, marquée exactement comme par un altimètre, de la profondeur d'une oeuvre.[73]

As soon as he paints the scene in words he is overcome by a sense of happiness, for he feels that he finally possesses the mystery which the steeples conceal, and by expressing it in a work of art he renders to the landscape its full significance.[74]

"Les arbres de Balbec"

Another time our young hero is riding along the Balbac road in Mme de Villeparisis's elegant carriage when the sudden apparition of three trees marking the entrance to a shady avenue evokes a profound happiness which he had not often felt since Combray. It is analogous to that given him by—among other things—the steeples of Martinville. But this time the impression remained incomplete:[75]

... je ne pouvais arriver à reconnaître le lieu dont ils étaient comme détachés mais je sentais qu'il m'avait été familier autrefois; de sorte que

[71] *TR. II.*, pp. 26-27. Cf. also *Ibid.* p. 50, quoted by Chernowitz, *op. cit.*, p. 225.
[72] Chernowitz, *op. cit.*, pp. 167-168.
[73] *TR. II.*, p. 52.
[74] Cf. *P. II.*, pp. 77-79, for Proust's explanation of the relation between the emotional revelation and the work of art.
[75] *JF. II.*, p. 161.

mon esprit ayant trébuché entre quelque année lointaine et le moment présent, les environs de Balbec vacillèrent et je me demandais si toute cette promenade n'était pas une fiction, Balbec un endroit où je n'étais jamais allé que par l'imagination, . . .[76]

Under the condition of this intense joy he makes such an effort to identify himself with the scene perceived that his present surroundings seem lost, and he begins to wonder if Balbec is only an imaginative place and the three old trees the reality which one recaptures on raising one's eyes from the book which describes an environment into which one believes that one has been bodily transported.[77] The fact that his mind wavers between some distant year and the present moment indicates that he seeks the source of his inspiration in the date of the " modèle interne." The date is the end of his inquiry.[78]

It is again by a sort of intuitive impression that he feels a sense of familiarity about trees.[79] But the problem of this impression of the " déjà vu " can only be solved by intellectual investgiation, and so he continues to search :

Je regardais les trois arbres, je les voyais bien, mais mon esprit sentant qu'ils recouvraient quelque chose sur quoi il n'avait pas prise, comme sur ces objets placés trop loin dont nos doigts allongés au bout de notre bras tendu, effleurent seulement par instants l'enveloppe sans arriver à rien saisir.[80]

As in his view of the steeples of Martinville he again feels that he is not penetrating the depth of his impression, and he has the confused notion of a hidden reality behind that which meets the eye : " mon esprit sentant qu'ils recouvraient quelque chose sur quoi il n'avait pas prise." [81] He knows that intense contemplation is necessary to reveal the essence of things. But he also believes that it is only during moments of repose. i. e. when the mind makes

[76] *Ibid.*, p. 161.
[77] *Ibid.*
[78] Dandieu, *op. cit.*, p. 133, points out that Proust seeks his inspiration in the date of an impression just as the romantics seek it in the name of God.
[79] This sentiment of the " déjà vu " of the Proustian revelation has been described by psychologists as " angoisse." Cf. Dandieu, *op. cit.*, p. 132.
[80] *JF. II.*, p. 162.
[81] *Ibid.*

no effort to establish a relation between a sensation and a memory that revelation produces itself.[82] For this reason he longs to be alone so that other preoccupations will not trouble the purity of his vision.

He remains for a long time thinking of nothing, and when his thoughts are collected and strengthened he can see the trees growing within himself. This projection of natural scenery within himself is a kind of literary empathy wherein he subjectifies the elements of landscape. They have become a part of him but they still refuse to betray their secret: " Je sentais de nouveau derrière eux le même objet connu mais vague et que je ne pus ramener à moi." [83] Contrary to his former experience the narrator cannot this time by any amount of intellectual effort penetrate the veil which hides from him the reality of the three trees. Instead of the intoxication which ensues as a result of possessing the contents of an object, he is overcome with discouragement at the feeling of not being able to attain that which he is seeking so earnestly. This great confusion in his mind leads to a sort of methodical skepticism—a process often used by Proust which consists of enumerating all the possible causes of an impression which he seeks to explain.[84] He questions himself:

Où les avais-je déjà regardés? Il n'y avait aucun lieu autour de Combray . . . Fallait-il croire qu'ils venaient d'années déjà si lointaines de ma vie que le paysage qui les entourait avait été entièrement aboli dans ma mémoire et que . . . ils surnageaient seuls du livre oublié de ma première enfance. N'appartenaient-ils au contraire qu'à ces paysages du rêve, toujours les mêmes, . . . N'étaient-ils qu'une image toute nouvelle détachée d'un rêve de la nuit précédente mais déjà si effacée qu'elle me semblait venir de beaucoup plus loin? Ou bien ne les avais-je jamais vus et cachaient-ils derrière eux comme tels arbres, telle touffe d'herbes que j'avais vus du côté de Guermantes un sens aussi obscur . . . de sorte que, sollicité par eux d'approfondir une pensée, je croyais avoir à reconnaître un souvenir. Ou encore ne cachaient-ils même pas de pensées et était-ce une fatigue de ma vision qui me les faisait voir doubles dans le temps comme on voit quelquefois double dans l'espace? [85]

The elaboration of these questions grows a bit monotonous but gives us an insight into the landscape of his mind. He even wonders if

---

[82] *S. I.*, pp. 71-72. Cf. *supra*, p. 19. Cf. also Dandieu, *op. cit.*, p. 130.
[83] *JF. II.*, p. 163.   [84] Dandieu *op. cit.*, p. 124.   [85] *JF. II.*, p. 163.

the intense mental effort of his strained vision makes him see the scene double in time as one occasionally sees things double in space. He does not know and he relates: " Cependant ils venaient vers moi; peut-être apparition mythique, ronde de sorcières ou de nornes qui me proposait ses oracles." [86]

This optical kinetic imagery in which the movement humanizes the trees is empathetic.[87] The spectator personifies because he can thus more easily identify himself with the object of perception. But he cannot answer any of these questions and finally his skepticism turns to despair and he chooses to believe that the trees are phantoms of the past . . . vanished friends who recall common memories:

Comme des ombres ils semblaient me demander de les emmener avec moi de les rendre à la vie. Dans leur gesticulation naïve et passionée, je reconnaissais le regret impuissant d'un être aimé qui a perdu l'usage de la parole, sent qu'il ne pourra nous dire ce qu'il veut et que nous ne savons pas deviner.[8]

The despair in his heart which results from the nebulosity of his vision is so keen that it brings on the idea of death, and thus the trees appear as ghosts appealing to him for life. Now in the movement of these illusory ghosts he discerns the helpless anguish of a beloved person who has lost the power of speech and therefore cannot convey his message. Here it seems that the narrator is haunted by the picture of his grandmother who had a stroke in the streets of Paris just before going to Balbec.

As his carriage bears him away from the scene, he feels that he is leaving what alone he believed to be true, what would have made him truly happy—it was like his life.[89] He watches the trees gradually withdraw waving their despairing arms and seeming to say to him:

. . . ce que tu n'apprends pas de nous aujourd'hui tu ne le sauras jamais. Si tu nous laisses retomber au fond de ce chemin d'où nous cherchions à

---

[86] *Ibid.*, p. 164.

[87] J. E. Downey, *Creative Imagination* (New York: Harcourt, Brace & Company, 1929), pp. 177-180.

[88] *JF. II.*, p. 164.

[89] *Ibid.*

nous hisser jusqu'à toi, toute une partie de toi-même que nous t'apportions tombera pour jamais au néant.[90]

This elucidation of his impression reveals an unusual self-projection into the scene. The lines of the trees release certain kinetic patterns of perception which are actually an integral part of his emotional complex, as in the lines, "leurs gesticulation . . . *passionnée*" and "agitant leurs bras *désespérés*." [91] Thus he has simultaneously subjectified the scene and objectified his own emotions. He has created a landscape of emotional objects.

This entire impression of the trees as dear companions of his childhood in possession of a part of his life reveals his propensity toward the Celtic belief that the souls of those whom we have lost are held captive in some inanimate object—an animal or a plant— and lost to us until the day when we happen to pass by or attain possession of the object which forms their prison. He earlier remarks that: "Alors elles tressaillent, nous appellent, et sitôt que nous les avons reconnues, l'enchantement est bris?. Délivrées par nous, elles ont vaincu la mort et reviennent vivre avec nous." [92] But in this event, though the trees appeal to him desperately, by no amount of insight or intellectual effort can he recognize their voice; and therefore as they do not reveal their essence to him, he cannot deliver them from death or know that part of his life which they possess.

This sentiment of death is associated with the author's aesthetics which stresses that poetic vision of the real is the only life worthy of being lived,[93] and that without art the reality of the exterior world which lies in the inner life of things and of ourselves remains forever unknown. The entire Proustian universe is built upon art and when he cannot give artistic expression to the life about him he has the feeling of ceasing to live himself. Consequently, as this landscape of the three trees disappears from his sight without

[90] *Ibid.*

[91] *Ibid.* Cf. Proust's description of "les trois arbres de Martinville," *S. I.*, p. 260, for a similar procedure.

[92] *S. I.*, p. 69.

[93] Cf. Pierre-Quint, *op. cit.*, p. 238, for an explanation of the similarity here with Bergson's philosophy of art.

revealing to him its poetic meaning he is as sad as though he had just lost a friend, had died within himself, or had denied his God.[94] That part of himself which he felt the trees to be, that which was actually nothing more than a " spiritual catastrophe of a tormenting oblivion " [95] he was never to know—it was forever dead.

In his impression of these three trees along the Balbec road spiritualization of the scene is not accomplished as the intellect cannot sufficiently penetrate the original emotion. The obstacle which prevents him from grasping the significance of the landscape is a tissue of ready-made visions which is a disposition of the mind rather than a reality. Beneath this veil dwells " reality, art and joy." [96]

This old road to Balbec over which he had traveled numerous times was a road little used but planted with old elm trees which he thought quite admirable. It was like many roads of the same kind which are to be found in France, climbing on a fairly steep gradient to its summit and then gradually falling for the rest of the way. At the time he traveled it he found no great attraction in it, he was only glad to be going home. But somehow a bond was established between it and his heart and later on it became for him a frequent source of joy by remaining in his memory as a loadstone to which all the similar roads that he traveled would at once attach themselves without breach of continuity, and would be able, thanks to it, to communicate with his heart:

Car dès que la voiture ou l'automobile s'engagerait dans une de ces routes qui auraient l'air d'être la continuation de celle que j'avais parcourue avec Mme de Villeparisis, ce à quoi ma conscience actuelle se trouverait immédiatement appuyée comme à mon passé le plus récent, ce serait (toutes les années intermédiaires se trouvant abolies) les impressions que j'avais eues par ces fins d'après-midi là, en promenade près de Balbec, quand les feuilles sentaient bon, que la brume s'élevait et qu'au delà du prochain village, on apercevrait entre les arbres le coucher du soleil comme s'il avait été quelque localité suivante, forestière, distante et qu'on n'atteindra pas le soir même.[97]

---

[94] *JF. II.*, p. 165. Cf. also Pierre-Quint, *op. cit.*, p. 128.

[95] Ortega y Gasset, " Le Temps, la distance et la forme chez Proust," *Nouvelle revue française*, XX (1923), p. 267.

[96] Pierre-Quint, *op. cit.*, p. 129.

[97] *JF. II.*, p. 166.

Harmonized with what he was feeling in another place, on a similar road surrounded by all the accessory sensations which were common to them both, these impressions took on the consistency of a particular type of pleasure, in which these awakened memories placed, amid the realities that his senses could perceive, no small part of a reality dreamed. It was this interpenetration of past impressions with the present scene that gave him, among those regions through which he was passing, more than an aesthetic feeling—a transient but exalted ambition to live there always. Often since then, the very odor of green leaves reminded him that returning over the old road with Mme de Villeparisis to the Grand Hotel was one of those indescribable happinesses which neither the present nor the future could restore and which one experiences only once in a lifetime.[98]

Because this road remained in the greenness of his memory, a similar road immediately awakened sentimental scenes from the past. It is the power of the awakened memory to place in present reality a part of a dreamed reality that characterizes the impression as an "indescribable happiness." And so again the sight of a landscape recaptures for Proust memories of the past.

" L'Eglise de Village "

The whole of Combray is revealed to the narrator in a moment of exalting plenitude, and as previously remarked the contents of the successive parts of this revelation is most often a landscape. Especially striking is his unforgettable representation of the church of Combray wherein he paints a series of landscapes rich in medieval history and culture, psychological nuance, and pictorial art.[99]

Proust's impression of this church which he had loved since his childhood was something entirely different from the rest of the town, and he pictures it first in a landscape of Time:

. . . un édifice occupant, s'il'on peut dire, un espace à quatre dimensions— la quatrième étant celle du Temps,—déployant à travers les siècles son

---

[98] *Ibid.*, pp. 166-167. This curious impression of the familiar scene does not allow only a reminiscense more or less authentic, but a certain emotional state which leads to a sort of " extase." Cf. Dandieu *op. cit.*, p. 140.

[99] Cf. *PM.*, pp. 103-112, for Proust's comments on Ruskin's guide for enjoying cathedrals.

vaisseau qui, de travée, de chapelle en chapelle, semblait vaincre et franchir non pas seulement quelques mètres, mais des époques successives d'où il sortait victorieux; dérobant le rude et farouche XIᵉ siècle dans l'épaisseur de ses murs . . .[100]

We have already observed Proust's preoccupation with spatial sensations in time and distance, and this geometrical use of time is explained by Murray as a sort of " spatial symbolism." [101] It is interesting to note in this connection that the narrator is not so much concerned with what Time has done to the church, as one might expect, but rather with what the church has done to Time. By a unique personification he has pictured it as having *sailed* the centuries with that old nave which seemed to *conquer* each epoch from which the whole building *emerged* triumphant. This is almost a philological fable reducing *nef* to its original meaning *bateau*.

Next he creates a supernatural atmosphere about the scene by picturing, in a tone of awe and reverence, the interior of the church as a fairy-haunted valley, where the rustic sees with amazement on a rock, a tree, a marsh, the tangible proof of the supernatural passage.[102]

The historical background of this church characterizes his impression to such a degree that he even gives to the tower a " temps perdu " (" avait contemplé saint Louis ") and a " temps retrouvé " (" semblait le voir encore ") :

. . . élevant dans le ciel au-dessus de la Place, sa tour qui avait contemplé saint Louis et semblait le voir encore; et s'enfonçant avec sa crypte dans une nuit mérovingienne où, nous guidant à tâtons sous la voûte obscure et puissamment nervurée comme la membrane d'une immense chauve-souris de pierre . . .[103]

Furthermore, he gives the oldest part of the church (" crypte ") its roots in the oldest historical epoch of France (" mérovingienne ") picturing the then undeveloped architectonic style (pre-romanesque) by a " chauve souris " flying in the dark.

The special life that Ruskin rendered to the stones of churches

---

[100] *S. I.*, p. 92.
[101] Cf. J. Murray, *op. cit.* Cf. also *supra*, p. 37.
[102] *S. I.*, p. 92.
[103] *Ibid.*, p. 93.

4

Proust gives to French cathedrals.[104] Though he views the church with a conventionally reverent attitude, he makes of it a living thing by representing it as "familière et mitoyenne"—a dear familiar friend. Because it is closely pressed between the houses of the town, he describes it as a "simple citoyenne de Combray," who might have had her number in the street had the streets of Combray borne numbers, and at whose door one felt that the postman ought to stop on his morning rounds. Like Verhaeren he vivifies through an animistic process everything that he touches. But for all that there existed, between the church and everything in Combray that was not the church, a clear line of demarcation which he never eliminated from the picture.[105]

The historical background and setting carefully established, he next presents a panoramic view of the whole countryside as it is dominated by the church. One may observe how every change of perspective is a source of fresh inspiration to the spectator: [106]

On reconnaissait le clocher de Saint-Hilaire de bien loin, inscrivant sa figure inoubliable à l'horizon où Combray n'apparaissait pas encore; quand du train qui, la semaine de Pâques, nous amenait de Paris, mon père l'apercevait qui filait tour à tour sur tous les sillons de ciel, faisant courir en tous sens son petit coq de fer, il nous disait: "Allons, prenez les couvertures, on est arrivé." Et dans une des plus grandes promenades que nous faisions de Combray, il y avait un endroit où la route resserrée découchait tout à coup sur un immense plateau fermé à l'horizon par des forêts déchiquetées que dépassait seule la fine pointe du clocher de Saint-Hilaire, mais si mince, si rose, qu'elle semblait seulement rayée sur le ciel par un ongle qui aurait voulu donner à ce paysage, à ce tableau rien que de nature, cette petite marque d'art, cette unique indication humaine. Quand on se rapprochait et qu'on pouvait apercevoir le reste de la tour carrée et à demi détruite qui, moins haute, subsistait à côté de lui, on était frappé surtout du ton rougeâtre et sombre des pierres; et, par un matin brumeux d'automne, on aurait dit, s'élevant au-dessus du violet orageux des vignobles, une ruine de pourpre presque de la couleur de la vigne vierge.[107]

---

[104] Dandieu, *op. cit.*, p. 104. Cf. also *S. I.*, p. 260.

[105] *Ibid.*, p. 94.

[106] M. Moore, "Les arts plastiques dans l'oeuvre de Marcel Proust" (University of Chicago, 1928), p. 19 writes: "Comme Ruskin, il associe la beauté des cathédrales gothiques au charme du paysage français."

[107] *S. I.*, p. 95. Cf. also *Ibid.*, p. 260, for a similar use of perspective in his description of "les clochers de Martinville."

First the steeple is distinguished from a distance inscribing its unforgettable form upon a horizon and again it is caught sight of from a train as it slips into every fold of the sky, always in dynamic motion projecting itself and creating various illusory perspectives for the transient spectator.[108] Another time viewed from an immense plain, closed at the horizon by strips of forest over which rose the steeple, the effect of remoteness gives to the scene the fantastic impression of a sketch in the sky.[109] Furthermore, this illusion is so delicate that it appears to be sketched by the fingernail, not the brush, of a painter anxious to give to such a landscape this little sign of art. The beauty of a natural scene Proust intuitively places in the realm of art.

This elevated poetic effect is made even more emphatic through contrast as the angle of perspective changes. We are suddenly taken near the church where the reddish and sombre tones of its stone tower are perceptible and seem to symbolize the rugged barbarities of the eleventh century. In the next clause his unrestricted poetic mind adds a tone of mystery to the scene by picturing it on a misty morning in autumn as " une ruine de pourpre." His use of the color adjective red connotates something of the unknowable— the Holy of Holies.[110]

Often in the Square, on their way home from church, his grandmother would make him stop and look up at the steeple. It was during those days that he first became aware of the geometrical beauty of a scene. The following picture is an excellent illustration of this aspect of his art:

Souvent sur la place, quand nous rentrions, ma grand'mère me faisait arrêter pour le regarder. Des fenêtres de sa tour, placées deux par deux les unes au-dessus des autres, avec cette juste et originale proportion dans les distances qui ne donne pas de la beauté et de la dignité qu'aux visages humains, il lâchait, laissait tomber à intervalles réguliers des volées de corbeaux qui, pendant un moment, tournoyaient en criant, comme si les vieilles pierres qui les laissaient s'ébattre sans paraître les voir, devenues tout d'un coup inhabitables et dégageant un principe d'agitation infinie,

---

[108] Chernowitz, *op. cit.*, p. 166.

[109] Cf. *S. I.*, p. 260, for other effects created by the remoteness of church spires.

[110] Downey, *op. cit.*, p. 87.

les avait frappés et repoussés. Puis, après, avoir rayé en tous sens le
velours violet de l'air du soir, brusquement calmés ils revenaient s'absorber
dans la tour, de néfaste redevenue propice, quelques-uns posés çà et là,
ne semblant pas bouger, mais happant peut-être quelque insecte, sur la
pointe d'un clocheton, comme une mouette arrêtée avec l'immobilité d'un
pêcheur à la crête d'une vague.[111]

It is notable that he even perceived regular intervals in the flight
of the crows which were flying about the steeple and which appeared
to receive an aspect of kindliness through their contact with the
stones of the church.

Having already subjectified the scene by portraying Saint Hilaire
as a citizen of Combray, he furthermore gives to this church a conscience of its own (conscience d'elle-même) and depicts the steeple
as that which speaks for it. In this way he accents his impression
of it as a living being with head and brains. To render more
intelligible the optical side of this psycho-sensorial description he
compares the inclination of its stony slopes, which draw together
as they rise, to hands joined in prayer—a comparison used before
him for Gothic windows. The effect produced by all this is
pictorial:

Et sans doute, toute partie de l'église qu'on apercevait la distinguait de
tout autre édifice par une sorte de pensée qui lui était infuse, mais c'était
dans son clocher qu'elle semblait prendre conscience d'elle-même, affirmer
une existence individuelle et responsable. C'était lui qui parlait pour elle.[112]

Memory of his grandmother's devotion to Saint Hilaire gives
sentimental perspective to the landscape, and for this reason she
remains a vital part of his impression of it. He delights in
picturing her impassioned gaze at its spire and he expresses her
feelings with a vividness that evokes our admiration and a sympathy
which wins our heart:

Sans trop savoir pourquoi, ma grand'mère trouvait au clocher de Saint-
Hilaire cette absence de vulgarité, de prétention, de mesquinerie, qui lui
faisait aimer et croire riches d'une influence bienfaisante, la nature, quand
la main de l'homme ne l'avait pas, comme faisait le jardinier de ma
grand'tante, rapetissée, et les oeuvres de génie . . . Je crois surtout que,
confusément, ma grand'mère trouvait au clocher de Combray ce qui pour
elle avait le plus de prix au monde, l'air naturel et l'air distingué.[113]

---

[111] *S. I.*, pp. 95-96.   [112] *Ibid.*, p. 96.   [113] *Ibid.*

In a confused way she finds her aristocratic culture reflected in this noble art of the past. She sees in the steeple a distinguished and natural air. Because she views it as an element of landscape, its lack of vulgarity and pretention is that which makes her love nature when unadorned by the works of man. Thus nature preaches aristocracy and delicacy. In this connection it is interesting to note that as his grandmother fervently contemplates the steeple, she projects herself so completely into the outpouring of its spire that her gaze seems to leap upward with it; and at the same time there is a devout smile upon her face:

Et en le regardant, en suivant des yeux la douce tension, l'inclinaison fervente de ses pentes de pierre qui se rapprochaient en s'élevant comme des mains jointes qui prient, elle s'unissait si bien à l'effusion de la flèche, que son regard semblait s'élancer avec elle; et en même temps elle souriait amicalement aux vieilles pierres usées dont le couchant n'éclairait plus que le faîte et qui, à partir du moment où elles entraient dans cette zone ensoleillée, adoucies par la lumière, paraissaient tout d'un coup montées bien plus haut, lointaines, comme un chant repris " en voix de tête " une octave au-dessus.[114]

This scene recalls the fusion of landscape and man which so many generations of Frenchmen used spontaneously when the churches had the form of headgear and dress. The old stones seem to feel rejuvenated in the sun just as grandmother does in the light of her recollections of the youth of France.

The deceptive height of the steeple caused by the effect of sunlight bathing its topmost pinnacles he likens to a song whose singer breaks into a falsetto, an octave above the accompanying air. It is a favorite device of Proust to clarify an impression by elements borrowed from the various arts. Here his spontaneous analogy to a song gives height to his visual impression and " en voix de tête " emphasizes its fallaciousness. The effect produced is almost a duality of sensory impressions.

Because the steeple remains to present time and to the narrator himself what it was to generations past, Proust represents it as an " ange gardien " in stone for the practical purposes of life:

C'était le clocher de Saint-Hilaire qui donnait à toutes les occupations, à toutes les heures, à tous les points de vue de la ville, leur figure, leur couronnement, leur consécration.[115]

---

[114] *Ibid.*, pp. 96-97.   [115] *Ibid.*, p. 97.

And it even served to tell him the hour of the day:

De ma chambre, je ne pouvais apercevoir que sa base qui avait été recou-
verte d'ardoise; mais quand, le dimanche, je les voyais, par une chaude
matinée d'été, flamboyer comme un soleil noir, je me disais: "Mon Dieu!
neuf heures. il faut se préparer pour aller à la grand'messe . . ."[116]

In a thoroughly interesting metaphor he shows that not only
historical associations, multiple effects of perspective, sentimental
analogies, etc. color his memory of this steeple but also his most
humble domestic activities. For instance, one fine day after Mass
when he stops at the bakery he perceives the steeple in front of
him as baked and brown like a large loaf of "holy bread" with
flakes and sticky drops on it:

Quand après la messe, on entrait dire à Théodore d'apporter une brioche
plus grosse que d'habitude parce que nos cousins avaient profité du beau
temps pour venir de Thiberzy déjeuner avec nous, on avait devant soi le
clocher qui, doré et cuit lui-même comme une plus grande brioche bénie,
avec des écailles et des égouttements gommeux de soleil, piquait sa pointe
aiguë dans le ciel bleu.[117]

Though "doré" may easily have been suggested by the heat of the
sun, his errand at the bakery seems to have called up this impression of the steeple as "cuit . . . comme une . . . grande brioche
bénie, avec . . . des égouttements gommeux . . ." Furthermore,
anything connected with the church is "béni." Even today the
church in France distributes "du pain béni." Thus we find our
narrator in a turmoil of sacred, domestic and poetic associations
psychologically reflected into a "prisma" of beauty.

This view, newly transposed, ends in Proust's most tender mother-
child relation—a really fairylike Oedipus complex:

Et le soir, quand je rentrais de promenade et pensais au moment où il
faudrait tout à l'heure dire bonsoir à ma mère et ne plus la voir, il était
au contraire si doux, dans la journée finissante, qu'il avait l'air d'être posé
et enfoncé comme un coussin de velours brun sur le ciel pâli qui avait cédé
sous sa pression, s'était creusé légèrement pour lui faire sa place et
refluait sur ses bords . . .[118]

Obviously it is the painful thought of having to bid his mother
good-night that accents the kindliness of the steeple. Its trans-

[116] *Ibid.*   [117] *Ibid.*, pp. 97-98.   [118] *Ibid.*, p. 98.

formation into a velvet cushion discloses a subtle patterning of thought which follows his fear of the contrary unpleasantness of his own pillow after her last kiss.

Even in places behind the church, from which it cannot be seen, the landscape seems always composed with reference to the steeple which would stand up here and there among the houses. Proust pictures it as even more effective when it appears this way without the church. This effect of the steeple dominating the landscape reminds him that there are many others which look best this way, and he recalls vignettes of housetops with surmounting steeples in quite another category of art than those formed by the dreary streets of Combray.[119] He recollects, for instance, the similar scene of a quaint Norman town whose Gothic spire creates a charming picture by its contrast to the houses it crowned:

Je n'oublierai jamais, dans une curieuse ville de Normandie voisine de Balbec, deux charmants hôtels du XVIIIᵉ siècle, qui me sont à beaucoup d'égards chers et vénérables et entre lesquels, quand on la regarde du beau jardin qui descend des perrons vers la rivière, la flèche gothique d'une église qu'ils cachent s'élance, ayant l'air de terminer, de surmonter leurs façades, mais d'une matière si différente, si précieuse, si annelée, si rose, si vernie, qu'on voit bien qu'elle n'en fait pas plus partie que de deux beaux galets unis, entre lesquels elle est prise sur la plage, la flèche purpurine et crénelée de quelque coquillage fuselé en tourelle et glacé d'émail.[120]

This jewel-like quality of the steeple which Proust's poetic pen carefully describes in a series of interesting epithets is that which distinguishes it from the more domestic material of the houses. It should be understood that this showering of epithets is not a matter of coquetry but the progressive climax to a more subtle but clear impression. Furthermore, his analogy of this splendid appearance of the spires above the houses to the effect of two pebbles, between which had been washed on the beach, the purple crinkled spire of some seashell spun into a turret gay with glossy color, is an even more delicate refinement of his impression. Whether or not the object of perception lends itself to equivocal illusions, the spectator's poetic mind often forms mental images which diversify his vision of the scene.

[119] *Ibid.*   [120] *Ibid.*, pp. 98-99.

In this connection Proust recalls that in one of the ugliest parts of Paris there is a window from which one can see, across layers of roofs, a violet dome (St. Augustine's), sometimes ruddy and sometimes of an ashy black solution:

Même à Paris, dans un des quartiers les plus laids de la ville, je sais une fenêtre où on voit après un premier, un second et même un troisième plan fait des toits amoncelés de plusieurs rues, une cloche violette, parfois rougeâtre, parfois aussi, dans les plus nobles " épreuves " qu'en tire l'atmosphère, d'un noir décanté de cendres, laquelle n'est autre que le dôme Saint-Augustin et qui donne à cette vue de Paris le caractère de certaines vues de Rome par Piranesi.[121]

The imperious air of the cupola above the houses seems to give an aesthetic quality to this otherwise ugly part of town. The variegated color-tones of what is actually the dome of Saint-Augustine sketched by the atmosphere is that which imparts to the view the character of Piranesi's views of Rome. The dome of Saint-Augustine becomes the dome of Saint Peter. His representation of the steeple as violet seems a bit far-fetched but it perhaps symbolizes the approaching sunset whose crepuscular rays accent its more ruddy tones. On the other hand its ashy black appearance is most likely due to its contrast when outlined against a brightly illuminated sky. This substantive use of the color adjective such as " un noir " is one of Proust's favorite pictorial devices.

But since none of these little etchings are surrounded in his memory by the feeling which makes one not merely regard a thing as a spectacle, but believe in it as a being without parallel, so none of them possess a whole section of his inmost life as does the memory of those aspects of the steeple of Combray from the streets behind the church.[122] It is always to the steeple that one must return:

Qu'on le vît à cinq heures, quand on allait chercher les lettres à la poste, à quelques maisons de soi, à gauche, surélevant brusquement d'une cime isolée la ligne de faîte des toits; que si, au contraire, on voulait entrer demander des nouvelles de Mme Sazerat, on suivit des yeux cette ligne redevenue basse après la descente de son autre versant en sachant qu'il faudrait tourner à la deuxième rue après le clocher; soit qu'encore, poussant plus loin, si on allait à la gare, on le vît obliquement, montrant de profil des arêtes et des surfaces nouvelles comme un solide surpris à un moment inconnu de sa

[121] *Ibid.*, p. 99.   [122] *Ibid.*

révolution; ou que, des bords de la Vivonne, l'abside musculeusement ramassée et remontée par la perspective semblât jaillir de l'effort que le clocher faisait pour lancer sa flèche au coeur du ciel: c'était . . . toujours lui qui dominait tout, sommant les maisons d'un pinacle inattendu, levé devant moi comme le doigt de Dieu dont le corps eût été caché dans la foule des humains sans que je le confondisse pour cela avec elle.[123]

Our hero seems never to have wearied of the sight of this peaceful landscape and every change of perspective awakened new joy in his heart. This method of presenting a series of impressions of a single element of landscape reveals again the influence of the impressionist painter. For instance, Renoir painted the cathedral of Rouen as blue and yellow representing the atmosphere of different hours of the day. It is curious to note that these multiple aspects of a landscape are analogous to the fashion in which Proust's multiple personality is pursued.[124] His conception of the church as a guardian angel is further accented in his comparison of its steeple to " le doigt de Dieu." Incidentally, " *le doigt de Dieu* " is also one of Rodin's sculptures and is reminiscent of concepts of Victor Hugo. Also the Holy Spirit is designated as *digitus dextri patris* in the *Veni creator*.

Just as the old Balbec road remained in his memory as a loadstone to which all similar roads attached themselves, likewise, many years later the sight of a steeple bearing any resemblance to Saint Hilaire awakens sentimental analogies which his impassioned contemplation seeks to clarify:

Et aujourd'hui encore si, dans une grande ville de province ou dans un quartier de Paris que je connais mal, un passant qui m'a " mis dans mon chemin " me montre au loin, comme un point de repère, tel beffroi d'hôpital, tel clocher de couvent levant la pointe de son bonnet ecclésiastique au coin d'une rue que je dois prendre, pour peu que ma mémoire puisse obscurément lui trouver quelque trait de ressemblance avec la figure chère et disparue, le passant, s'il se retourne pour s'assurer que je ne m'égare pas, peut, à son étonnement, m'apercevoir qui, oublieux de la promenade entreprise ou de la course obligée, reste là, devant le clocher, pendant des heures, immobile, essayant de me souvenir, sentant au fond de moi des terres reconquises sur l'oubli qui s'assèchent et se rebâtissent; et sans doute alors, et plus anxieusement que tout à l'heure quand je lui demandais de me

[123] *Ibid.*   [124] Chernowitz, *op. cit.*, p. 148.

renseigner, je cherche encore mon chemin, je tourne une rue . . . mais . . . c'est dans mon coeur.[125]

Startled by impressions which he had formerly transformed poetically, haunted by memories which he enhanced into an ubiquity, Proust creates an introverted cosmos in his heart and mind.[126]

" Les aubépines "

Proust has been proclaimed a true poet of nature. Poets, like landscape painters, often display an instinctive preference for certain aspects of nature, but Proust like Turner has landscape at his command from the " meanest flower " to all the majesty of heaven. Evidence of this may be found in his delightful descriptions of the hawthorn blossoms which, though they are not landscapes as such, are " tableaux vivants " of the individual aspects of a garden town and merit attention in this study. In these colorful frescoes, painted with romantic, realistic, psychological, sentimental and imaginative elements, one may discern another phase of spiritualization. It is the poet's exalted adoration of the scenes observed that inspires their artistic recreation. He sings the praises of this newly found delight in a succession of inimitable pictures in which the magic of his poetry transfigures the hawthorns " à l'ombre des jeunes filles en fleurs." [127] Let us observe how his ecstatic imagination metaphorically transcribes their youthful, spiritual and feminine qualities:

C'est au mois de Marie que je me souviens d'avoir commencé à aimer les aubépines. N'étant pas seulement dans l'église si sainte, mais où nous avions le droit d'entrer, posées sur l'autel même, inséparables des mystères

---

[125] *S. I.*, p. 100.

[126] Cf. Robert Proust, *op. cit.*, pp. 114-122, for Proust's original sketch of " L'eglise de Village," cf. also *Ibid.*, pp. 94-96, for Proust's description of " La Cathédrale de Lisieux." Cf. also Polanscak's comments on Proust's representation of the Gothic church, *op. cit.*, pp. 65-67. Cf. Clermont-Tonnere, *Robert de Montesquiou et Marcel Proust* (Paris: Flammarion, 1925), p. 231, for Proust's letter to Montesquiou in which he elaborates his method of painting churches.

[127] Cf. Jean Pommier, *La Mystique de Marcel Proust* (Paris: Droz, 1939), pp. 35-38, for an explanation of Proust's symbolic transformation of flowers.

à la célébration desquels elles prenaient part, elles faisaient courir au milieu des flambeaux et des vases sacrés leurs branches attachées horizontalement les unes aux autres en un apprêt de fête, et qu'enjolivaient encore les festons de leur feuillage sur lequel étaient semés à profusion, comme sur une traîne de mariée, de petits bouquets de boutons d'une blancheur éclatante. Mais, sans oser les regarder qu'à la dérobée, je sentais que ces apprêts pompeux étaient vivants et que c'était la nature elle-même qui, en creusant ces découpures dans les feuilles, en ajoutant l'ornement suprême de ces blancs boutons, avait rendu cette décoration digne de ce qui était à la fois une réjouissance populaire et une solennité mystique. Plus haut s'ouvraient leurs corolles çà et là avec une grâce insouciante, retenant si négligemment comme un dernier et vaporeux atour le bouquet d'étamines, fines comme des fils de la Vierge, qui les embrumait tout entières, qu'en suivant, qu'en essayant de mimer au fond de moi le geste de leur efflorescence, je l'imaginais comme si ç'avait été le mouvement de tête étourdi et rapide, au regard coquet, aux pupilles diminuées, d'une blanche jeune fille, distraite et vive.[128]

It was during the month of Mary that he first fell in love with the hawthorn blossoms and it is probably for this reason that, in his mind, they became forever linked with religious ceremonies. This start is tremendous because it puts these flowers under the aspect of Eternity. In the first sentence, which gives the keynote to his entire impression, several themes are introduced simultaneously. "Le mois de Marie" suggests at once spring (nature), religion (the Virgin Mary), and woman in her purest aspect (the Virgin Mary). The hawthorns link the "secular glories of the one and the holy rites of the other."[129] Appearing on the church altar, they are inseparable from the mysteries in whose celebration they are taking part. They are dressed for the festival of nature, in white buds and scalloped leaves and, likewise, they are dressed by nature for the festival of religion. "Nature has wrought the miracle of spring and blossom time mysteriously, in preparation for the religious mysteries which are being celebrated. Moreover, the hawthorns' dress is likened to the train of a bride thus echoing the Virgin theme, and symbolizing spring, the bride time of the year."[130] This metaphoric imagery suggests the collaboration of the nature festival

---

[128] *S. I.*, pp. 163-164.

[129] D. Adelson, "Proust's Styles," *Romanic Review*, XXXIV (1943), p. 135.

[130] *Ibid.*

of spring and the religious festival of Easter elaborated in the following sentence:

Mais sans oser les regarder qu'à la derobée, je sentais que ces apprêts pompeux étaient vivants et que c'était la nature elle-même qui, en creusant ces découpures dans les feuilles en ajoutant l'ornement suprême de ces blancs boutons, avait rendu cette décoration digne de ce qui était à la fois une réjouissance populaire et une solennité mystique.[131]

In a sort of pantheistic fervor he vivifies the scene by representing the vitality of nature as inextricably mingled with supernatural powers (religious mysteries). It is nature herself who by trimming the shape of the foliage and adding the crowning ornament of those snowy buds makes the decorations worthy of what is at once a public rejoicing and a solemn mystery. The narrator finds the mysteries of religion mirrored in nature. This "paganism" involves morè than Francis Jammes' method of superposing simply the ecclesiastical year upon the natural year.

Proust sees in this spectacle an interpenetration of natural and supernatural phenomena but he appears insensitive to the real significance of their collaboration. He does not seek any cause for these effects but simply presents nature and religion as entities which for some mysterious reason appear inseparable upon this occasion. He could have added a truly great spiritual import to the scene, had he traced the origin of both to a common source—a superior being in the realm of the supernatural. Instead, nature as such appears to be the superior force and the mysteries wrought by it apparently have not stimulated an investigation of their cause.

However, " because a young bride too is a mysterious creature, with something of the same miracle about her as surrounds spring and the Resurrection, the hawthorn in the last sentence, with a final leap of the imagination, is transformed into a lovely young girl in white, symbolizing, in the half-shy, half-daring coquetry of an innocence just about to burst out of the bud—the recurring mysteries of life—spring, religion and woman." [132] Here there is also the interplay of chastity and motherhood as introduced in the

---

[131] *S. I.*, p. 164.

[132] D. Adelson, *op. cit.*, p. 135. Cf. also I. Tiedtke, *Symbole und Bilder in Werke Marcel Prousts* (Hamburg: Ewert, 1936).

beginning in the Virgin Mary motif. This transfiguration of the hawthorn into a young bride was previously hinted in his description of its dress as " la traîne de mariée " and which he now pictures as " les fils de la Vierge." His concept of an occasion simultaneously a public festivity and a solemn mystery carries the bridal theme to the celebration of the wedding, all of which justifies his image of " une blanche jeune fille." The carelessly graceful movement of the blossoms is that which animates the scene and accents the impression of an enticing young girl indifferent and alive. There is alliterative value in his unique simile " fine comme des fils de la Vierge."

Now it is interesting to observe how the various motives (spring, religion and woman) are constructively illuminated from different angles which show the object of comparison in new ways. Sometime later when walking with his parents the young boy finds a whole path throbbing with the odor of hawthorns:

La haie formait comme une suite de chapelles qui disparaissaient sous la jonchée de leurs fleurs amoncelées en reposoir; au-dessous d'elles, le soleil posait à terre un quadrillage de clarté, comme s'il venait de traverser une verrière; leur parfum s'étendait aussi onctueux, aussi délimité en sa forme que si j'eusse été devant l'autel de la Vierge . . .[133]

Because the beauty of the hawthorns first attracted his attention and affection during the month of Mary's services, the sight of a whole hedge of them now suggests a series of chapels whose walls are no longer visible under the mountains of flowers heaped upon their altars. This architectural effect is accented by the play of light which gives the illusion of shining in through a window: " le soleil posait à terre un quadrillage de clarté, comme s'il venait de traverser une verrière." Furthermore, the scent of the flowers, " aussi onctueux," he finds reminiscent of the incense burned during certain religious ceremonies and all this gives him the impression of standing before " l'autel de la Vierge." He has borrowed the religious motif from the previous scene and by a connecting of metaphors renders visible the plastic beauty of his impression—a musical way of interweaving motives. The architectural aspect of this floral array is discernible even in the flowers themselves, whose

[133] *S. I.*, p. 200.

flamboyant style is comparable to those which in church frame the stair to the rood-loft or close the perpendicular tracery of the windows:

> . . . les fleurs, ainsi parées, tenaient chacune d'un air distrait son étincelant bouquet d'étamines fines et rayonnantes nervures de style flamboyant comme celles qui à l'église ajouraient la rampe du jubé ou les meneaux du vitrail et qui s'épanouissaient en blanche chair de fleur de fraisier.[134]

The epithets—étincelant, fin, rayonnant—which glorify the stamens, mirror the concept of the florid and showy French late Gothic " style flamboyant." In the last sentence the use of " chair " to specify the unusual character of the white of the strawberry blossom gives a sensuous quality to the substance of the hawthorn.[135] The effect produced by this last comparison is pictorial.

Antithesis is a favorite device used by Proust to make more striking the object portrayed; thus he emphasizes the elegance of the hawthorns by contrasting them to the simple and rustic dog-roses which would be climbing the same path in a few weeks:

> Combien naïves et paysannes en comparaison sembleraient les églantines qui dans quelques semaines, monteraient elles aussi en plein soleil le même chemin rustique, en la soie unie de leur corsage rougissant qu'un souffle défait.[136]

Proust's landscapes are never represented through observation alone but in conjunction with his sensitive and penetrating introspection and retrospection. In the following passage his effort to project himself and his imagination into this floral spectacle reveals his empathetic attitude toward the scene: [137]

> Mais j'avais beau rester devant les aubépines à respirer, à porter devant ma pensée qui ne savait ce qu'elle devait en faire, à perdre, à retrouver leur invisible et fixe odeur, à m'unir au rythme qui jetait leurs fleurs, ici et là, avec une allégresse juvénile et à des intervalles inattendus comme certains intervalles musicaux, elles m'offraient indéfiniment le même charme avec

---

[134] *Ibid.*

[135] Cf. *S. I.*, p. 244, for a similar use of the " gustatory " image to describe a flower. Paul Souday, *Marcel Proust* (Paris: Simon Kra, 1927), p. 14, says that this perception is eminently Ruskinian.

[136] *S. I.*, p. 200.

[137] Cf. *supra*, pp. 44, 54, for other unusual examples of literary empathy.

une profusion inépuisable, mais sans me le laisser approfondir davantage, comme ces mélodies qu'on rejoue cent fois de suite sans descendre plus avant dans leur secret. Je me détournais d'elles un moment, pour les aborder ensuite avec des forces plus fraîches.[138]

In order to recapture the enchanting fragrance of these blossoms, he tries to absorb himself in the rhythm which their flowers emitted here and there. But a wall of darkness shrouds from him the still unknown for though this charm of the flowers offers itself indefinitely in an inexhaustible profusion, it occurs at intervals as unexpected as certain intervals of music and will not allow him to delve into it any more deeply than those melodies which one can play over a hundred times in succession without coming any nearer to their secret.[139]

Proust's elaboration of an olfactory experience in auditory terms suggests an imaginative use of the sense analogies rather than a genuine duality of sensory impressions. Such synaesthetic phrasing gives a more intimate understanding of the poet's inner perception and emotive patterns.

But since Proust's aesthetics preaches that a complete interpenetration of the exterior world and the interior vision, i. e. subject and object, is necessary to reach the totality of an impression, he makes a still greater effort to unveil the mysterious charm of these flowers by turning away from them for a moment so as to gather renewed strength and return to them as a "tabula rasa." The psychological pattern here is similar to his perception of the landscape of the three trees along the Balbec road.[140] When he returns, he contemplates the scene as one contemplates a masterpiece of painting which, one imagines, one will be better able to absorb when one has looked away for a moment.[141] Even for Proust, the real lover of nature, the interpretation of nature through art and culture is a thing very normal just as it was for all French writers from Charles d'Orléans to Honoré de Balzac. But it is in vain that he shapes his fingers into a frame so as to have nothing but the hawthorns before his eyes: the sentiment which they arouse in him remains obscure and vague and refuses to project itself and to

---

[138] *S. I.*, p. 200.
[139] Cf. *supra*, p. 42.
[140] *Ibid.* Cf. also *JF. II.*, p. 162.
[141] *S. I.*, p. 201.

become one with the flowers. They themselves offer him no enlight-
enment and he cannot yet penetrate the depth of his impression.[142]
But Proust's art-parallelism transcends that of his predecessors.
Art for him is synonymous with immortality; therefore, by placing
nature in the realm of art he receives unique joy in the contemplation
of its beauty.[143]

The poet's mysterious longing is not satisfied until suddenly the
apparition of a particularly lovely pink hawthorn excites a " véritable extase "—a spontaneous overflow of emotion in which the
lyrical impulses of his soul seek and find expression.[144] Proust
renders this joy in its essential quality by analyzing it into its
personal elements:

Alors me donnant cette joie que nous éprouvons quand nous voyons de notre
peintre préféré un oeuvre qui diffère de celles que nous connaissions, ou
bien si l'on nous mène devant un tableau dont nous n'avions vu jusque-là
qu'une esquisse au crayon, si un morceau entendu seulement au piano nous
apparaît ensuite revêtu des couleurs de l'orchestre, mon grand-père m'ap-
pelant et me désignant la haie de Tansonville, me dit: " Toi qui aimes les
aubépines, regarde un peu cette épine rose; est-elle jolie! [145]

Even the singularity of the sensation evoked by the sight of this
pink flower he interprets through art associations.   For instance,
he explains that he was inspired with a rapture analogous to the
feeling he has at seeing the work of a favorite painter different
from any already known, or a picture of which he has seen only the
pencilled sketch, or at hearing the full orchestration of a piece of
music heard only on the piano. This emotional parallelism indicates
that the diverse individualities of music and painting increased
Proust's capacity for enjoying life intellectually and emotionally.[146]

[142] *Ibid.*

[143] Cf. Pierre-Quint, *op. cit.*, pp. 253-265, for Proust's conception of " L'art
et le sentiment du divin."

[144] Here again the psychological significance of the scene is in the
" révélation " of the unique beauty of the " épine rose " which puts the
spectator in a sort of trance.

[145] *S. I.*, p. 201.

[146] Cf. Irving Babbitt, *The New Laokoon* (New York: Houghton Mifflin Company, 1910), p. 146, for remarks on the emotional complex of the
different sense impressions.

At the same time it elaborates his impression of the scene as a work of art—one of Nature's masterpieces.

In the passage above cited the writer also communicates the impression that the pink hawthorn is the apotheosis of the species already observed. It is his favorite flower but different from those previously admired. The other flowers were merely the sketch: this is the finished picture. It is the full orchestration of a piece heard on the piano. He thus minimizes the beauty of the white hawthorn which remained silent to his musings and exalts this pink blossom whose fullness and splendour immediately reveals itself to him. The fact that he cannot do as much with the white blossom is proof that taste and emotion belong to a series of higher passive sensations of the " souvenir " type which one cannot evoke but which are evoked in one by a mysterious force. This " Bildnis " of reality is virtual poetry and its inspiration parallels that of the mystic which Bremond treats in his *Prière et Poésie*. His inner vision thus unclouded he transposes the " épine rose " into a series of poetic images:

En effet c'était une épine, mais rose, plus belle encore que les blanches. Elle aussi avait une parure de fête,—de ces seules vraies fêtes que sont les fêtes religieuses, puisqu'un caprice contingent ne les applique pas comme les fêtes mondaines à un jour quelconque qui ne leur est pas spécialement destiné, qui n'a rien d'essentiellement férié,—mais une parure plus riche encore, car les fleurs attachées sur la branche, les unes au-dessus des autres, de manière à ne laisser aucune place qui ne fût décorée, comme des pompons qui enguirlandent une houlette rococo, étaient " en couleur," par conséquent d'une qualité supérieure selon l'esthétique de Combray, si l'on en jugeait par l'échelle des prix dans le " magasin " de la Place ou chez Camus où étaient plus chers ceux des biscuits qui étaient roses. Moi-même j'appréciais plus le fromage à la crème rose, celui où l'on m'avait permis d'écraser des fraises.[147]

His heart warm with thoughts of the hawthorn whose blossoms were pink and lovelier than the white, his mind rockets back to the " sub specie aeternitatis " of his first impression to which he gives an even more elevated poetic effect. In the main sentence " aussi " indicates the comparative element of the scene and " une parure de fête " strikes a familiar chord whose overtones will elaborate the fullness of his original vision. Again he depicts the flower in terms

[147] *S. I.*, pp. 201-202.

5

of imagery drawn from religious and sentimental associations; again it is metaphorically treated as gowned in holiday attire—this time he distinguishes the celebration as exclusively religious. His reference to " les fêtes religieuses " gives a double connotation to the spectacle—one festive, the other religious—each of which blossoms into all manner of images. The festal aspect of the picture is well supported by his repetition of the key word " fête " and the religious nature of the occasion is accented in the ecclesiastical word " férié."

Now this picture of the hawthorn carries with it the author's idea that the only true holidays are holy days of religion because they are not appointed by a capricious accident, as secular holidays are appointed, upon days which are not especially ordained for such observances, and which have nothing about them essentially festal.[148] Since this particular flower appears created for such a special event, it is attired even more richly than the rest. His representation of the blossoms clinging to their branches one above the other like the tassels wreathed about the crook of a rococo shepherdess gives a perspective into the history of France and indicates a certain voluptuous lightness of Proust's mind in the midst of an almost " sacred " experience.

Even more curious in his evaluation of the quality of the flowers according to the aesthetic standards of Combray which he judged by the scale of prices at the stores where the most expensive biscuits were those whose sugar was pink. His use of color to estimate the value of the flowers is sentimental rather than decorative. Ever since his childhood the environment in which he lived and loved influenced greatly his feelings for the simplest things of life. Therefore, now in this impression he disengages certain features from their compositional context (in this case color) and gives to their beauty a value in terms of past associations. As, for example, he places a higher value on this pink hawthorn blossom than on the white one because at Combray he had placed a higher value on cream cheese when it was pink, when he had been allowed to tinge it with crushed strawberries.[149] Such sentimental color analogy links the scene more intimately with his past life.

The fact that he places such a special value on these flowers which have chosen the color of edible and delicious things reflects his acute interest in gastronomy. The festal theme gains monmentum here as good food is usually part of any festive occasion. But also he finds the color of the floral display comparable to some exquisite addition to one's costume whose beauty is most striking to the eye. In this confusion of sense impressions he writes that because of their superiority these colors always seem more vivid and more natural than any other tints, even after the mind has realized that they offer no gratification to the appetite and have not been selected by the dressmaker.[105] Proust revels in this vitality of nature mingled with one's personal life.

The unusual loveliness of this pink flower he attributes to the " évolution créatrice " of nature :

Et certes, je l'avais tout de suite senti, comme devant les épines blanches, mais avec plus d'émerveillement, que ce n'était pas facticement, par un artifice de fabrication humaine, qu'était traduite l'intention de festivité dans les fleurs, mais que c'était la nature qui, spontanément, l'avait exprimée avec la naïveté d'une commerçante de village travaillant pour un reposoir, en surchargeant l'arbuste de ces rosettes d'un ton trop tendre et d'un pompadour provincial.[151]

Again nature has spontaneously prepared itself for the festivities in which it takes part. Furthermore, he adds a charming note of simplicity to the scene by perceiving in the work of nature the " naïveté " of a country woman decorating a street altar for some procession. At the end of the sentence, the phrase " un pompadour provincial " accents this simplicity and merges the earlier rococo theme (houlette) and the rural theme (aesthetics of Combray). In the next sentence with a rather voluptuous splash of color he again fuses the leading motifs in the expression " fêtes religieuses " and pictures the hawthorns as something artistic, rural and ecclesiastical :

Au haut des branches, comme autant de ces petits rosiers aux pots cachés dans des papiers en dentelles, dont aux grandes fêtes on faisait rayonner sur l'autel les minces fusées, pullulaient milles petits boutons d'un teint plus pâle qui, en s'entr'ouvrant, laissaient voir, comme au fond d'une coupe de marbre rose, de rouges sanguines et trahissaient plus encore que les fleurs, l'essence particulière, irrésistible, de l'épine, qui, partout où elle bourgeonnait, où elle allait fleurir, ne le pouvait qu'en rose.[152]

---

[150] *Ibid.*   [151] *Ibid.*, pp. 202-203.   [152] *Ibid.*, p. 203.

The " pots cachés dans des papiers en dentelles " indicates their
dress for the " grandes fêtes " and " l'autel " connotes the place and
the religious aspect of the celebration about to take place.   The
artistic effect of the buds disclosing, as they open, blood red stain
as at the bottom of a cup of pink marble, appears to mirror the
mysteries of the religious celebration.   Their form as " une coupe
de marbre rose " may have been suggested to him by thoughts of
the chalice and " rouge sanguine " by the Most Blessed Sacrament
(Precious Blood) worshipped upon the altar.   It may be, however,
also a remembrance of beautiful glasses of red marble with shades
of pink in them.   The special " rouge sanguine " gives a very strong
sensuous quality to the picture.   In addition to its rich poetic
quality this outburst of metaphoric eloquence is evidence of a
profound intellectual penetration into the scene.

Proust has tenderly built up and elaborated the spiritual loveliness of the hawthorns, and now in the last sentence he presents us
with a very vivid concrete picture.   He recapitulates all the earlier
motifs in a condensed kaleidoscope and ends " globally " with the
religious motif with which he started:

Intercalé dans la haie, mais aussi différent d'elle qu'une jeune fille en robe
de fête au milieu de personnes en négligé qui resteront à la maison tout
prêt pour le mois de Marie, dont il semblait faire partie déjà, tel brillait
en souriant dans sa fraîche toilette rose, l'arbuste catholique et délicieux.[153]

This " jeune fille en robe de fête " is reminiscent of the " blanche
jeune fille " of his first acquaintance with the hawthorns.   " Robe de
fête " carries the image of " une traîne de mariée " and their appearance as " tout prêt pour le mois de Marie, dont il semblait faire
partie déjà " supports his original conception that the flowers are
inseparable from the mysteries in whose celebration they are taking
part.   Their contrast to a crowd of dowdy women in everyday
clothes is just another expression of their elegance.

In this final personification his poetic patterns are crystallized
and welded forever into a spiritual impression.   He artfully blends
and gives finality to the religious-festal motif in the locution
" l'arbuste catholique et délicieux."   The religious motif is given
finality in " catholique " and the festive motif in " délicieux."

[153] *Ibid.*

Though the Catholic idea has been suggested throughout his portrayal of the " aubépines " it is not until the final rounding up of ideas that he specifies its religious significance as " catholique." Spiritualization thus has been accomplished again, for his artistic expression of this element of landscape is more than the pictorial transposition of a scene. It is the sonorous manifestation of a spiritual relation exactly executed.

Sometime later, when it was necessary for the narrator to leave Combray and the " aubépines," we find him in a state of intoxication pledging his eternal affection for them:

" O mes pauvres petites aubépines, . . . ce n'est pas vous qui voudriez me faire du châgrin, me forcer à partir. Vous, vous ne m'avez jamais fait de peine! Aussi je vous aimerai toujours." Et, essuyant mes larmes, je leur promettais, quand je serais grand, de ne pas imiter la vie insensée des autres hommes et, même à Paris, les jours de printemps, au lieu d'aller faire des visites et écouter des niaiseries de partir dans la campagne voir les premières aubépines.[154]

It is evident from the passages examined in this chapter that Proust first evokes a landscape, studies it, and then paints it in all its ephemeral details. It is notable also that in these landscapes he never makes a fundamental distinction between a present scene and the sudden reappearance in memory of a scene from the past. He projects the elements of a memory landscape to contemplate them as purely as he contemplates a scene under direct observation. Compare, for example, his intuitive contemplation of the steeples of Martinville with his meditation over the resurrection of Combray. The result of the psychological experience in both cases is the artistic reconstitution of a landscape, the difference being only a question of *impressions* in the one case and of *reminiscences* in the other.[155]

However, whether his landscape impressions were objective such as he received from the sight of the trees along the Balbec road and the hawthorns of Méséglise or subjective memories as those awakened by the unevenness of the two flagstones he tried to bring out the obscurity of what he had felt and convert it into a spiritual

---

[154] *Ibid.*, p. 210. Cf. also Robert Proust, *op. cit.*, pp. 92-99, for Proust's original sketch of the hawthorn blossoms.

[155] *TR. II.*, p. 24.

equivalent. This method was to him the creating of a work of art— [156] his key to immortality. The spontaneity with which these scenes came to his mind he felt was the mark of their genuineness:

Mais justement la façon fortuite, inévitable, dont la sensation avait été rencontrée, contrôlait la vérité d'un passé qu'elle ressuscitait, des images qu'elle déclenchait, puisque nous sentions son effort pour remonter vers la lumière, que nous sentons la joie du réel retrouvé." [157]

Thus through the involuntary resurrection of landscapes from the past Proust has " retrouvé le temps perdu " and eternalized it in the language of his novel.

[156] *Ibid.*
[157] *Ibid.*, p 25.

CHAPTER III

LANDSCAPE IN PAINTING

We have observed that the landscape of Proust's childhood days was the source and inspiration of much of his work. Now we shall examine how the painted landscape supplemented reality and became an important source of his interest in the various aspects of natural scenery. In his novel it is the medium for the expression and exhibition of many of his literary methods.

Elstir

In his portrayal of Elstir, Proust presents an artist " whose work, whose particular vision and sensibility has profoundly influenced his own way of experiencing life and provided the mode which was to guide his literary efforts." [1] Consequently, the scenes painted by Elstir represent Proust's own efforts as a landscape artist and reveal " an essential and organic relation to the entire novel and to the author's own view of life." [2] We are confronted here with a case similar to Zola's *L'Oeuvre*, where Manet's art is the inspiration for Zola's literary impressionism.

The identification of Elstir has evoked an enormous amount of controversy among literary and art critics. As it is not the purpose of this study to draw conclusions on this particular subject, we will note briefly the most interesting observations of Proustian scholars.

Chernowitz and Feuillerat appear to have made the most profound analyses of this subject. Feuillerat shows " that in the original manuscript version of *A la recherche du temps perdu* completed in 1912 Proust had already conceived Elstir and his art as very significant." [3] Chernowitz adds, after a study of this early version, that " although Elstir's commentary on the church at

---

[1] Chernowitz, *op. cit.*, p. 96.

[2] *Ibid.*

[3] Albert Feuillerat, *Comment Marcel Proust a composée son roman* (New Haven: Yale University Press, 1934), p. 55, quoted in Chernowitz, *op. cit.*, p. 100.

Balbec, showing the narrator the beauty of the façade, was characteristic of Ruskin and Emile Mâle, Elstir's dominant characteristic in the first version was almost without admixture that of an
Impressionist painter being a composite of Manet, Pissarro, Whistler, and Monet." [4]   Feuillerat further comments "that several
pictures described correspond exactly, at least in genre and general
impression, to some of the famous paintings of Monet." [5]   The
particular water color which he names " La Falaise Rose," and
which we will examine later, he says recalls Monet's " Les Hautes
Falaises d'Etretat." He adds " that in a general way Elstir's views
of the " mer pâlie " vaporized by the sun, the sensation of the
torpidity of things by intense heat, the opposition of " ombres
fraîches " and of " luminosité radieuse " are all very characteristic
of the seascapes of Monet." [6]   In fact Monet, Manet and other
Impressionist painters have pictured seascapes exactly like these. [7]
In this first manuscript, which has remained partly unpublished,
we may find that it was such pictures of Elstir which permitted
Proust to love " les choses naturelles " to which he had previously
paid no attention. [8]   " A water color instills in him the desire to
see again in real life scenes of the ocean where the bathers and the
yachts are an integral part of the view . . . furthermore, Elstir's
studies render the narrator less restricted in his tastes by bringing
out the charms of a provincial French town, such as ' des scènes
pittoresques de la vie populaire familièrement dominées au-dessus
du marché, du magasin de bonneterie ou du grand café, par deux
vieilles tours abbatiales . . .' [9]   Here Proust may have thought of
Pissarro's pictures, for the latter painted market scenes and fairs
in village squares in Rouen and elsewhere that show a perfect
knowledge of provincial life." [10]

On the other hand, Bussom in his article " Proust and Painting "

[4] Chernowitz, *op. cit.*, p. 100.

[5] Feuillerat, *op. cit.*, p. 61.

[6] *Ibid.*, cf. also Chernowitz, *op. cit.*, p. 102. Cf. also Polanscak, *op. cit.*,
pp. 21-27, for further comments on the identification of Elstir with the
Impressionist painters.

[7] Chernowitz, *op. cit.*, p. 101.

[8] *Ibid.*, p. 100, cf. also Feuillerat, *op. cit.*, p. 56.

[9] *Ibid.*, p. 55, cited in Chernowitz, *op. cit.*, p. 101.

[10] *Ibid.*, p. 101, cf. also footnote 41, p. 212.

writes that Elstir's attitude is more that of Cézanne who painted
nature from his own peculiar and individual vision and in the way
in which objects are "inter-related and fused in a more definitely
plastic organization."[11] He says that Proust was interested in the
colors but not the "smudging" or the "pointilleux" technique of
the impressionists.[12] Thus scholars have not only emphasized the
great significance of Elstir in Proust's novel, but also the influence
of the Impressionist and post-Impressionist painters in his creation
of this artist. In this way they have revealed the original source of
Proust's interest in these particular aspects of nature and his
literary methods of representing them.

Elstir's Pictorial Methods

It is important to know something of the characteristic elements
of Elstir's art before we can reach a sympathetic understanding and
appreciation of his landscapes. The narrator himself, upon entering
Elstir's studio, anticipates a poetical understanding of many forms
of nature which he had never isolated from the general spectacle
of reality.[13] Likewise, by a sort of reciprocal illumination, we may
anticipate a more poetical understanding of Proust's literary efforts
—especially in his landscapes—through an investigation of Elstir's
art. Chernowitz, in his *Proust and Painting,* has treated this
subject so thoroughly that it seems fitting at this point to refer the
reader to his analysis.[14] His chapter on Elstir has been of infinite
value to a study of this group of Proust's landscapes and also to an
understanding of his artistic ideas and methods. Therefore, much
of it merits repetition here.

Chernowitz points out that the outstanding characteristic of
"Elstir's art was the fact that although he was very learned, he
deliberately started with a *tabula rasa* in order to paint things as
they appeared at the first moment,—' le seul vrai, où notre intelligence n'était pas encore intervenue pour expliquer ce qu'elles sont,
nous ne substituons pas à l'impression qu'elles nous ont donnée les

[11] T. W. Bussom, "Proust and Painting," *Romanic Review,* XXXIV
(1943), p. 61.
[12] *Ibid.,* p. 62.
[13] *JF. III.,* p. 97.
[14] Chernowitz, *op. cit.,* pp. 89-119.

notions que nous avons d'elles." [15]   He adds that this is a fundamental of impressionist art. But apparently the idea was not exclusive to impressionism as Rousseau, Wordsworth and Wagner were
pervaded by the fear that the meddling intellect was fatal to
spontaneity.[16] "Moreover, Elstir would compose his pictures entirely 'avec des parcelles de realité, qui toutes avaient été person-
nellement senties,' so that everything seemed uniformly produced
by the same vision, responding furthermore to that unity of nature
which was imposing at that hour its optic law." [17]

"No subject is too humble for Elstir who discovers and reveals
the previously unperceived charm of simple things. He teaches
the narrator to see things anew." [18] Thus Elstir's studio impresses
the young poet as "le laboratoire d'une sorte de nouvelle création
du monde" [19] in which from the chaos of all the things we see, he
extracts, by painting them on various canvases, a wave of the sea
crushing angrily on the sand its lilac foam, or a young man in a
white linen suit leaning upon the rail of a vessel, etc., all of which
acquire a new dignity "in artistic life" from the fact that they
continue to exist.[20]

Almost all the discoveries made by the narrator in the studio
consisted of seascapes done at Balbec. He observed that the charm
of each of them lay in a sort of metamorphosis of the things represented in them, analogous to what in poetry one calls metaphor;
and that if God the Father had created things by naming them, it
was by taking away their names or giving them other names that
Elstir recreated them.[21] The names which denote things correspond
invariably to an intellectual notion, alien to our true impressions
and compelling us to eliminate from them everything that is not
in keeping with itself. As for example, the narrator explains that
from his hotel window at Balbec he had often been led by some
effect of sunlight to mistake what was only a darker stretch of sea

[15] *Ibid.*, p. 102, quoted from Feuillerat *op. cit.*, p. 56.
[16] I. Babbitt, *op. cit.*, p. 107.
[17] Chernowitz, *op. cit.*, p. 103.
[18] *Ibid.*, pp. 103-104.
[19] *JF. III.*, p. 97.
[20] *Ibid.* Cf. also Chernowitz, *op. cit.*, p. 111.
[21] *JF. III.*, p. 98.

for a distant coastline, or to gaze at a belt of liquid azure without knowing whether it belonged to sea or sky. But finally his reason would re-establish between the elements that distinction which in his first impression he had overlooked.[22] Now Elstir's work is taken from those rare moments in which one sees nature " poétique-ment." [23] " He abdicates his intellect and learning so as to abandon himself more completely to pure sensation and thus he sees things not as they are, but as they appear during the split second of his first glance at them." [24] Therefore, he makes an effort to reproduce things not as he knows them to be, but according to the optical illusions of which this first sight of them is composed.[25]

In this connection Chernowitz writes:

The ' équivoques ' of Elstir are of two kinds. One is the mirage type which makes us wonder whether we see a real tower or its reflection in the water, an effect which so fascinated Claude Monet that, as his art pro-gressed, the element of water became less and less visible as such and was there only to reflect the sky. Monet was indeed unusually sensitive to the interpenetrability of all elements, water, air, earth and stone. The other kind of ' équivoque ' is one of natural staging, where the deceptive illusion is due to the odd angle of perspective from which the scene is viewed. It is the second type of illusion that Proust elaborates in his last version of Elstir. He has found a felicitous epithet for both types of deceptive effects, which he now calls ' métaphore.' [26]

He occasionally combines these two types of illusion in a single sentence, as in the following harbor scene: " Des hommes qui poussaient des bateaux à la mer, couraient aussi bien dans les flots que sur le sable, lequel mouillé, réfléchissait déjà les coques comme s'il avait été de l'eau " [27]—and there are many other similar ex-amples. It should be noted that it is the pictorial rather than the literary metaphor that he employs to represent such scenes.

[22] *Ibid.*
[23] *Ibid.*, p. 99.
[24] Chernowitz, *op. cit.*, pp. 104-105. Cf. also Van Meter Ames, *Proust and Santayana* (New York: Willett Clark and Company, 1937), p. 78, for additional remarks on Elstir's pictorial representation of exterior reality.
[25] *JF. III.*, p. 103. Cf. also Chernowitz *op. cit.*, p. 105.
[26] *Ibid.*, p. 107.
[27] *JF. III.*, p. 100.

" Le Port de Carquethuit "

One of the metaphors observed most often in Elstir's seascapes is
that which comparing land and sea, suppresses every line of demarcation between them. He even goes so far as to interchange land
and sea in his pictorial technique. This actually is his metaphorism.
It is this comparison, untiringly repeated on a single canvas, which
gives it a multiform and powerful unity. It is for this type of
metaphor—in a picture of the harbor of Carquethuit—that Elstir
prepares the mind of the spectator by using only marine terms for
the little town, and urban terms for the sea.[28] Chernowitz points
out that " the painting may be imaginary, but it is described to the
reader in such skillful sequence as to reconstruct the visual experience of the spectator as he moves from one surprising aspect
to another." [29] His images are spontaneous but he does not stop
at his first impression:

Soit que les maisons cachassent une partie du port, un bassin de calfatage
ou peut-être la mer même s'enfonçant en golfe dans les terres ainsi que
cela arrivait constamment dans ce pays de Balbec, de l'autre côté de la
pointe avancée où était construite la ville, les toits étaient dépassés (comme
ils l'eussent été par des cheminées ou par des clochers) par des mâts
lesquels avaient l'air de faire des vaisseaux auxquels ils appartenaient,
quelque chose de citadin, de construit sur terre, impression qu'augmentaient
d'autres bateaux, demeurés le long de la jetée, mais en rangs si pressés que
les hommes y causaient d'un bâtiment à l'autre sans qu'on pût distinguer
leur séparation et l'interstice de l'eau, et ainsi cette flottille de pêche avait
moins l'air d'appartenir à la mer que, par exemple, les églises de Criquebec
qui, au loin, entourées d'eau de tous côtés parce qu'on les voyait sans la
ville, dans un poudroiement de soleil et de vagues, semblaient sortir des
eaux, soufflées en albâtre ou en écume et, enfermées dans la ceinture d'un
arc-en-ciel versicolore, former un tableau irréel et mystique. Dans le
premier plan de la plage, le peintre avait su habituer les yeux à ne pas
reconnaître de frontière fixe, de démarcation absolue, entre la terre et
l'océan. Des hommes qui poussaient des bateaux à la mer, couraient aussi
bien dans les flots que sur le sable, lequel mouillé, réfléchissait déjà les
coques comme s'il avait été de l'eau. La mer elle-même ne montait pas
régulièrement, mais suivait les accidents de la grève, que la perspective
déchiquetait encore davantage, si bien qu'un navire en pleine mer, à demi-
caché par les ouvrages avancés de l'arsénal semblait voguer au milieu de

---

[28] *Ibid.*, p. 99.   [29] Chernowitz, *op. cit.*, p. 108.

la ville; des femmes qui ramassaient des crevettes dans les rochers, avaient l'air parce qu'elles étaient entourées d'eau et à cause de la dépression qui, après la barrière circulaire des roches, abaissait la plage (des deux côtés les plus rapprochés de terre), au niveau de la mer, d'être dans une grotte marine surplombée de barques et de vagues, ouverte et protégée au milieu des flots écartés miraculeusement.[30]

One may observe that on the beach in the foreground the painter has arranged that the eye should discover no fixed frontier between land and sea—the two penetrate each other reciprocally. The whole picture gives the impression of harbors in which the sea enters into the land and in which the land is already subaqueous and the population amphibian. The marine element is everywhere apparent:

. . . et près des rochers, à l'entrée de la jetée, où la mer était agitée, on sentait aux efforts des matelots et à l'obliquité des barques couchées en angle aigu devant la calme verticalité de l'entrepôt, de l'église, des maisons de la ville, où les uns rentraient, d'où les autres partaient pour la pêche, qu'ils trottaient rudement sur l'eau comme sur un animal fougueux et rapide dont les soubresauts, sans leur adresse, les eût jetés à terre. Une bande de promeneurs sortaient gaiement en une barque secouée comme une carriole; une matelot joyeux mais attentif aussi la gouvernait comme avec des guides, menait la voile fougueuse, chacun se tenait bien à sa place pour ne pas faire trop de poids d'un côté et ne pas verser, et on courait ainsi par les champs ensoleillés dans les sites ombreux, dégringolant les pentes. C'était une belle matinée malgré l'orage qu'il avait fait. Et même on sentait encore les puissantes actions qu'avait à neutraliser le bel équilibre des barques immobiles, jouissant du soleil et de la fraîcheur, dans les parties où la mer était si calme que les reflets avaient presque plus de solidité et de réalité que les coques vaporisées par un effet de soleil et que la perspective faisait s'enjamber les unes les autres. Ou plutôt on n'aurait pas dit d'autres parties de la mer. Car entre ces parties, il y avait autant de différence qu'entre l'une d'elles et l'église sortant des eaux, et les bateaux derrière la ville. L'intelligence faisait ensuite un même élément de ce qui était, ici noir dans un effet d'orage, plus loin tout d'une couleur avec le ciel et aussi verni que lui, et là si blanc de soleil, de brume et d'écume, si compact, si terrien, si circonvenu de maisons, qu'on pensait à quelque chaussée de pierres ou à un champ de neige, sur lequel on était effrayé de voir un navire s'élever en pente raide et à sec comme une voiture qui s'ébroue en sortant d'un gué, mais qu'au bout d'un moment, en y voyant sur l'étendue haute et inégale du plateau solide, des bateaux titubants, on comprenait, identique en tous ces aspects divers, être encore la mer.[31]

---

[30] *JF. III.*, pp. 99-100.

[31] *Ibid.*, pp. 101-102, quoted also by Chernowitz, *op. cit.*, pp. 108-109.

This world of mirages and optical tricks recurring in nature offers ample opportunity for Proust to indulge in his impulse towards metaphoric expression which was always irresistible within him and contains the literary value of an otherwise too " literal " *transposition d'art*. The fact that nature so often proved to be the exact contrary of what it appeared was a constant source of delight to him.[32]

The spectator sees masts of boats moored at the jetty as so many pinnacles built on dry land, while the church of Criquebec seems to emerge from the water. Also a ship actually at sea appears to be sailing across the middle of town. Chernowitz has made a penetrating analysis of this scene which merits citation here. He writes :

Like a painter, Proust breaks up what we are accustomed rationally to envisage as a single element—the sea—into many disparate units: here a dark portion in a storm effect, there something that matches the color and smoothness of the sky, and elsewhere a light patch, bright with sunshine, mist, and foam, and encompassed by land structures. This divisional approach reveals a remarkable understanding of the nature of painting and pictorial vision. The description also shows Proust's keen appreciation and analysis of the organic interlacing, the multiple unity, of the picture's double motif—land and sea.

Just as the little phrase of Vinteuil's is according to Proust a fusion of parts from works of Saint-Saëns, Wagner, and Fauré, so *Le Port de Carquethuit* can be expected to be a fusion of several paintings. It seems to be based at least in part on Edouard Manet's *Port de Bordeaux*, where we find a similar setting, a semicircular shore in perspective, and a similar projection of land elements (the church and other buildings) far into what seems to be the sea. Few have equalled Manet in rendering the sea in its many moods; seascapes, according to the *catalogue raisonné* of his works, constitute by far the largest category of the scenes he painted . . . Though the effects of mirage in the painting remind one of Claude Monet, they are less apparent and less numerous. The ocean still retains substantiality—the fishermen are " riding on the rough water as they might on a swift and fiery animal "—and recalls the relative firmness with which, in spite of his Impressionism, Manet molds his elements. Although Proust does not mention Eugène Boudin, painter of French harbors and beaches, several elements in the *Port de Carquethuit*, such as the bustling activity at the harbor, the accumulation of masts, the women gathering sea food,

---

[32] R. Ironside, " The Artistic Vision of Proust," *Horizon*, IV (July, 1941), 28-41.

as well as the general precision of descriptive detail, all suggest typical aspects depicted by this forerunner of Impressionism.[33]

Chernowitz, however, did not consider a closer pattern as for example Signac's *Entrée du Port Marseilles* in the Musée de Luxembourg. Bussom remarks that the scene appears intentionally distorted to fit into the form of composition that the artist had in mind and that the realistic details of the scene serve merely as elements of composition brought into close relationship so that things pertaining to the sea are presented as if they were a part of the land. " The elements are recognizable but are arranged arbitrarily into a form that arrests the attention and holds it in suspense by the sudden challenge made to the eye to adapt itself to the new design." [34] This new pattern along with its unique composition displays a charm unprecedented in the art of literary landscape.

The narrator further remarks that since Elstir began to paint he has come to know what are called " admirable " photographs of scenery and towns.[35] This epithet is generally applied to some unusual picture of a familiar object, a picture different from those we often see, unusual and yet true to nature, and for that reason doubly impressive because it startles us, makes us emerge from our habits and at the same time brings us back to ourselves by recalling an earlier impression. For example:

. . . celle de ces photographies "magnifiques," illustrera une loi de la perspective, nous montrera telle cathédrale que nous avons l'habitude de voir au milieu de la ville, prise au contraire d'un point choisi d'où elle aura l'air trente fois plus haute que les maisons et faisant éperon au bord du fleuve d'où elle est en réalité distante.[36]

Now the effort made by Elstir to reproduce things not as he knows them but according to the illusion of his first impression of them leads to this point: he gives special emphasis to certain of these laws of perspective which are all the more striking, since his art is their first interpreter: [37]

---

[33] Chernowitz, *op. cit.*, pp. 109-110. Cf. Jacques Henri Bornecque, *Peintres et écrivains* (Paris: Arts et Métiers graphiques, 1947), p. 73, for a comparison of Manet's *Le Port de Bordeaux* with Proust's text quoted above.

[34] T. W. Bussom, *op. cit.*, p. 63.   [36] *Ibid.*, pp. 102-103.

[35] *JF. III.*, p. 102.   [37] *Ibid.*, p. 103.

Un fleuve, à cause du tournant de son cours, un golfe à cause du rapproche-
ment apparent des falaises, avaient l'air de creuser au milieu de la plaine
ou des montagnes un lac absolument fermé de toutes parts. Dans un
tableau pris de Balbec par une torride journée d'été en rentrant de la mer,
semblait enfermé dans des murailles de granit rose, n'être pas la mer,
laquelle commençait plus loin. La continuité de l'océan n'était suggérée que
par des mouettes qui, tournoyant sur ce qui semblait au spectateur de la
pierre, humaient au contraire l'humidité du flot.[38]

Proust's metaphoric vision here is comparable to that found in
Valéry's *Cimetière marin*. Other laws are discernible in the same
canvas:

. . . au pied des immenses falaises, la grâce lilliputienne des voiles blanches
sur le miroir bleu où elles semblaient des papillons endormis, et certains
contrastes entre la profondeur des ombres et la pâleur de la lumière.[39]

This play of light and shade interests Elstir so much that at times
he paints what are " véritables mirages." For example, a palace
mirrored in the water becomes under his transmuting lens a symmetrical object because the identity between it and its reflection
is so deceptive: [40]

. . . où un château coiffé d'une tour apparaissait comme un château circulaire complètement prolongé d'une tour à son faîte, et en bas d'une tour
inverse, soit que la pureté extraordinaire d'un beau temps donnât à l'ombre
qui se reflétait dans l'eau la dureté et l'éclat de la pierre, soit que les
brumes du matin rendissent la pierre aussi vaporeuse que l'ombre.[41]

One may note in the above the sensitivity of the artist's retina to
the most ephemeral effects of atmosphere. In a similar fashion, the
houses clustered beneath the spires of a riverside town, seem to be
held in suspense like pendulums:

Un fleuve qui passe sous les ponts d'une ville était pris d'un point de vue
tel qu'il apparaissait entièrement disloqué, étalé ici en lac, aminci là en
filet, rompu ailleurs par l'interposition d'une colline couronnée de bois où
le citadin va le soir respirer la fraîcheur du soir; et le rythme même de
cette ville bouleversée n'était assuré que par la verticale inflexible des
clochers qui ne montaient pas, mais plutôt, selon le fil à plomb de la

---

[38] *Ibid.*
[39] *Ibid.*
[40] Cf. Ironside, *op. cit.*, pp. 28-41, for remarks on Proust's visual acuity.
[41] *JF. III.*, p. 104.

pesanteur marquant la cadence comme dans une marche triomphale, semblaient tenir en suspens au-dessous d'eux toute la masse plus confuse des maisons étagées dans la brume, le long du fleuve écrasé et décousu.[42]

" The study of sharp contrasts between deep shadows and the blinding spaces of sunlight interested Monet and all the Impressionists, in whose work light was the chief character, since its decomposition into vibrant local contrasts was the basis of their technique." [43] Decomposition of light is strikingly evident in the following passage:

De même au delà de la mer, derrière une rangée de bois une autre mer commençait, rosée par le coucher du soleil et qui était le ciel. La lumière inventant comme de nouveaux solides, poussait la coque du bateau qu'elle frappait, en retrait de celle qui était dans l'ombre, et disposait comme les degrés d'un escalier de cristal la surface matériellement plane, mais brisée par l'éclairage de la mer au matin.[44]

Chernowitz writes that these effects of mirage are due to the fact that the Impressionist artist cannot grasp details in his first impression but rather a general view of the whole which necessarily renders the scene somewhat vague. " Since the brush stroke here serves no longer to designate form but merely optic value, it naturally makes form appear indefinite and easily interchangeable." [45]

The narrator mentions other pictures in which " sur la falaise ou dans la montagne, le chemin cette partie à demi humaine de la nature," [46] underwent, like river or ocean, the eclipse of perspective:

Et soit qu'une arête qu'une arête montagneuse, ou la brume d'une cascade, ou la mer, empêchât de suivre la continuité de la route, visible pour le promeneur mais non pour nous, le petit personnage humain en habits démodés perdu dans ces solitudes semblait souvent arrêté devant un abîme, le sentier qu'il suivait finissant là, tandis que, trois cents mètres plus haut dans ces bois de sapins, c'est d'un oeil attendri et d'un coeur rassuré que nous voyions reparaître la mince blancheur de son sable hospitalier au pas du voyageur, mais dont le versant de la montagne nous avait dérobé, contournant la cascade ou le golfe, les lacets intermédiaires.[47]

In his analysis of Elstir's seascapes " Proust does not describe

[42] *Ibid.*
[43] Chernowitz, *op. cit.*, p. 106.
[44] *JF. III.*, pp. 103-104.

[45] Chernowitz, *op. cit.*, pp. 106-107.
[46] *JF. III.*, p. 104.
[47] *Ibid.*, pp. 104-105.

6

the external actions of the artist or the technical means at his disposal. Instead, we are given insight into the psychological processes of the painter at work." [48] We are informed, for instance, of the effort made by Elstir to strip himself of every intellectual concept so that he might recreate his own visualization. This effort was all the more admirable in that this man, who before sitting down to paint made himself deliberately ignorant of everything he knew, had in reality an exceptionally cultivated mind.[49]

These illusory effects as observed in the water colors of Elstir are apparent in some of Proust's scenes of Balbec and the " équivoque " according to various angles of perspective is found often in scenes which are built around Gothic church spires, but there are many other landscapes which do not reveal either kind of optical illusion or any trace of the Impressionist's technique, as, for example, scenes of Combray, Paris, Doncières and Venice.

" Les Creuniers "

Elstir's painting of the harbor of Carquehuit teaches Proust to visualize nature pictorially but his portrait of the cliffs at Creuniers inspires in him the desire to see in real life scenes in which hitherto he had not been interested. Elstir had previously spoken of the Balbec church as giving the impression of a great cliff, a huge breakwater built of the stone of the country.[50] Now the reversed situation presents a comparable illusion, i. e. a water color of the cliffs suggests the form of a cathedral: " regardez ces falaises, regardez comme ces rochers puissamment et délicatement découpés font penser à une cathédrale." [51] Here again the painter represents a scene viewed " poétiquement ":

En effet, on eût dit d'immenses arceaux roses. Mais peints par un jour torride, ils semblaient réduits en poussière, volatilisés par la chaleur,

---

[48] Chernowitz, *op. cit.*, p. 98.

[49] *JF. III.*, p. 105. In *PM.*, p. 169, Proust refers to Turner's statement: " Mon affaire est de dessiner ce que je vois, non ce que je sais."

[50] *JF. III.*, p. 187. Cf. André Maurois, " Proust et Ruskin," *Essays and Studies by Members of the English Association*, XVII (1932), p. 28, for remarks on the source of Proust's interest in the architectural aspects of natural scenery.

[51] *JF. III.*, p. 187.

laquelle avait à demi bu la mer, presque passée, dans toute l'étendue de la toile, à l'état gazeux. Dans ce jour où la lumière avait comme détruit la réalité, celle-ci était concentrée dans des créatures sombres et transparentes qui par contraste donnaient une impression de vie plus saisissante, plus proche: les ombres. Altérées de fraîcheur, la plupart, désertant le large enflammé s'étaient réfugiées au pied des rochers, à l'abri du soleil, d'autres nageant lentement sur les eaux comme des dauphins s'attachaient aux flancs de barques en promenade dont elles élargissaient la coque, sur l'eau pâle, de leur corps verni et bleu. C'était peut-être la soif de fraîcheur communiquée par elles qui donnait le plus la sensation de la chaleur de ce jour et qui me fit m'écrier combien je regrettais de ne pas connaître les Creuniers.[52]

This perception of the cathedral is reminiscent of Renoir's numerous sketches of the Rouen Cathedral, particularly the pink one, as well as Monet's cliffs painted at Etretat. As previously remarked the fallacious effects of the pale sea vaporized by the torpidity of the sun are characteristic of the seascapes of Monet.[53]

Ortega y Gasset defines impressionism as a pictorial style which consists of " the denial of the external form of realities and of the reproduction of their inward form, their inward chromatic complexity." [54] Elstir seems to follow just such a technique, which is actually more of a " perspectivism " than impressionism, in this representation of the cliffs at Creuniers. In quite a technical manner he gives the picture a color-light perspective rather than a linear perspective. The scene was sketched on such a hot day that the cliffs seemed to have crumbled into dust and the whole picture appears " volatilized and misty through the decomposition of light." [55]

The atmospheric intention of the scene having been introduced in the first sentence the painter next focuses his attention on the pictorial effect of chiaroscuro on transparent substances:

Dans ce jour où la lumière avait comme détruit la realité, celle-ci était concentrée dans des créatures sombres et transparentes qui par contraste donnaient une impression de vie plus saisissante, plus proche: les ombres.[56]

---

[52] *Ibid.*
[53] Feuillerat, *op. cit.*, p. 56. Cf. also Chernowitz p. 100, 102. M. Moore, *op. cit.*, writes that " Elstir devant l'église de Balbec c'est Ruskin devant la cathédrale de Rouen."
[54] Ortega y Gasset, *op. cit.*, p. 276.
[55] Chernowitz, *op. cit.*, p. 111.
[56] *JF. III.*, p. 187.

It is the element of light in his perception of these transparent and dark " créatures " which by its contrast gives a certain quantity of life to the picture. Technically, Proust's *ombres* are depicted in colors complementary to *lumière* and therefore living—not dead black or brown shadows.[57] At the end of the sentence the locution " les ombres " seems added to concretize his metaphorical " expressionism."

In this landscape of aerial and diffused vibrations the animated shadows appear to be seeking coolness at the foot of the rocks or swimming gently over the tide, close to the moving vessels whose hulls they extend upon the pale waters with their glossy blue forms. The narrator comments that it was perhaps " la soif de fraîcheur communiquée par elles " that gave him the sensation of the heat of the day and made him regret so much not knowing the Creuniers.[58] It appears to this writer that the sensation of heat would have been communicated first.

And so it was that the sight of these rocks in the water color of Elstir suggested to Proust new aspects of nature. It inspired him with a thirst for beauty, not exactly natural beauty such as he sought among the cliffs at Balbec, but rather an architectural beauty in nature.[59] The young man having come to Balbec to see the kingdom of storms and never having seen the ocean sufficiently tempestuous, now after observing this sketch, is amazed to find himself dreaming of a sea which is no more than a whitish vapor that has lost its consistency and color [60]—a dream which not only suggests intimate acquaintance with the seascapes of the Impressionist painters but is also reminiscent of the literary descriptions of the pale motionless sea, vaporous and white, in Pierre Loti's *Pêcheur d'Islande*. Furthermore, the narrator is enchanted by the idea that the artist has fixed forever upon the painted canvas the imperceptible reflux of the tide, the pulsation of one happy moment. He becomes so enamored at the sight of this magic portrait that

[57] Chernowitz, *op. cit.*, p. 111, writes that Proust's " shadows are blue, as can be seen in the works of the Impressionists who no longer used black, not considering it a color, but regarding it technically speaking only as the absence of light."

[58] *JF. III.*, p. 187.

[59] *Ibid.*

[60] *Ibid.*, pp. 187-188. Cf. also *S. I.*, p. 240.

he thinks only of recapturing the vanished day in its instantaneous and slumbering beauty, and he seems to experience an intoxication similar to that of the artist after the creation of a work of art.[61] He must seek in reality this painted scene which has so powerfully aroused his imagination but in order to receive the impression in its primtiive form, atmospheric and other conditions must be identical to those rendered visible in the picture and so he hopes that the weather will be favorable enough for him to see from the height of the cliffs the same blue shadows as are represented by Elstir.[62]

Sometime later when the narrator finally sees these famous Creuniers at just the time of the day and when the light was the same as when Elstir painted them, due to an unfortunate event, which had no connection at all with his desire to see the cliffs, he finds himself incapable of experiencing the pleasure he had anticipated by the sight of them.[63] In this case it was not a matter of reality disillusioning him but that of a previous emotional disturbance conditioning his reaction. However, his word painting of the scene is noteworthy and should be compared with Elstir's water color.

In portraying the same effects he seems to have created an even finer pictorial language:

. . . je pus distinguer tout d'un coup à mes pieds, tapis entre les roches où elles se protégeaient contre la chaleur, les Déesses marines qu'Elstir avait guettées et surprises, sous un sombre glacis aussi beau qu'eût été celui d'un Léonard, les merveilleuses Ombres abritées et furtives, agiles et silencieuses, prêtes au premier remous de lumière à se glisser sous la pierre, à se cacher dans un trou et promptes, la menace du rayon passée, à revenir auprès de la roche ou de l'algue sous le soleil émietteur des falaises, et de l'Océan décoloré dont elles semblent veiller l'assoupissement, gardiennes immobiles et légères, laissant paraître à fleur d'eau leur corps gluant et le regard attentif de leurs yeux foncés.[64]

In this clair-obscure impression though the poet does not mention

---

[61] *JF. III.*, p. 188.
[62] *Ibid.* Cf. also André Maurois, *op. cit.*, p. 28, for remarks on Proust's propensity for seeking in reality that which is exalted in pictures.
[63] *JF. III.*, p. 219.
[64] *Ibid.*

the arched effect of the cliffs, he pictures the same diversity of light
and shadow, the same volatile diffusion of atmospheric elements and
the same sensation of intense heat symbolized as threatening the
existence of "les merveilleuses Ombres" and crumbling the cliffs
into dust, but this time transposed into a mythological-pantheistic
scene. Light struggles against shadow with the force of primitive
mythological divinities.[65] The ravaging sun produces the effect of
an "Océan décoloré" and the bluishness of the shadows which he
was so anxious to see he portrays as the "yeux foncés" of these
atmospheric creatures. Their transparent beauty under a dark glaze
represented as resembling the loveliness of that of a Leonardo
painting shows that a knowledge of painting aids both his perception and reproduction of natural scenery. The smallest details
of nature recall to him the old masters.

This time in order to emphasize the superiority and charm of
these illusory creatures he transposes them into marine goddesses,
thus clothing his impression with poetic associations. His capi-
talization of the "Ombres" and their dwelling place, the "Océan,"
enhances them as objects of supreme regard. Again it is the play
of light on the marvelous shadows which animates the scene and
communicates an impression of life. We see, for instance, the
shadows ready at the first glimmer of light to slip behind the
stones, to hide in a cave or to glide over the surface of the waves.
In the water color as well as in reality these shadows are dramati-
cally pictured as creatures seeking shelter from the torpidity of the
sun and consequently displaying human sensitivity. In both pictures their thirst for coolness indicates their sense of touch and in
the latter they even reveal a sense of sight as he depicts them attentively watching the slumbers of the ocean with their dark blue eyes.
To their inward complexity he gives a concrete form ("leur
corps") which he characterizes by the abstract epithet "gluant."
For Proust the impression of something human was to be found in
all aspects of nature and thus his scenery is as living as his people.
His personification of meteorological phenomena is especially striking
and unique.

In these sketches Proust unveils nature so as to make us see it

---

[65] Polanscak, *op. cit.*, p. 42.

according to his own unique vision. He not merely describes a scene but conveys an impression. He portrays " une qualité de la vision, la révélation de l'univers particulier que chacun de nous voit et que ne voient pas les autres," [66] to which he adds his sentiment, art experience and selective taste.

" Fêtes nautiques "

After several visits to Elstir's studio, during which he was introduced to sketches of water tournaments, the narrator confesses that everything that previously he had shut out of his field of vision, not only the effects of sunlight on the sea and shore but even the regattas and race meetings, he will seek with ardor, for the reason that these are now associated in his mind with an aesthetic idea.[67] The splash of color and luminous vastness of a racecourse, where one is constantly surprised by fresh lights and shades, now charms his ecstatic imagination. For during these visits he comes to realize, through the artist's own enthusiasm, that the regattas where exquisitely dressed women are seen bathed in the greenish light of a marine racecourse, might be for a modern artist as interesting a subject as were the revels that Veronese and Carpaccio loved to depict.[68]

It is apparently Elstir's description of Carpaccio's *Legend of Saint Ursula* which instills in him the " desire to see in real life ' these aquatic revels ' where men and boats are one with the ocean and the multicolored passengers are treated as if they are part of the landscape " : [69]

Les navires étaient massifs, construits comme des architectures, et semblaient presque amphibies comme des moindres Venise au milieu de l'autre, quand amarrés à l'aide de ponts volants, recouverts de satin cramoisi et de tapis persans ils portaient des femmes en brocart cerise ou en damas vert, tout près des balcons incrustés de marbres multicolores où d'autres femmes se penchient pour regarder, dans leurs robes aux manches noires à crevés blancs serrés de perles ou ornés de guipures. On ne savait plus où finissait

---

[66] Dreyfus, *op. cit.*, p. 292.   Cf. Pierre-Quint, *op. cit.*, pp. 257-258, for an explanation of the artist's " univers particulier."

[67] *JF. III.*, p. 182.

[68] *Ibid.*, p. 183.

[69] Feuillerat, *op. cit.*, p. 55, also quoted by Chernowitz, *op. cit.*, p. 101.

la terre, où commençait l'eau, qu'est-ce qui était encore le palais ou déjà le navire, la caravelle, la galéasse, le Bucentaure.[70]

Here is a Venetian masterpiece in which the beauty of colorful costumes rivals the architectural splendors of the setting. Elstir explains that the beauty of shipping in those days was in its solidity and the complication of its structure.[71] In this scene as in Elstir's own water colors land and water penetrate each other reciprocally. There is the same overlapping of elements in odd perspective due to the angle from which the scene is viewed. Here the vast vessels appear to be part of the Venetian palaces under whose balconies they are moored and it is scarcely perceptible whether the elegantly gowned ladies are situated on the balconies or on the hanging stages decked with crimson satin and Persian carpets.

Similar subjects have been of interest to artists through the ages but Elstir points out that the greater charm of such scenes in his day is due to a modern simplicity of yachting fashions versus the elaborate decorum of Carpaccio's time. He notes: " ce qui est gracieux, ce sont ces toilettes légères, blanches et unies, en toile, . . . qui au soleil et sur le bleu de la mer font un blanc aussi éclatant qu'une voile blanche." [72] He discloses an obvious preference for soft colors versus the bright and multicolors of the Venetians. In his colorful description of the ladies' fashions and the types of vessels used in those days Proust recreates " la couleur temporelle " of the 16th century.[73]

Before these visits to Elstir, Marcel had taken care when he stood by the sea to expel from his field of vision the bathers in the foreground and the yachts with their dazzling sails, everything which prevented him from contemplating what in his mind was " le flot immémorial qui déroulait déjà sa même vie mystérieuse avant l'apparition de l'espèce humaine." [74] But now since he has seen Elstir's sea pictures, a young woman dressed in white, on the deck of a

[70] *JF. III.*, p. 184.
[71] *Ibid.*, p. 183.
[72] *Ibid.*, p. 185.
[73] François Fosca, " La couleur temporelle chez Marcel Proust," *Nouvelle revue française* XX (1923), p. 240, writes that " la couleur temporelle . . . est au temps ce que la couleur locale est à l'espace."
[74] *JF. III.*, pp. 188-189.

yacht flying the American Flag, duplicates itself in his imagination and at once breeds in him an insatiable desire to visit the spot and see there with his own eyes white linen dresses and flags against the sea.

After acquainting himself with Elstir's seascapes our young hero no longer conceives nature as " en opposition avec tous ces fastidieux perfectionnements de l'industrie " [75] nor regards the sea as immemorial and still contemporary with the ages in which it had been set apart from the land.[76] It is evident from these passages that landscapes seen in painting not only suggested to Proust new aspects of natural beauty, but likewise orientated his aesthetic ideas.

In another sea picture by Elstir it is the innumerable reflections of the same light on the various elements of the scene, crowded into a small square of beauty which the painter has cut out of a marvelous afternoon, that enchants our narrator and brings him closer to the realization that there are no degrees of value and beauty and that the value is in the painter's eye:

Cette fête au bord de l'eau avait quelque chose d'enchanteur . . . Ce qui ravissait dans la robe d'une femme cessant un moment de danser à cause de la chaleur et de l'essoufflement, était chatoyant aussi, et de la même manière, dans la toile d'une voile arrêtée, dans l'eau du petit port, dans le ponton de bois, dans les feuillages et dans le ciel . . . La dame un peu vulgaire qu'un dilettante en promenade éviterait de regarder, excepterait du tableau poétique que la nature compose devant lui, cette femme est belle aussi, sa robe reçoit la même lumière que la voile du bateau, et il n'y a pas de choses plus ou moins précieuses, la robe commune et la voile en elle-même jolie sont deux miroirs du même reflet, tout le prix est dans les regards du peintre. Or celui-ci avait su immortellement arrêter le mouvement des heures à cet instant lumineux, où la dame avait eu chaud et avait cessé de danser, où l'arbre était cerné d'un pourtour d'ombre, où les voiles semblaient glisser sur un vernis d'or. Mais justement parce que l'instant pesait sur nous avec tant de force, cette toile si fixée donnait l'impression la plus fugitive, on sentait que la dame allait bientôt s'en retourner, les bateaux disparaître, l'ombre changer de place, la nuit venir, que le plaisir finit, que la vie passe et que les instants, montrés à la fois par tant de lumières qui y voisinent ensemble, ne se retrouvent pas.[77]

---

[75] *Ibid.*, p. 189. Cf. also *S. I.*, p. 240-241.
[76] *JF. III.*, p. 189.
[77] *G. II.*, p. 102.

Proust is again fascinated by the painter's ability to arrest for all time the motion of the hours at this luminous instant. Because the depicted moment is so obvious, this so permanent canvas gives one a most fleeting impression. He recognizes now that many of Elstir's landscapes are rendered with an exactitude which tells one to the very minute what time of day it is, thanks to the precise angle of the setting sun or to the fleeting fidelity of the shadows. " Par-là l'artiste donne, en l'instantanéisant, une sorte de réalité historique vécue ou symbole de la fable, le peint, et le relate du passé défini." [78]

Thus through Elstir's landscape art Proust reveals his own literary methods and technical excellencies. A pronounced impressionistic concept of nature is discernible in these sketches but Proust's greatest originality as a landscape artist lies in his own unique vision of the world represented by the pictorial metaphor. It is also significant that the architectural splendors of nature, the enchantment of a pale and vaporous sea and the aesthetic possibilities of water festivals were revealed to Proust by means of the *painted* landscape.

[78] *Ibid.*, p. 103.

CHAPTER IV

THE PICTORIAL LANDSCAPE

In the beginning of his novel, Proust writes that he has spent a great deal of his time recalling places and their surrounding landscapes—Combray, Balbec, Paris, Doncières, Venice and others—before the people he had known or seen in these places.[1] The very fact that he took the trouble to indicate that his memory of these landscapes survived all other memories is evidence of the significance that he wanted to give them in his work. The pictorial representation of these landscapes as they were recorded in the mind of the writer is so complicated that it calls for an examination. Proust above all needs a sympathetic mind if we would receive all that he can give, but we are slow in understanding what came to him in a flash and we have to penetrate the charm of his literary landscapes by a sort of running commentary on his texts.

The term "pictorial" is hardly sufficient to describe any of Proust's landscapes as a study of most of his passages will reveal more than the mere picturesque. However, the expression seems appropriate to differentiate certain landscapes from those which disclose a primarily psychological or literary function. These landscapes in addition to exhibiting Proust's skill as a descriptive artist function also as a medium for the portrayal of the realistic setting of his story as sublimated by a dream world. If we neglect either of these two aspects, we will never grasp the individuality of a Proustian pictorial landscape.

Landscape Miniatures

"Le village de Combray"

An examination of Proust's passages devoted to Combray and its surroundings will reveal a little of the seduction which inspired his poetic genius. Landscapes drawn by the hand of one who has from childhood loved the places of which he writes have a peculiar

---

[1] *S. I.*, p. 19.

attraction, and such is the unique charm of Proust's Combray recreated to the image of " son esprit." Combray, as the narrator represents it, is " une ville de rêve " and by penetrating this region of dreamy grace one can arrive at a better understanding of " l'âme proustienne." Proust gives to this " petite cité " all the glory of its past.

In the reconstruction of his adolescent poetic visions Proust gives us first his impression of Combray viewed from a distance:

Combray de loin, à dix lieues à la ronde, vu du chemin de fer quand nous y arrivions la dernière semaine avant Pâques, ce n'était qu'une église résumant la ville, la représentant, parlant d'elle et pour elle aux lointains, et, quand on approchait, tenant serrés autour de sa haute mante sombre, en plein champ, contre le vent, comme une pastoure ses brebis, les dos laineux et gris des maisons rassemblées qu'un reste de remparts du moyen âge cernait çà et là d'un trait aussi parfaitement circulaire qu'une petite ville dans un tableau de primitif.[2]

In recreating the atmosphere of his youth he reconstructs for posterity and the world of art the atmosphere of another epoch. This provincial town whose houses are clustered about its Gothic church he places in its medieval setting and he portrays its circular outline in the manner of the primitive masters.[3] A scene such as this, viewed from a distance both in time and space is the beginning of a kind of impressionism, which was dear to Velasquez and Flaubert.

Next he takes us into the town itself and shows us the strange and pious sadness so characteristic of Combray:

A l'habiter, Combray était un peu triste, comme ses rues dont les maisons construites en pierres noirâtres du pays, précédées de degrés extérieurs, coiffées de pignons qui rabattaient l'ombre devant elles, étaient assez obscures pour qu'il fallût dès que le jour commençait à tomber, relever les rideaux dans les " salles." [4]

Here Proust seems to consciously create the impression that this " tristesse " is a result of certain geographical characteristics of the country which in the course of years have marked the atmosphere of the town and the life of its inhabitants.

[2] *Ibid.*, p. 74.   Cf. *Ibid.*, pp. 97, 99; cf. *supra*, p. 55.
[3] Chernowitz, *op. cit.*, p. 127.
[4] *S. I.*, p. 74.

The streets of the city, though a little sad, blaze with historic and cultural associations. Their names are documents of the early history of Combray when the Church reigned supreme. His recollection of them is characterized by " un sentiment d'angoisse qui naît d'une sorte de volupté intellectuelle ": [5]

. . . des rues aux graves noms de saints (desquels plusieurs se rattachaient à l'histoire des premiers seigneurs de Combray) : rue Saint-Hilaire, rue Saint-Jacques où était la maison de ma tante, rue Sainte-Hildegarde, où donnait la grille, et rue de Saint-Esprit sur laquelle s'ouvrait la petite porte latérale de son jardin; et ces rues de Combray existent dans une partie de ma mémoire si reculée, peinte de couleurs si différentes de celles qui maintenant revêtent pour moi le monde, qu'en vérité elles me paraissent toutes, et l'église qui les dominait sur la place, plus irréeles encore que les projections de la lanterne magique; et qu'à certains moments il me semble que pouvoir encore traverser la rue Saint-Hilaire, pouvoir louer une chambre rue de l'Oiseau—à la vieille hôtellerie de l'Oiseau flesché, des soupiraux de laquelle montait une odeur de cuisine qui s'élève encore par moments en moi aussi intermittente et aussi chaude,—serait une entrée en contact avec l'Au-delà plus merveilleusement supernaturelle que de faire la connaissance de Golo et de causer avec Geneviève de Brabant.[6]

It is the immateriality of his visionary memories which causes him to believe that a visit to these places again would secure a supernatural contact with the unseen world. It is not simply the act of revisiting these streets that would bring contact with the supernatural but the traversing of the milieu in which his childhood had been spent would be a means of recapturing the past. This seems to be his idea of communion with " l'Au-delà " because at the moment that this occurs he becomes a timeless person and is living out of this world, so to speak.[7]

His recollection of " la rue Saint Jacques " discloses his early interest in the architectural aspects of a scene. Nothing was trivial or insignificant to his acute powers of observation:

. . . unie, grisâtre, avec les trois hautes marches de grès presque devant chaque porte, semblait comme un défilé pratiqué par un tailleur d'images gothiques à même la pierre où il eût sculpté une crèche ou un calvaire.[8]

---

[5] Larcher, *op. cit.*, p. 36.
[6] *S. I.*, pp. 74-75.
[7] *TR. II.*, p. 14. Cf. also *supra*, p. 25.
[8] *S. I.*, p.75.

And, on the other hand, the " rue de l'Oiseau " is a reminder of seventeenth century elegance:

> On passait, rue de l'Oiseau, devant une vieille hôtellerie de l'Oiseau flesché dans la grande cour de laquelle entrèrent quelquefois au XVIIᵉ siècle les carrosses des duchesses de Montpensier, de Guermantes et de Montmorency quand elles avaient à venir à Combray pour quelque contestation avec leurs fermiers, pour une question d'hommage.[9]

His representation of the streets after the passing of the cavalry stationed in Combray reveals his impulse toward metaphoric expression:

> Longtemps après que l'accalmie était venue, un flot inaccoutumé de promeneurs noircissait encore les rues de Combray. Et devant chaque maison, même celles où ce n'était pas l'habitude, les domestiques ou mêmes les maîtres, assis et regardant, festonnaient le seuil d'un liséré capricieux et sombre comme celui des algues et des coquilles dont une forte marée laisse le crêpe et la broderie au rivage, après qu'elle s'est éloignée.[10]

The vacuity of the streets dotted with people after the passing of the soldiers is felicitously compared to the border of shells and sea-weed on the beach after a strong tide has retreated.

His memory of moonlight over Combray invites comparison to the art of Hugh Robert and by this specific pictorial analogy he communicates its impression of the beauty of immortal ruins:

> Dans chaque jardin le clair de lune, comme Hubert Robert, semait ses degrés rompus de marbre blanc, ses jets d'eau, ses grilles entr'ouvertes. Sa lumière avait détruit le bureau du télégraphe. Il n'en subsistait plus qu'une colonne à demi brisée, mais qui gardait la beauté d'une ruine immortelle.[11]

This effect of ruins is apparently created by the capricious play of light and shadow on the dark masses.

For two consecutive summers the young boy used to sit in the heat of their Combray garden sick with a longing, inspired by the book he was reading, for a land of mountains and rivers:

> . . . où je verrais beaucoup de scieries et où, au fond de l'eau claire, des morceaux de bois pourrissaient sous des touffes de cresson; non loin montaient le long de murs bas, des grappes de fleurs violettes et rougeâtres. Et

---

[9] *Ibid.*, p. 239.   [10] *Ibid.*, p. 132.   [11] *Ibid.*, p. 167.

comme le rêve d'une femme qui m'aurait aimé était toujours présent à ma pensée . . . ce rêve fut imprégné de la fraîcheur des eaux courantes; et quelle que fût la femme que j'évoquais, des grappes de fleurs violettes et rougeâtres s'élevaient aussitôt de chaque côté d'elle comme des couleurs complémentaires.[12]

He recalls with tender affection the Sunday afternoons spent in this garden during which were awakened his desires for adventure and travel:

Beaux après-midi du dimanche sous le marronnier du jardin de Combray, soigneusement vidés par moi des incidents médiocres de mon existence personnelle que j'y avais remplacés par une vie d'aventures et d'aspirations étranges au sein d'un pays arrosé d'eaux vives, vous m'évoquez encore cette vie quand je pense à vous et vous la contenez en effet pour l'avoir peu à peu contournée et enclose—tandis que je progressais dans ma lecture et que tombait la chaleur du jour—dans le cristal successif, lentement changeant et traversé de feuillages, de vos heures silencieuses, sonores, odorantes et limpides.[13]

There is a nostalgic delight in his reflection of these hours lived in the realm of pure fantasy for the memory of them still recalls to him those adventures and strange aspirations. Longing for travel is bound to evoke picturesque scenery as was the case with Watteau, Baudelaire, Rimbaud, Gauguin and many others. This passage discloses reading as at least a partial source of his interest in mountainous and fluvial scenery. The country in which a story that he was reading took place made a far stronger impression upon his mind than the actual landscape that would meet his eyes when he raised them from his book.[14]

Associated with souvenirs of that charming garden at Combray are impressions left upon him by the sound of chimes from the village square. These recollections disclose another old custom characteristic of the town.[15] It was during those same inspired

[12] *Ibid.*, p. 127. Cf. also *infra*, p. 191, for explanation of the "erotical" aspect of this passage.
[13] *Ibid.*, pp. 129-130.
[14] *Ibid.*, p. 127.
[15] Cf. *PM.*, p. 237, for a description of garden scenery in which Proust refers to "les cloches qu'on entendait faire voler le son en éclats sur la place pour le bien de la terre."

Sunday afternoons that he first discovered pleasure in the sonorous notes chimed from the steeple of Saint Hilaire. There appears a synaesthetic quality in this delightful sensation, the memory of which he records in the following citation:

> . . . une heure sonnait au clocher de Saint-Hilaire, . . . après lequel, le long silence qui le suivait, semblait faire commencer, dans le ciel bleu, toute la partie qui m'était encore concédée pour lire . . .[16]

The hour is indicated by sound after which the following silence becomes a measure of time observed in the sky. Thus his knowledge of the time is determined by an imaginative collaboration of sound and sight, i. e. by the sound of chimes seen in the sky above him.

He gives the impression of looking at a skyscape whose dominant feature is sound when he writes that as each hour sounded it inscribed itself on the surface of the sky. Each note seems to ascend the sky and there exhibit itself visibly:

> . . . à chaque heure il me semblait que c'étaient quelques instants seulement auparavant que la précédente avait sonné; la plus récente venait s'inscrire tout près de l'autre dans le ciel et je ne pouvais croire que soixante minutes eussent tenu dans ce petit arc bleu qui était compris entre leurs deux marques d'or.[17]

His concretization of an abstract phenomenon ("soixante minutes") by placing it in a tiny arc of blue, where he sees it, is an interesting twist of his sense impressions not free perhaps from classical recollections of the *horae*.

His spontaneous transposition of sound into visual terms—two golden figures—is not without poetic associations. Such tonal vision is a rare form of synaesthesia and enriches Proust's imagery by all manner of delicate connotations. One might receive the impression that this tiny arc of blue which he contemplates is a visible phenomenon, but if the text is read carefully one will find that it is rather his mental vision of time between the sounding of the chimes.[18]   Another impression of the sound of chimes

---

[16] *S. I.*, p. 129.   These sensations were discovered by Georges Rodenbach in *Bruges-la-morte*.

[17] *S. I.*, p. 129.

[18] Cf. *PM.*, p. 236, for Proust's reference to "le son d'or des cloches." A

ascending the sky to become a part of it and thereby indicating there the hour of the day, appears in the following passage:

Le visage du ciel même semblait changé. Après le déjeuner, le soleil, conscient que c'était samedi, flânant une heure de plus au haut du ciel, et quand quelqu'un pensant qu'on était en retard pour la promenade, disait: "Comment, seulement deux heures?" en voyant passer les deux coups du clocher de Saint-Hilaire (qui ont l'habitude de ne rencontrer encore personne dans les chemins désertés à cause du repas de midi ou de la sieste, le long de la rivière vive et blanche que le pêcheur même a abandonnée, et passent solitaires dans le ciel vacant où ne restent que quelques nuages paresseux), tout le monde en chœur lui répondait: "Mais ce qui vous trompe, c'est qu'on a déjeuné une heure plus tôt, vous savez bien que c'est samedi!" [19]

Still another time the narrator reflects his adolescent desire to remain all day reading and listening to those bells whose dulcet notes create an atmosphere of inviting tranquility and charm:

On gagnait le mail entre les arbres duquel apparaissait le clocher de Saint-Hilaire. Et j'aurais voulu pouvoir m'asseoir là et rester toute la journée à lire en écoutant les cloches; car il faisait si beau et si tranquille que, quand sonnait l'heure, on aurait dit non qu'elle rompait le calme du jour mais qu'elle le débarrassait de ce qu'il contenait et que le clocher avec l'exactitude indolente et soigneuse d'une personne qui n'a rien d'autre à faire, venait seulement—pour exprimer et laisser tomber les quelques gouttes d'or que la chaleur y avait lentement et naturellement amassées—de presser, un moment voulu, la plénitude du silence.[20]

This impression suggests a sort of magical suffusion wherein the pianissimo of the chimes blends itself with the prevailing silence to enrich the day. At this point we must stress emphatically how much superior the writer is to the painter simply by outdoing the latter's proper means of expression.

After representing the various urban aspects of Combray—its streets, houses, church, gardens, moonlit evenings and sunny afternoons—Proust pictures its surrounding countryside. He writes that there were in the environs of Combray two ways which one took for walks and so opposite:

similar impression is created by Francis Jammes in *De l'Angelus de l'aube à l'Angelus du soir.*

[19] *S. I.*, p. 162.
[20] *Ibid.*, p. 239.

7

. . . qu'on ne sortait pas en effet de chez nous par la même porte, quand on voulait aller d'un côté ou de l'autre: le côté de Méséglise-la-Vineuse, qu'on appelait aussi le côté de chez Swann parce qu'on passait devant la propriété de M. Swann pour aller par là, et le côté de Guermantes.[21]

Of " Méséglise-la-Vineuse " he tells us that he never knew anything more than the way there. During his whole boyhood it was to him something as inaccessible as the horizon, which remained hidden from sight however far one went, by the folds of a country which did not bear the least resemblance to the country around Combray. Guermantes, on the other hand, was the ultimate goal, ideal rather than real, of the Guermantes way, a sort of abstract geographical term.[22] Since his father used to speak of the Méséglise way as comprising the finest view of a plain that he knew and of the Guermantes way as typical of river scenery, he had invested each of them, while conceiving them as two distinct entities, with that unity which belongs only to the creations of the mind.[23] An examination of his pictorial representations of these two ways will disclose the fact that the smallest detail of either of them appeared to him as a precious thing which exhibited the special excellence of the whole. Above all, it is interesting how he set between these walks, far more distinctly than the mere distance in space which separated them, the distance that there was between the two parts of his brain in which he used to think of them—one of those distances of the mind which separates things irremediably from one another, keeping them forever upon different planes.[24] In *Du Côté de chez Swann* Proust has restored the scenery of both places in a succession of inimitable word pictures.

" Le côté de Méséglise "

Poets sing their sweetest songs when filled with the ecstasy of spring and so it is with a rapturous exaltation that Proust gives expression to his reminiscences of the glories of the plains and woods, the lilacs, hawthorns, and apple blossoms which while decorating the Méséglise way in the spring enchanted his adolescent soul.

[21] *Ibid.*, p. 194.
[22] *Ibid.*, p. 195.
[23] *Ibid.*
[24] *Ibid.*, pp. 195-196.

He first pictures a bit of the local color about Méséglise in his impression of the lilacs whose scent welcomed strangers along the way. Let us examine how Proust completes a creative impression by a metaphorical transformation of its most picturesque elements:

> Quand on voulait aller du côté de Méséglise . . . on sortait de la ville par le chemin qui passait le long de la barrière blanche du parc de M. Swann. Avant d'y arriver, nous rencontrions, venue au-devant des étrangers, l'odeur de ses lilas. Eux-mêmes, d'entre les petits coeurs verts et frais de leurs feuilles, levaient curieusement au-dessus de la barrière du parc, leurs panaches de plumes mauves ou blanches qui lustrait, même à l'ombre, le soleil où elles avaient baigné. Quelques-uns, à demi cachés par la petite maison en tuiles appelée maison des Archers, où logeait le gardien, dépassaient son pignon gothique de leur rose minaret. Les Nymphes du printemps eussent semblé vulgaires, auprès de ces jeunes houris qui gardaient dans ce jardin français les tons vifs et purs des miniatures de la Perse. Malgré mon désir d'enlacer leur taille souple et d'attirer à moi les boucles étoilées de leur tête odorante, nous passions sans nous arrêter . . .[25]

This personification of the flowers suggests their amiable character and at the same time gives us an idea of the painter's attitude toward the scene. These " geishas " in the form of flowers with their little green hearts and white and purple blossoms display an ethereal quality characteristic of lovely young girls. Especially interesting is the luminosity of their blossoms which he paints as glowing with sunlight even in the shade.

Proust's poetic use of " rose minaret " to depict the form of the bushes overtopping the gable of the Archer's lodge introduces an oriental tone which gains momentum in his transfiguration of their blossoms into " jeunes houris," the general effect of which he pictures in terms of a Persian miniature. It is obviously their multiplicity of blossoms and richness of color which invite this comparison of the lilacs to a kind of Persian art.

This portrait of young " houris "—those dark-eyed nymphs of the Mohammedan paradise, allegedly beautiful virgins endowed with perpetual youth—emphasizes the depth of color, beauty and perpetual freshness of the flowers whose vivacity he accentuates through contrast to the ordinary " Nymphs du printemps "— perhaps those of Botticelli. We have already seen that it is a

[25] *Ibid.*, pp. 196-197.

favorite device of Proust's to personify nature and especially to liken beautiful flowers to young ladies.[26] Here he draws his analogies from the far and near east showing that there also the poetic-erotical mind is " à l'ombre des jeunes filles en fleurs." This rather exotic representation of the lilacs whose pliant bodies are elegantly gowned and whose fragrant heads are crowned with starry locks, is certainly the impression of an ardent feminist treated with affection and discloses a melancholy undertone of the ubiquity and eternity of Goethe's *Das ewig Weibliche.* In the eighteenth century Diderot and Buffon did similar things.

In another passage Proust subtly pictures his impression of " le temps des lilas " in marine terms:

Le temps des lilas approchait de sa fin; quelques-uns effusaient encore en hauts lustres mauves les bulles délicates de leurs fleurs, mais dans bien des parties du feuillage où déferlait, il y avait seulement une semaine, leur mousse embaumée, se flétrissait, diminuée et noircie, une écume creuse, sèche et sans parfum.[27]

Curtius has made a penetrating analysis of this passage, a part of which merits consideration here. He points out how Proust succeeds by a connecting of metaphors in rendering visible the substance of the lilacs. Proust depicts the rhythm of the growth of the plant and compares the starry flowers of each thyrsus to bubbles born on the surface of a liquid. Such an impression inspires the suite of comparisons borrowed from the marine element—the play of waves on the shore. These metaphors serve to depict the evolution and the death of the flowers—to express the coefficient of real duration which enters into the impression. Curtius further notes that the evocative power of the description does not come from an accumulation of suggestive terms but from an extraordinarily precise reproduction of the most characteristic forms of the object— our memory is filled with sensations of touch and smell characteristically evoked by lilacs. This passage represents both the conception and realization of a work of art. Again the style is nothing

---

[26] Cf. *Ibid.*, pp. 163-164, 200-203, for Proust's transfiguration of the " aubépines," and *SG. II.(1).*, pp. 111-112, for his transfiguration of the " pommiers."

[27] *S. I.*, p. 197.

of the exterior but the manifestation of a spiritual relation between man and nature.[28]

These lilacs which adorned the Méséglise way invested it with a charm and significance which was for him alone, the memory of which remained with him through the ages:

Quand par les soirs d'été le ciel harmonieux gronde comme une bête fauve et que chacun boude l'orage, c'est au côté de Méséglise que je dois de rester seul en extase à respirer, à travers le bruit de la pluie qui tombe, l'odeur d'invisibles et persistants lilas.[29]

It is through sound that the memory of the odor of lilacs is evoked and conveys to him the "déjà-vu" experience. His imaginary state of ecstasy indicates the emotional intensity of the evocation.

The narrator next recalls that this same park stretched way into the distance and that there was an artificial lake there constructed by Swann's parents. His description of this "pièce d'eau" is especially significant for the reason that it contains Proust's philosophical theories concerning the power of nature in the work of man:

Devant nous, une allée bordée de capucines montait en plein soleil vers le château. A droite, au contraire, le parc s'étendait en terrain plat. Obscurcie par l'ombre des grands arbres qui l'entouraient, une pièce d'eau avait été creusée par les parents de Swann; mais dans ses créations les plus factices, c'est sur la nature que l'homme travaille; certains lieux font toujours régner autour d'eux leur empire particulier, arborent leurs insignes immémoriaux au milieu d'un parc comme ils auraient fait loin de toute intervention humaine, dans une solitude qui revient partout les entourer, surgie des nécessités de leur exposition et superposée à l'oeuvre humaine. C'est ainsi qu'au pied de l'allée qui dominait l'étang artificiel, s'était composée sur deux rangs, tressée de fleurs de myosotis et de pervenches, la couronne naturelle, délicate et bleue qui ceint le front clair-obscur des eaux, et que le glaïeul, laissant fléchir ses glaives avec un abandon royal, étendait sur l'eupatoire et la grenouillette au pied mouillé, les fleurs de lis en lambeaux, violettes et jaunes, de son sceptre lacustre.[30]

In a rather classical manner this picture carries with it the idea that even in his most artificial creations nature is the material

[28] Ernst Robert Curtius, *Marcel Proust* (Paris: Les Editions de la revue nouvelle, 1928), pp. 70-74. Cf. *supra*, p. 74.

[29] *S. I.*, p. 266.

[30] *Ibid.*, pp. 197-198.

upon which man has to work and therefore certain places will persist in remaining surrounded by the vassals of their own particular empire and will raise their immemorial standards, in the midst of artificially created scenery, independent of any human interference.

In two short clauses a series of metaphoric expressions gives to the picture a regal tone whereby the work of man appears subordinate to the work of nature. For instance, the verb " régner " connotes the power of nature, " leur empire particulier " distinguishes it from any human sovereignty and its " insignes immémoriaux " suggests the mysterious eternity common to the French soil.

Such sovereignty of nature he finds manifesting itself around this artificial lake where one sees, in two tiers woven of trailing forget-me-nots and periwinkle, the natural delicate blue garland which binds the luminous shadowed brows of water-nymphs and where the iris sweeping in regal profusion appear as vassals which raise their standards and superimpose themselves upon the work of man. The lake, though constructed by the hands of man, is of the stuff of nature and therefore remains under its power.

One may receive the impression in this picture that the artist is not painting precisely " d'après nature " but after a unique impression of his own conditioned by the idea that nature is independent of man and that, in a sort of " évolution créatrice," manifests its power and superority, i. e. it has created this profusion of flowers as an emblem of the kingdom of the lake. Such regal bearing of this floral array suggests analogy to the royal emblem of monarchial France. Here again Proust seems to see culture and nature woven together and his picture represents a historical and philosophical rather than a botanical interest in the scene.

It is noteworthy that Proust has reconstructed this regal display of nature on a rising scale of intensity. He reveals its power to *reign* in its own *empire,* he portrays the *regal profusion* of its emblems and his final description of its " *sceptre lacustre* " serves as a climax in which his ironical intention is crystallized. So this picture which has some of the atmosphere of another age—the monarchial age of France—creates the impression that traditional historical France corrects the voluntary artistic " nouveaux riches " aspirations of Swann's parents.[31]

It was near this garden along a small path which mounted toward the fields that Proust first fell in love with the hawthorns. We have already observed in Chapter II his impassioned contemplation of these flowers which kindled his poetic ardour and became themselves the subject of artistic expression.[32] Larcher in his charming pamphlet *Le Parfum de Combray* aptly expresses, concerning Proust's passages devoted to the hawthorns, that:

. . . dans ce parfum de mois de Marie, nous nous étions senti entraînés dans un rythme qui nous berçait et faisait communier les sens et la pensée. Nous touchons au grand secret de l'art proustien qui suscite en nous, comme dans une révélation religieuse, un sentiment d'amour où la musique et la poésie relient notre organisme animé de désirs et notre intelligence qui pressent l'infini.[33]

As previously noted the narrator's memory of the Month of Mary reappears several times, since around the hawthorns floated an atmosphere of former springs which Larcher believes " lui ont inspiré le titre d'*A l'Ombre des jeunes filles en fleurs*," but which is most improbable.[34]

Later we will find that it was in this same park that his love for a young girl was born.[35]

It was also along Méséglise that he first came to admire apple trees outlined against a gleaming expanse:

A intervalles symétriques, au milieu de l'inimitable ornementation de leurs feuilles qu'on ne peut confondre avec le feuille d'aucun autre arbre

---

[31] In this connection Proust writes: . . . il n'y avait pour moi de beaux spectacles que ceux que je savais qui n'étaient pas artificiellement combinés pour mon plaisir, mais étaient nécessaires, inchangeables,—les beautés des paysages ou du grand art . . . D'ailleurs la nature par tous les sentiments qu'elle éveillait en moi, me semblait ce qu'il y avait de plus opposé aux productions mécaniques des hommes. Moins elle portait leur empreinte et plus elle offrait d'espace à l'expansion de mon coeur. *S. II.*, pp. 240-241.

[32] Cf. *supra*, pp. 60-74.

[33] Larcher, *op. cit.*, p. 72.

[34] *Ibid.*, p. 31. Cf. Clermont-Tonnère, *op. cit.*, p. 232, for other ideas concerning Proust's inspiration for the title *A l'Ombre des jeunes filles en fleurs*.

[35] Cf. *infra*, p. 192.

fruitier, les pommiers ouvraient leurs larges pétales de satin blanc ou
suspendaient les timides bouquets de leurs rougissants boutons. C'est du
côté de Méséglise que j'ai remarqué pour la première fois l'ombre ronde que
les pommiers font sur la terre ensoleillée, et aussi ces soies d'or impalpable
que le couchant tisse obliquement sous les feuilles, et que je voyais mon
père interrompre de sa canne sans les faire jamais dévier.[36]

The geometric beauty of the scene appears to have charmed his
sight for he pictures the trees at regular intervals casting circular
shadows upon the ground. But his poetic mind is still " à l'ombre
des jeunes filles en fleurs " for he describes the apple blossoms by a
suite of epithets which again suggests the bride theme—an echo
of a similar theme portrayed in his picture of the hawthorns.[37] The
time of the year is determined by the nature of the scene. Their
large petals of white satin are suggestive of the young bride in
white and symbolize spring, the bride time of the year.[38] Their
" timides bouquets " and their " rougissants boutons " lend the impression of a shyness and innocence about to burst out of the bud.
This sentence is especially reminiscent of the imagery pictured in
his portrayal of the hawthorns. The fusion of social and botanical
elements is characteristic of his representation of many flowers that
he loved and which he saw from a biological angle.

It is interesting to note that he mixes the abstract and concrete
in developing the image—" satin blanc " and " rougissants " are
blended with " timides "—and that it is the abstract " timides "
which lends the human touch and completes the image. In the
next sentence he paints a suffusion of light and shadow as the sun
descends to blend itself with the circular shadows cast by the trees.
He gives the impression that even the shadows are made luminous
by the ever returning glow of the sun. His use of " satin " and
" soies " to make more exact his description of " blanc " and " or "
emphasizes the sensorial quality of the colors and indicates an
artistic interest in the picturesque elements of the scene. Great

[36] *S. I.*, p. 211.

[37] Cf. *supra*, pp. 62-64, 74.

[38] Friedrich von Logau in the seventeenth century wrote:

Dieser Monat (May) ist ein Kuss, den der Himmel gibt der Erde
Dass sie, jetzo eine Braut nunmehr eine Mutter werde.

Cf. *supra*, p. 62, also cf. *JF. II.*, pp. 147-148. Cf. Adelson, *op. cit.*, p. 135.

Venetian painters from Tintoretto to Paolo Veronese were once well aware of this technique.

At Balbec the apple trees in full bloom, outlined against the sea, create an even more splendorous spectacle in which our poet sees the effects of a refined art and which he contemplates in breathless adoration:

> Là où je n'avais vu avec ma grand'mère au mois d'août que les feuilles et comme l'emplacement des pommiers, à perte de vue ils étaient en pleine floraison, d'un luxe inouï, les pieds dans la boue et en toilette de bal, ne prenant pas de précautions pour ne pas gâter le plus merveilleux satin rose qu'on eût jamais vu et que faisait briller le soleil; l'horizon lointain de la mer fournissait aux pommiers comme un arrière-plan d'estampe japonaise; si je levais la tête pour regarder le ciel entre les fleurs, qui faisaient paraître son bleu rasséréné, presque violent, elles semblaient s'écarter pour montrer la profondeur de ce paradis. Sous cet azur une brise légère mais froide faisait trembler légèrement les bouquets rougissants. Des mésanges bleues venaient se poser sur les branches et sautaient entre les fleurs, indulgentes, comme si ç'eût été un amateur d'exotisme et de couleurs qui avait artificiellement créé cette beauté vivante. Mais elle touchait jusqu'aux larmes parce que, si loin qu'on allât dans ses effets d'art raffiné, on sentait qu'elle était naturelle, que ces pommiers étaient là en pleine campagne comme des paysans, sur une grande route de France.[39]

One by one each element of landscape wins special attention from Proust, and thereby is pictured as the predominating feature of a scene. The white moon sharply carved upon an afternoon sky captures the poet's fancy and its stealthy movement suggests to him an actress not yet ready to make an appearance and therefore wishing to avoid attention:

> Parfois dans le ciel de l'après-midi passait la lune blanche comme une nuée, furtive, sans éclat, comme une actrice dont ce n'est pas l'heure de jouer et qui, de la salle, en toilette de la ville, regarde un moment ses camarades, s'effaçant, ne voulant pas qu'on fasse attention à elle.[40]

Then in his description of the vast expanse of plains seen from Méséglise he displays particular interest in the natural movement of air. In the following passage the entire scene is built on the play of wind over the fields and is interfused with the personal spiritual view of the poet:

---

[39] *SG. II.(1).*, pp. 211-212.   [40] *S. I.*, p. 211.

Ils étaient perpétuellement parcourus, comme par un chemineau invisible, par le vent qui était pour moi le génie particulier de Combray. Chaque année, le jour de notre arrivée, pour sentir que j'étais bien à Combray je montais le retrouver qui courait dans les sayons et me faisait courir à sa suite. On avait toujours le vent à côté de soi du côté de Méséglise, sur cette plaine bombée où pendant des lieues il ne recontre aucun accident de terrain. Je savais bien que Mlle Swann allait souvent à Laon passer quelques jours et, bien que ce fût à plusieurs lieues, la distance se trouvant compensée par l'absence de tout obstacle, quand, par les chauds après-midi, je voyais un même souffle, venu de l'extrême horizon, abaisser les blés les plus éloignés, se propager comme un flot sur toute l'immense étendue et venir se coucher, murmurant et tiède, parmi les sainfoins et les trèfles, à mes pieds, cette plaine qui nous était commune à tous deux semblait nous rapprocher, nous unir, je pensais que ce souffle avait passé auprès d'elle, que c'était quelque message d'elle qu'il me chuchottait sans que je pusse le comprendre, et je l'embrassais au passage.[41]

This concept of the wind as the tutelary genius of Combray simultaneously gives tactual and visual kinaesthetic imagery to the scene. The idea of its running through his clothing gives to the wind a tactual quality while his picture of " le génie " which sets him running in its wake is the visual kinaesthetic representation of his impressions. He is describing a thing seen and felt at the same time, therefore the appropriateness of the double imagery. Proust is here a realistic myth writer, a kind of French Shelley. His visual acuity is further evident in his perception of the wind from a distance as it manifests itself by bowing the heads of corn in far-off fields.

Proust's portrayal of the wind and plains as a sort of spiritual bond between two young people lends a very pleasant emotional coloring to the picture—a psychological nuance which in this particular case might justify Ferré's explanation of Proust's landscape as an accessory circumstance of love.[42] This liaison created by nature is represented as a charm immaterial but none the less intimate and absolutely true, because it is conceivable to anyone disposing of an artistic mind and a sentiment of nature.

There is much literary and classic schooling behind this vague personification of the wind as genius and pander. The concept

[41] *Ibid.*, pp. 210-211.
[42] Cf. *infra*, p. 199, cf. also *Ferré, op. cit.*, pp. 52-53.

is certainly something like Virgil's *Vos ego* and also has affinities
with Shelley's *Ode to the West Wind*.

A similar representation of the wind is found in *Sodome et
Gomorrhe* where the passing of gentle breezes is represented as
extending a double tie between Albertine and Marcel:

> Quand Albertine trouvait plus sage de rester à Saint-Jean-de-la-Haise
> pour peindre, je prenais l'auto, et ce n'était pas seulement à Gourville et à
> Féterne, mais à Saint-Mars-le-Vieux et jusqu'à Criquetot que je pouvais
> aller avant de revenir la chercher. Tout en feignant d'être occupé d'autre
> chose que d'elle, et d'être obligé de la délaisser pour d'autres plaisirs, je ne
> pensais qu'à elle. Bien souvent je n'allais pas plus loin que la grande
> plaine qui domine Gourville et comme elle ressemble un peu à celle qui
> commence au-dessus de Combray, dans la direction de Méséglise, même à
> une assez grande distance d'Albertine, j'avais la joie de penser que si mes
> regards ne pouvaient pas aller jusqu'à elle, portant plus loin qu'eux, cette
> puissante et douce brise marine qui passait à côté de moi, devait dévaler,
> sans être arrêtée par rien jusqu'à Quetteholme, venir agiter les branches des
> arbres qui ensevelissent Saint-Jean-de-la-Haise sous leur feuillage, en
> caressant la figure de mon amie, et jeter ainsi un double lien d'elle à moi
> dans cette retraite indéfiniment agrandie, mais sans risques, . . .[43]

A description of " le bois de Roussainville " as it appeared from
a distance along the Méséglise way shows Proust again viewing
landscape from a point which lets the scene appear to best advantage,
i. e. emphasizes the harmony of its various details, for example:

> Souvent le soleil se cachait derrière une nuée qui déformait son ovale et
> dont il jaunissait la bordure. L'éclat, mais non la clarté, était enlevé à la
> campagne où toute vie semblait suspendue, tandis que le petit village de
> Roussainville sculptait sur le ciel le relief de ses arêtes blanches avec une
> précision et un fini accablants. Un peu de vent faisait envoler un corbeau
> qui retombait dans le lointain, et, contre le ciel blanchissant, le lointain
> des bois paraissait plus bleu, comme peint dans ces camaïeux qui décorent
> les trumeaux des anciennes demeures.[44]

An interpenetration of natural elements wherein the clouds impinge
upon the roundness of the sun which in turn momentarily adorns
their edges is portrayed in the first sentence. In the next sentence
the simpler and nobler elements of the landscape assert themselves,
but only after the blaze of the sun's magnificence has disappeared.[45]

---

[43] *SG. II.(3).*, pp. 74-75.
[44] *S. I.*, p. 216.
[45] This little village carved in relief upon the sky is what eighteenth-

Proust's portrayal of the little village carving in relief upon the sky the white masts of its gables with a startling precision of detail reveals his interest in the superb " craftsmanship " of nature as seen in the various elements of a landscape.

A bird in flight is represented as being driven by the wind and its graceful movement gives not only life but aesthetic unity to the scene. Although there is a wealth of harmony in the picture, it is the delicate contrast represented by the pale sky above the deeper blue of the distant woods that the artist finds analogous to those cameos which decorate the walls of old houses. This infinite and dynamic variety of a Proustian landscape makes the heart of the reader literally throb.

The climate of Méséglise, the narrator tells us, had an unduly high rainfall and it is perhaps for this reason that his memory has retained some delightful pictures of spring showers in this vicinity. The following passage though not a landscape as such is the depiction of the predominating feature of a scene, i. e. rain, at a specific time. One may observe, however, that Proust displays as much pictorial skill when his attention is focused upon a single object as when it is unbounded in extensive ranges. It is his skill in describing the movement of raindrops that is of interest in this animated scene:

> Mais d'autres fois se mettait à tomber la pluie . . . les gouttes d'eau comme des oiseaux migrateurs qui prennent leur vol tous ensemble, descendaient à rangs pressés du ciel. Elles ne se séparent point, elles ne vont pas à l'aventure pendant la rapide traversée, mais chacune tenant sa place, attire à elle celle qui la suit et le ciel en est plus obscurci qu'au départ des hirondelles.[46]

He first gives both form and movement to the drops of water likening them to migrating birds. Once the movement is indicated kinetic imagery is developed in a series of qualifying phrases. For instance, he pictures the drops flying off together, coming out of the sky in close marching order and making no movement at random in their rapid course. The swiftness of the movement is made visible,

century garden artists termed the " accidents heureux " of the scene. von Jan, *op. cit.*, p. 49.

[46] *S. I.*, p. 217.

in addition to being compared to the flight of birds, by the impression that each drop is drawing after it the one which is following. Their movement is so rapid that the motion in every direction seems equal.

It was certainly with a geometric eye that Proust perceived the movement of these drops and pictured it in a spatial language, thus making his impression more visible to the reader. Note, for instance, how the drops " ne se séparent point . . . elles ne vont pas à l'aventure . . . chacune tenant sa place . . . attire à elle celle qui la suit . . ." This series of spatial sensations—four phrases all of which express the same idea—creates an impression of a symmetrical fall.

The movement of rain under direct observation awakened Proust's visual powers but another time the sound of rain from without reminds him that in summer bad weather is only a passing fit of superficial ill-temper expressed by the permanent underlying fine weather.[47] His imagination excited by these reflections he pictures this " beau temps " of summer as firmly established in the soil on which it has taken solid form in dense masses of foliage over which the rain may pour in torrents without weakening the resistance offered by their real and lasting happiness. In the village streets, on the walls of the houses and in their gardens he visualizes its silken banners, violet and white:[48]

Assis dans le petit salon, où j'attendais l'heure du dîner en lisant, j'entendais l'eau dégoutter de nos marronniers, mais je savais que l'averse ne faisait que vernir leurs feuilles et qu'ils promettaient de demeurer là, comme des gages de l'été, toute la nuit pluvieuse, à assurer la continuité du beau temps; qu'il avait beau pleuvoir, demain, au-dessus de la barrière blanche de Tansonville, onduleraient, aussi nombreuses, de petites feuilles en forme de coeur; et c'est sans tristesse que j'apercevais le peuplier de la rue des Perchamps adresser à l'orage des supplications et des salutations désespéreés; c'est sans tristesse que j'entendais au fond du jardin les derniers roulements du tonnerre roucouler dans les lilas.[49]

And so these passing summer showers and storms were not destructive forces but rather decorative elements. They glazed the foliage that they touched and accentuated its stability. Mme Colette is

[47] *Ibid.*, p. 219.   [48] *Ibid.*   [49] *Ibid.*, p. 220.

the only other great contemporary writer who paints this type of "rainy landscape."

Finally when our hero comes to summon up all that he owes the Méséglise way he realizes that it had been either the accidental setting of many intellectual discoveries or the direct inspiration of much artistic thought.[50] He reflects, for instance, that it was during one of those walks that he first discovered that his feelings for the phenomena of nature were often stimulated by amorous desires, i. e. by a desire for a peasant girl of whatever region he was observing.[51]

Thus Proust has converted his memory of Méséglise into living landscapes which captivate the reader and expose him—at least emotionally—to their metamorphosis.

The importance of this garden scenery for which Proust has shown such predilection is easy to judge by the numerous descriptions he has given of it both in *A la recherche du temps perdu* and in the preface of his translation of Ruskin's *Sesame and Lilies.* His representation of a park in *Sésame et les lys* which has been reproduced in *Pastiches et mélanges* can be identified with both " le côté de Méséglise " and " le côté de Guermantes " and because of completeness merits citation in its entirety: [52]

Un peu plus loin, dans certains fonds assez incultes et assez mystérieux du parc, la rivière cessait d'être une eau rectiligne et artificielle, couverte de cygnes et bordée d'allées où souriaient des statutes, et, par moments, sautelante de carpes, se précipitait, passait à une allure rapide la clôture du parc, devenait une rivière dans le sens géographique du mot—une rivière qui devait avoir un nom et ne tardait pas à s'épandre (la même vraiment qu'entre les statues et sous les cygnes) entre des herbages où dormaient des boeufs et dont elle noyait les boutons d'or sortis de prairies rendues par elle assez marécageuses et qui, tenant d'un côté au village par des tours informes, restées disait-on du moyen âge, joignaient de l'autre, par des chemins montants d'églantines et d'aubépines, la "nature" qui s'étendait à l'infini des villages qui avaient d'autres noms, l'inconnu, . . . Je laissais les autres finir de goûter dans le bas du parc, au bord des cygnes et je montais en courant dans le labyrinthe jusqu'à telle charmille

---

[50] *Ibid.*, p. 224.

[51] Cf. *infra*, pp. 191, 199-201, for an explanation of this " erotical " function of landscape in the works of Proust.

[52] Larcher, *op. cit.*, p. 61.

où je m'asseyais, introuvable, adossé aux noisetiers taillés, apercevant le plant d'asperges, les bordures de fraisiers, le bassin où certains jours les chevaux faisaient monter l'eau en tournant, la porte blanche qui était la " fin du parc " en haut, et, au-delà, les champs de bleuets et de coquelicots.[53]

This passage though varying in detail from his descriptions in *Du Côté de chez Swann* is evidence of his early interests in this type of scenery. Apparently it was this literary landscape that furnished starting points for Proust's description of the scenery around Combray. The paths decorated with dog-roses and hawthorns and the fields of corn flowers and poppies we have seen reproduced in his pictures of the Méséglise way whereas the river flowing between banks covered with buttercups on one side and emblems of the Middle Ages on the other must have inspired his descriptions of the river scenery along the Vivonne.

Larcher identifies Swann's park in *Du Côté de chez Swann* with a park in the town of Illiers, France, called " le Pré Catélan " which was owned by Proust's uncle, M. Jules Amiot, who had put it at the disposition of the population of the town thereby making of it " un jardin public." [54]

" Le côté de Guermantes "

The scenery which adorned the Guermantes way also afforded our neurasthenic hero ample opportunity to indulge the lyric impulses of his soul. In another succession of adolescent reveries we find him giving artistic expression to its abundant poetic associations. He pictures first the quaint Rue des Perchamps which one took to go the Guermantes way:

On partait tout de suite après déjeuner par la petite porte du jardin et on tombait dans la rue des Perchamps, étroite et formant un angle aigu, remplie de graminées au milieu desquelles deux ou trois guêpes passaient la journée à herboriser, aussi bizarre que son nom d'où me semblaient dériver ses particularités curieuses et sa personnalité revêche . . .[55]

He explains that because a school now rises upon its site this is a street for which one might search in vain through the Combray of today. But in the elaboration of his reverie he obliterates the

---

[53] *PM.*, pp. 236-237.   [54] Larcher, *op. cit.*, p. 60.   [55] *S. I.*, p. 238.

present and leaves not a stone of the modern edifice standing; he pierces through it to restore " la rue des Perchamps." For such reconstitution he believes that memory furnishes him with more detailed guidance than is generally at the disposal of restorers. He seems to believe also that the pictures which his memory has preserved of what Combray looked like in his childhood days are perhaps the last surviving in the world. This restoration of a Combray which no longer exists, he says, is as moving as those old engravings of the *Last Supper* or that painting by Gentile Bellini in which one sees in a state in which they no longer exist, the masterpiece of Da Vinci and the portico of Saint Mark's.[56] They are " émouvant " because they are part of the past and their memory gives one a sense of contact with a world no longer seen by living men. His explanation of his pictorial memory discloses an atmosphere of dreamy remoteness and a longing for a kind of pseudo-immortality as is elaborated also in Jules Romains', *Mort de quelqu'un.*

The great charm of the Guermantes way was due to the fact that it was followed by the course of the Vivonne and Proust represents its river scenery in a series of exquisite word paintings. Under his impassioned gaze it ripples through the soul and eyes of a genius. The following picture portrays first the joy of a perennial friendship in its freshening flow:

On la traversait une première fois, dix minutes après avoir quitté la maison, sur une passerelle dite le Pont-Vieux. Dès le lendemain de notre arrivée, le jour de Pâques, après le sermon s'il faisait beau temps, je courais jusque-là, voir . . . la rivière qui se promenait déjà en bleu-ciel entre les terres encore noires et nues, accompagnées seulement d'une bande de coucous arrivés trop tôt et de primevères en avance, cependant que ça et là une violette au bec bleu laissait fléchir sa tige sous le poids de la goutte d'odeur qu'elle tenait dans son cornet.[57]

Under the magic of his pen the meanderings of the sky-blue water flowing past banks dotted with daffodils, primroses and hazel-nut trees receive a human interest:

Le Pont-Vieux débouchait dans un sentier de halage qui à cet endroit se tapissait l'été du feuillage bleu d'un noisetier sous lequel un pêcheur en chapeau de paille avait pris racine . . .[58]

[56] *Ibid.*, p. 238.   [57] *Ibid.*, p. 240.   [58] *Ibid.*

The trees having been battered down, the blue foliage of the hazel-nut seems to have been that of a willow. He continues to describe more precisely the geographic aspects of the course of the Vivonne:

Nous nous engagions dans le sentier de halage qui dominait le courant d'un talus de plusieurs pieds; de l'autre côté la rive était basse, étendue en vastes prés jusqu'au village et jusqu'à la gare qui en était distante.[59]

Also this river scenery was ablaze with the romance of history and again Proust becomes a memorialist depicting an epoch of the past. He has already painted the background and set the stage for the historical drama he is about to unfold:

Ils étaient semés des restes, à demi enfouis dans l'herbe, du château des anciens comtes de Combray qui au moyen âge avait de ce côté le cours de la Vivonne comme défense contre les attaques des sires de Guermantes et des abbés de Martinville. Ce n'étaient plus que quelques fragments de tours bossuant la prairie, à peine apparents, quelques créneaux d'où jadis l'arbalétrier lançait des pierres, d'où le guetteur surveillait Novepont, Clairefontaine, Martinville-le-Sec, . . . toutes terres vassales de Guermantes entre lesquelles Combray était enclavé, aujourd'hui au ras de l'herbe, dominés par les enfants de l'école des frères qui venaient là apprendre leurs leçons ou jouer aux récréations;—passé presque descendu dans la terre, couché au bord de l'eau comme un promeneur qui prend les frais, mais me donnant fort à songer, me faisant ajouter dans le nom de Combray à la petite ville d'aujourd'hui une cité très différente, retenant mes pensées par son visage incompréhensible et d'autrefois qu'il cachait à demi sous les boutons d'or.[60]

Such was the scene of the castle of the old counts of Combray, who during the Middle Ages had had the course of the Vivonne as a barrier and defense against attack from the Lords of Guermantes and the Abbots of Martinville. This historical aspect of the landscape reflects Proust's preoccupation with the role of duration and time. He pictures the destruction of time which has left on the broad meadows only a few stumps of towers and broken battlements—emblems of a past that had sunk down and nearly vanished under the earth, but that did not destroy the eternal aristocracy of the Guermantes whose renowned dignity and elegance emitted psychological elements over the landscape. It was these aspects of the past which gave to Proust as a child food for thought and made

[59] *Ibid.*   [60] *Ibid.*, pp. 240-241.

8

the name of Combray connote not the little town which it is today but a historic city vastly different, seizing and holding his imagination by the remote, incomprehensible features which it half concealed beneath a veil of buttercups.

The real significance of this romantic scene lies in the fact that it was a source of inspiration to the adolescent whose impression of it remained forever a part of his life and later became material for artistic expression. The aesthetic miracle is the child's intuitive localizing of all these imponderable events beneath the " boutons d'or." After presenting the historical and psychological aspects of the landscape, by a spontaneous turn of thought, he stops to paint a charming picture of the meadow concealed beneath a veil of buttercups. This feature of the landscape he depicts as an entity in itself but actually it is a logical addition to the background upon which the previous scene was painted.

The color tone of the picture is extended. Until now Proust has been a kind of literary miniaturist like Pol de Limbourg but suddenly he becomes the luminarist painter with modern eyes and expresses the vivid coloring of an additional impression:

Ils étaient fort nombreux à cet endroit qu'ils avaient choisi pour leurs jeux sur l'herbe, isolés, par couples, par troupes, jaunes comme un jaune d'oeuf, brillants d'autant plus me semblait-il, que ne pouvant dériver vers aucune velléité de dégustation le plaisir que leur vue me causait, je l'accumulais dans leur surface dorée, jusqu'à ce qu'il devînt assez puissant pour produire de l'inutile beauté; et cela dès ma plus petite enfance, quand du sentier de halage je tendais les bras vers eux sans pouvoir épeler complètement leur joli nom de Princes de contes de fées français, venus peut-être il y a bien des siècles d'Asie, mais apatriés pour toujours au village, contents du modeste horizon, aimant le soleil et le bord de l'eau, fidèles à la petite vue de la gare, gardant encore pourtant comme certaines de nos vieilles toiles peintes, dans leur simplicité populaire, un poétique éclat d'orient.[61]

This scene which is full of a kind of intellectual voluptuousness receives graphic value through the poet's form and color vocabulary, as in his description of the buttercups: ". . . isolés, par couples, par troupes, jaunes comme un jaune d'oeuf, brillants d'autant plus . . ." The simplicity of his color vocabulary is evident in his use of a color adjective (" jaune d'oeuf ") whose

[61] *Ibid.*, p. 241.

meaning is inherent to the noun qualified. Yellow is the dominant color tone of the picture and his use of the adjectives "brillants" and "dorée" gives the impression of an added lustre coming from the sun.

The pleasure which these flowers give to his sight is so keen that he seems to have the desire that his gustatory organs receive the same sensation, i. e. the same pleasure. His desire for a gustatory pleasure at this moment may have had its source in the fact that the color of the "boutons d'or" suggested a thing edible, or in the general sensorial quality of the scene. But since he is powerless to consummate with his palate the pleasure which the sight of them affords him, he will let it accumulate as his eyes range over their gilded expanse, until it acquires the strength to create in his mind a fresh example of absolutely unproductive beauty. The poetic color of the buttercups allows them a double connotation. In their name he fancies an elegantly robed legendary prince and their color being that of the sacred emblem of oriental races, his impression receives some of the enchantment of the golden East—of the Arabian Nights.

There is a delightful blending of simplicity and poetic exoticism in his symbolic representation of the flowers as foreigners from Asia, from a distant century and endowed with human emotions, such as "contents . . . aimants . . . et fidèles." The latter procedure was already known to naturalists from Zola to Lemonnier. His abstract epithets seem to be in harmony with the color of the scene. The "dorée" of their exterior appearance has perhaps suggested the "content" and "fidèle" of his subjective impression. The plebeian simplicity of the scene, by nature of its contrast, seems to retain for it "un poétique éclat d'orient" where "orient" continues implicitly the motive of Asia and assures the splendour of his impression.

Proust's landscapes are often inseparable from his own interior preoccupations and his dramatic representation of a water lily under the whirling currents of the Vivonne reveals the fact more than ever that his ideas and imagination are seriously affected by his physical and psychological ailments.[62] At a point where the course

[62] Edmund Wilson, *Axel's Castle* (New York: Scribners, 1943), p. 165.

of the Vivonne becomes choked with water plants, he pictures a
single water lily continually straining to follow the current and
continually jerked back by its stem. In one of his most extravagant
fancies he likens this spectacle to the futile attempts of the neurasthenic to break the habits which are eating his life.[63] His observations of the scene and the analogies which ensue appear to be the
reflection of his own state of chronic neurasthenia:

> Bientôt le cours de la Vivonne s'obstrue de plantes d'eau. Il y en a
> d'abord d'isolées comme tel nénufar à qui le courant au travers duquel il
> était placé d'une façon malheureuse laissait si peu de repos que comme un
> bac actionné mécaniquement il n'abordait une rive que pour retourner à
> celle d'où il était venu, refaisant éternellement la double traversée. Poussé
> vers la rive, son pédoncule se dépliait, s'allongeait, filait, atteignait
> l'extrême limite de sa tension jusqu'au bord où le courant le reprenait, le
> vert cordage se repliait sur lui-même et ramenait la pauvre plante à ce
> qu'on peut d'autant mieux appeler son point de départ qu'elle n'y restait
> pas une seconde sans en repartir par une répétition de la même manoeuvre.
> Je la retrouvais de promenade en promenade, toujours, dans la même situ-
> ation, faisant penser à certains neurasthéniques . . . Tel était ce nénufar,
> pareil aussi à quelqu'un de ces malheureux dont le torment singulier, qui
> se répète indéfiniment durant l'éternité, excitait la curiosité de Dante et
> dont il se serait fait raconter plus longuement les particularités et la cause
> par le supplicié lui-même, si Virgile, s'éloignant à grands pas, ne l'avait
> forcé à le rattraper au plus vite . . .[64]

Proust knew that his asthma was of a neurotic character and his
attempts to escape it only actuated the fatal habits which were
ruining his life. As he perceived this lily so he saw himself caught
"dans l'engrenage" of his own eccentricities. The apparent auto-
matic movement of the lily from one bank to the other, caused by
the current, invites comparison to "un bac actionné mécaniquement." This reference to "un bac" illuminates the optical side
of the picture and "actionné mécaniquement" renders more intelligible the psychological aspect of the complex impression, i. e. it
accents the helpless state of the lily caught in a current over which
it has no control just as the neurasthenic is caught in the treadmill
of his maladies. Also this "mécaniquement" seems to emphasize
the futility of trying to overcome an irremediable force created by

[63] *Ibid.*   [64] *S. I.*, p. 242.

habit. In this way the picture carries with it the idea that a force having become mechanical through habit cannot be overcome.

Overwhelmed by the pathos of the scene it is with a feeling of compassion that he further likens the ill-fated lily to those wretches whose peculiar torments, repeated indefinitely throughout eternity, aroused the curiosity of Dante. In an indirect way he endows this natural object with human emotion. This additional literary comparison possesses the power of communicating more explicitly the impression of unrest—the morbid fascination of the scene.

The above landscape obviously was drawn under a spell of deep dejection and so it is with a change of mood that he paints the water lilies in their more seductive form. These vividly colored scenes, still along the Vivonne, give the impression that the retouching brush of a genius has gone over the true and original features of nature, as for example in the following passage which reads:

Mais plus loin le courant se ralentit, il traverse une propriété dont l'accès était ouvert au public par celui à qui elle appartenait et qui s'y était complu à des travaux d'horticulture aquatique, faisant fleurir, dans les petits étangs que forme la Vivonne, de véritables jardins de nymphéas. Comme les rives étaient à cet endroit très boisées, les grandes ombres des arbres donnaient à l'eau un fond qui était habituellement d'un vert sombre mais que parfois quand nous rentrions par certains soirs rassérénés d'après-midi orageux, j'ai vu d'un bleu noir et cru tirant sur le violet, d'apparence cloisonnée et de goût japonais. Çà et là, à la surface, rougissait comme une fraise une fleur de nymphéa au coeur écarlate, blanc sur les bords.[65]

It is by a refined optic art that he represents shadows which partake of the nature of their surroundings. The color of the trees interpenetrates the reflection of the water and both are subject to the ephemeral effects of atmosphere and light which are constantly altering their harmonies. Note for instance that with a change of atmosphere the " vert sombre " background of the scene becomes a " bleu noir " that is almost violet. We have already observed that in the description of colors Proust—outdoing the feeble attempts of Bernardin de Saint-Pierre—never hesitates to use allusions or comparisons taken from the human world or the world of art. The vivid coloring of this scene he accentuates through comparison to Japanese cloisonné.

[65] *Ibid.*, p. 243.

Chernowitz repeats the truism that this painting of shadows in brighter tones, such as dark green, deep blue and violet, " immediately recalls Impressionist painting which partly under the influence of vividly colored Japanese prints did away with the conventional black." [66]   In such a bright scene a singularly scattered lily portrayed as blushing like a strawberry, " au coeur écarlate, blanc sur les bords," adds to the picture a brilliant depth of color.

The magic of poetry transfigures any landscape and the following passage is characteristic of how the humblest details of nature lift our hero as on wings into realms of unimaginable beauty. In this scene which is colored by his personal imaginative insight and interfused with his vital social and intellectual preoccupations there is a sort of magical suffusion wherein the heavens descend to blend themselves with this more familiar earth of ours. Let us examine the component parts of the picture:

> Plus loin, les fleurs plus nombreuses étaient plus pâles, moins lisses, plus grenues, plus plissées, et disposées par le hasard en enroulements si gracieux qu'on croyait voir flotter à la dérive, comme après l'effeuillement mélancolique d'une fête galante, des roses mousseuses en guirlandes dénouées. Ailleurs un coin semblait réservé aux espèces communes qui montraient le blanc et rose proprets de la julienne, lavés comme de la porcelaine avec un soin domestique . . .[67]

Proust's social attitudes are so much a part of his mental disposition that they even characterize his impressions of nature. As he distinguishes human beings according to their social status so his flowers lend themselves to similar classifications. In the same manner that he describes fair ladies of Parisian society he pictures these ladies of the floral world as " plus pâles, moins lisses . . . en enroulements si gracieux." Not even the casual reader of Proust can fail to be struck by his constant fusion of the social and botanical. He then pictures the commoner types of lily which he places in a corner especially reserved for themselves. In his mind the two classes—the commoners and the aristocrats are definitely and distinctly divided. The idea of the commoner species is elaborated in appropriate terms evoking the frugal carefulness of a typical bourgeois world, as in the line: " lavés comme de la por-

---

[66] Chernowitz, *op. cit.*, p. 75.   [67] *S. I.*, p. 244.

celaine avec un soin domestique." Having catagorized the flowers
socially he next paints them in a charming vignette:

. . . un peu plus loin, pressées les unes contre les autres en une véritable
plate-bande flottante, on eût dit des pensées des jardins qui étaient venues
poser comme des papillons leurs ailes bleuâtres et glacées, sur l'obliquité
transparente de ce parterre d'eau; de ce parterre céleste aussi: car ils
donnait aux fleurs un sol d'une couleur plus précieuse, plus émouvante que
la couleur des fleurs elles-mêmes; et, soit que pendant l'après-midi il fît
étinceler sous les nymphéas le kaléidosocope d'un bonheur attentif, silencieux, et mobile ou qu'il s'emplît vers le soir, comme quelque port lointain,
du rose et de la rêverie du couchant, changeant sans cesse pour rester
toujours en accord autour des corolles de teintes plus fixes, avec ce qu'il y a
de plus profond, de plus fugitif, de plus mystérieux,—avec ce qu'il y a
d'infini,—dans l'heure, il semblait les avoir fait fleurir en plein ciel.[68]

Here the infinite diversity of Proust's illustrative imagery manifests
itself as he represents the interpenetration of the various elements of
nature with processes of thinking in the manner of Paul Valéry.
Proust detects in the features of a landscape new charms which the
ordinary aphilosophical eye cannot see. His unusual acuity to every
detail of color, light and form is displayed in this representation of
a " plate-bande," as creating the impression of " des pensées des
jardins qui étaient venues poser comme des papillions leurs ailes
bleuâtres et glacées." It is notable that his use of " transparent "
to qualify " l'obliquité " is not a matter of shading but an attempt
to attain a more exact expression of what he sees and a kind of
equation of pensée-flower = pensée-thought.

In the development of his imagery he proceeds from the concrete
to the abstract both in terminology and in thought. As he sees the
phenomena of nature integrate, his thoughts swing from the earthly
to the heavenly (heavenly being a term of value) and the " parterre
d'eau " becomes a " parterre céleste." The reflection of the bluish
flowers in the water has given to the landscape a celestial hue more
precious and more moving than the colors of the flowers themselves.
The poet might have thought of that curious clarity of objects when
mirrored in water as well as in thought.

The epithet " émouvant " gives to the scene an almost human
emotion due perhaps to its latent sublimation. The celestial garden

[68] *Ibid.*

endowed with " un bonheur attentif, silencieux " is abstract but alive, and a setting sun which dreams or inspires dreams is a slight personification, the result of Proust's unconscious nature pantheism.

In the next clause we may again observe close connection between the man and his art. His description of the kaleidoscopic garden as incessantly changing and ever remaining in harmony about the more permanent colors of the flowers themselves could be interpreted as a reflection of his psychology of duration and time. As Proust would have our ego modified every hour, so this " parterre d'eau " is pictured as " changeant sans cesse." Nature seems to undergo a metamorphosis analogous to that of persons. According to Proust, people or things do not change only in themselves but in relation to other people or other things. So it is that this watery garden is incessantly changing to remain in harmony with the more permanent color of the flowers. His visual acuity here perceives the " évolution créatrice " of nature.

Proust teaches that the universe and mankind are made subject to the category of time [69] and on the strength of this precept by a series of abstract epithets—" plus profond . . . plus fugitif . . . mystérieux . . . infini "—he portrays an impression of infinity in the constant change of the garden. This conception of the infinite in nature must have assured Proust of the reality of the scene, as for him only that which was independent of time was real.[70]

Proust was determined to prove that he believed not in mechanical evolution but in creative progress, in nature as well as in human activity. And so he represents this garden as symbolizing the " progress " of nature—progress meaning " creative sublimation."

In the midst of this enchanted scenery one may observe that Proust possessed a spontaneous aesthetic color vision discernible in a delicately drawn cloudscape wherein mist and warm hues evoke phantasmal colors against the celestial expanse. The representation of the play of color in clouds is indicative of the color intoxication of his youth. Let us observe how Proust's unique metaphoric pen transforms floral colors into celestial bouquets:

Il y a dans les nuages ce soir des violets et des bleus bien beaux, n'est-ce pas, . . . un bleu surtout plus floral qu'aérien, un bleu de cinéraire, qui

[69] Pierre-Quint, *op. cit.*, p. 153.   [70] *TR. II.*, pp. 20-21.

surprend dans le ciel. Et ce petit nuage rose n'a-t-il pas aussi un teint de fleur, d'oeillet ou d'hydrangéa. Il n'y a guère que dans la Manche, entre Normandie et Bretagne, que j'ai pu faire de plus riches observations sur cette sorte de règne végétal de l'atmosphère. Là-bas près de Balbec, près de ces lieux sauvages, il y a une petite baie d'une douceur charmante où le coucher du soleil du pays d'Auge, le coucher de soleil rouge et or que je suis loin de dédaigner, d'ailleurs, est sans caractère, insignifiant; mais dans cette atmosphère humide et douce s'épanouissent le soir en quelques instants de ces bouquets célestes, bleus et roses, qui sont incomparables et qui mettent souvent des heures à se faner. D'autres s'effeuillent tout de suite et c'est alors plus beau encore de voir le ciel entier que jonche la dispersion d'innombrables pétales soufrés ou roses.[71]

The poetic image here is not revealed through any single word. The impression of a vegetable kingdom in the clouds is suggested by the loveliness of floral tints in the sky. The floral motif is carried by the verb " s'épanouissent " and culminates in the color word " bouquets célestes " which conveys a full aesthetic impression in itself. Furthermore, his description of these heavenly flowers as shedding their leaves and scattering their petals over the sky is a poetic overtone which completes the creative formation of his impression. In this scene Proust obviously attempts to evoke value by color and his distinction of a red and gold sunset as insignificant and without character when compared to the soft blue and rose of a more gentle atmosphere reveals his own highly refined aesthetic " color sense."

After masterfully picturing the harmonious blending of the color phenomena of nature—the red and gold sunset and the blue and rose clouds—he lends a mysterious and illusive charm to the scene by painting its contrasting elements—the golden sands against the funereal shores of the Opal Bay:

Dans cette baie, dite d'opale, les plages d'or semblent plus douces encore pour être attachées comme de blondes Andromèdes à ces terribles rochers des côtes voisines, à ce rivage funèbre, fameux par tant de naufrages, où tous les hivers bien des barques trépassent au péril de la mer. Balbec! la plus antique ossature géologique de notre sol, vraiment Ar-mor, la Mer, la fin de la terre, la région maudite qu'Anatole France . . . a si bien peinte, sous ses brouillards éternels, comme le véritable pays des Cimmériens, dans l'Odyssée.[72]

---

[71] *S. I.*, p. 189.   [72] *Ibid.*, pp. 189-190.

It is difficult to imagine that the sunless gloom suggested by his analogy to the Cimmerians could exist in an atmosphere of such iridescent and resplendent colors.

But sooner or later Proust reminds us of the very worldliness of his " céleste " and transfigured landscapes as in the following scene wherein food is as eligible for sublimation as sex. He writes that once after a long walk at the end of the day the reflection of the western sky from the windows of his aunt Léonie's house cast a fiery glow which evoked more than a single sensory impression. This reflected glow of the setting sun was associated in his mind with the glow of the fire over which at that moment was roasting the chicken that was to furnish him, in place of the poetic pleasure he had found in the scenery, with the sensual pleasures of good food, warmth and rest:

> Au commencement de la saison où le jour finit tôt, quand nous arrivions rue du Saint-Esprit, il y avait encore un reflet du couchant sur les vitres de la maison et un bandeau de pourpre au fond des bois du Calvaire qui se reflétait plus loin dans l'étang, rougeur qui, accompagnée souvent d'un froid assez vif, s'associait, dans mon esprit, à la rougeur du feu au-dessus duquel rôtissait le poulet qui ferait succéder pour moi au plaisir poétique donné par la promenade, le plaisir de la gourmandise, de la chaleur et du repos.[73]

This kind of sensorial vision of natural scenery we will find scattered throughout Proust's landscape pictures.

It was during these childhood walks around the countryside of Combray that Proust first foresaw happiness and peace in communion with nature. Note, for instance, how he anticipated a true bond between nature and man's heart in the swift flow of the Vivonne:

> Au sortir de ce parc, la Vivonne redevient courante. Que de fois j'ai vu, j'ai désiré imiter quand je serais libre de vivre à ma guise, un rameur, qui, ayant lâché l'aviron, s'était couché à plat sur le dos, la tête en bas, au fond de sa barque, et la laissant flotter à la dérive, ne pouvant voir que le ciel qui filait lentement au-dessus de lui, portrait sur son visage l'avant-goût du bonheur et de la paix.[74]

---

[73] *Ibid.*, p. 193.
[74] *Ibid.*, p. 245.

But never in the course of these walks did he penetrate as far as the source of the Vivonne which had in his mind so ideal an existence that he was greatly surprised when he learned that it was in the same department and at a given number of miles from Combray.

He never reached the other goal which he longed to attain— Guermantes itself. The Duke and Duchess of Guermantes he knew were real personages who did actually exist but they remained for him wrapped in the mystery of the Merovingian Age and bathed, as in a sunset, in the orange light which glowed from the resounding syllable " antes." Their ducal personality was enormously distended so as to encircle that Guermantes of which they were Duke and Duchess ". . . tout ce côté de Guermantes' ensoleillé, le cours de la Vivonne, ses nymphéas et ses grands arbres, et tant de beaux après-midi." [75]

These fragments of a riverside country remained for Proust a sort of storybook land intersected by little gardens of the ducal park. It was while indulging in dreams of imaginary walks with Mme de Guermantes in this ducal park that he was reminded, that since he wished some day to become a writer, it was high time to decide what sort of books he was going to write. But when he tried to discover some subject to which he could impart a philosophical significance of infinite value, his mind would stop like a clock and he was devastated by his lack of talent.[76] Many times afterwards it was from the Guermantes way that he sadly reflected his lack of literary talent:

. . . dans mes promenades du côté de Guermantes, il me parut plus affligeant encore qu'auparavant de n'avoir pas de dispositions pour les lettres, et de devoir renoncer à être jamais un écrivain célèbre. Les regrets que j'en éprouvais, tandis que je restais seul à rêver un peu à l'écart, me faisaient tant souffrir, que pour ne plus les ressentir, de lui-même par une sorte d'inhibition devant la douleur, mon esprit s'arrêtait entièrement de penser aux vers, aux romans, à un avenir poétique sur lequel mon manque de talent m'interdisait de compter.[77]

---

[75] *Ibid.*, p. 247. Cf. *infra*, pp. 229-235.
[76] *S. I.*, p. 248-249.
[77] *Ibid.*, p. 256.

Much later in life Proust returned to Combray and repeated the walks which he used to take when he went the Méséglise way:

Au plaisir de jadis qui était de voir en rentrant le ciel pourpre encadrer le calvaire ou se baigner dans la Vivonne, succédait celui de partir à la nuit venue, quand on ne rencontrait plus dans le village que le triangle bleuâtre irrégulier et mouvant des moutons qui rentraient. Sur une moitié des champs le coucher s'éteignait; au-dessus de l'astre était déjà allumée la lune qui bientôt les baignerait tout entiers.[78]

Now when he found the little interest he took in Combray he felt more keenly than in the past the conviction that he would never be able to write anything—that his imagination and sensibility had grown feeble. It distressed him to find how little he relived his early years especially when he found the Vivonne thin and ugly. He did not notice material discrepancies of any magnitude in what he remembered, but separated from the places which he was visiting by the whole expanse of a different life, there was not between them and himslf that contiguity from which is born the immediate and total deflagration of memory. One of his greatest surprises was finding the source of the Vivonne—which he had always imagined as something extra-terrestrial—merely a sort of rectangular basin in which bubbles rose to the surface.[79]

In this connection it is interesting to note his impression of Tansonville during a visit there many years later. This time it is with only a vague sense of pleasure that he looks out upon the beautiful verdure of the estate, the lilacs at the entrance, the tall trees at the water's edge, and the forest of Méséglise in the background:

... c'est joli d'avoir tant de verdure dans la fenêtre de ma chambre jusqu'au moment où dans le vaste tableau verdoyant, je reconnus, peint lui au contraire en bleu sombre, simplement parce qu'il était plus loin, le clocher de l'église de Combray, non pas une figuration de ce clocher, ce clocher lui-même, qui mettant ainsi sous mes yeux la distance des lieues et des années, était venu, au milieu de la lumineuse verdure et d'un tout autre ton, si sombre qu'il paraissait presque seulement dessiné, s'inscrire dans le carreau de ma fenêtre.[80]

---

[78] *AD. II.*, p. 203.   [79] *Ibid.*, pp. 204-205.   [80] *TR. I.*, pp. 7-8.

So it was that each of these landscape fragments in and about Combray were the realities which framed the unfolding of Proust's childhood days and inspired his artistic genius. To further point out how these landscapes formed his entire existence he indicates that the truths which in the course of his life had changed the meaning and aspect of his thoughts remained enclosed in the milieu of their apparition:

Les fleurs qui jouaient alors sur l'herbe, l'eau qui passait au soleil, tout le paysage qui environna leur apparition continue à accompagner leur souvenir de son visage inconscient ou distrait . . .[81]

In other words this countryside around Combray because it served as environment to the apparition of new truths was to survive for him in all its ephemeral details. Furthermore, the proof that these landscapes are not accessory elements but aspects of an essential reality, is that their memory can survive other circumstances of the apparition of these truths, perhaps to the truths themselves:

. . . ce parfum d'aubépine qui butine le long de la haie où les églantiers le remplaceront bientôt, un bruit de pas sans écho sur le gravier d'une allée, une bulle formée contre une plante aquatique par l'eau de la rivière et qui crève aussitôt, mon exaltation les a portés et a réussi à leur faire traverser tant d'années successives, tandis qu'alentour les chemins se sont effacés et que sont morts ceux qui les foulèrent et le souvenir de ceux qui les foulèrent.[82]

By linking the survival of their memory to a state of " exaltation " born of the landscape itself he seems to indicate a true bond between nature and his emotional life. He has taken nature into his soul and there it has dwelt in ecstasy.

As we have noted in Proust's various psychological experiences, it is the involuntary memory which in the course of time reveals these scenes from the past.[83] He writes that sometimes a fragment of landscape transported into the present will detach itself in such isolation from all associations that it floats uncertainly upon his mind like a flowering isle of Délos and that he is unable to say from

[81] *S. I.*, p. 264.
[82] *Ibid.*
[83] Cf. *supra*, p. 21, for an explanation of Proustian revelation through the involuntary memory.

what place or from what time it comes—again he is stressing the fact that the memory of landscape survives all other truths. His comparison of landscape souvenirs to " une Délos fleurie " emphasizes their profundity in his mind and the process of their revelation as coming up from an interior world into an exterior world. He continues:

Mais c'est surtout comme à des gisements profonds de mon sol mental, comme aux terrains résistants sur lesquels je m'appuie encore, que je dois penser au côté de Méséglise et au côté de Guermantes. C'est parce que je croyais aux choses, aux êtres, tandis que je les parcourais, que les choses, les êtres qu'ils m'ont fait connaître, sont les seuls que je prenne encore au sérieux et qui me donnent encore de la joie. Soit que la foi qui crée soit tarie en moi, soit que la réalité ne se forme que dans la mémoire, les fleurs qu'on me montre aujourd'hui pour la première fois ne me semblent pas de vraies fleurs.[84]

It is singularly important that he identifies the memory of these landscapes as preeminently the deepest layer of his mental soil. He reflects also that the people and things he thought of when roaming these ways are today those alone which can still give him joy. Again nature becomes paralleled to and inserted into sociological structures. Furthermore, he recalls the landscape around Combray as the country where he would feign pass his life:

Le côté de Méséglise avec ses lilas, ses aubépines, ses bleuets, se coquelicots, ses pommiers, le côté de Guermantes avec sa rivière à têtards, ses nymphéas et ses boutons d'or, ont constitué à tout jamais pour moi la figure des pays où j'aimerais vivre, où j'exige avant tout qu'on puisse aller à la pêche, se promener en canot voir des ruines de fortifications gothiques et trouver au milieu des blés, ainsi qu'était Saint-André-des-Champs, une église monumentale, rustique et dorée comme une meule.[85]

It is because the lilacs, hawthorns, corn flowers, etc., which he may encounter again in the fields, are situated on the same level of his past as the two ways that they at once established contact with his heart. And it may be concluded that it is as a mechanism for evoking this past that these fragments of natural scenery which occupy such a profound place in his emotional and intellectual life give pleasure to the narrator.

[84] *S. I.*, p. 264.   [85] *Ibid.*, p. 265.

Now when he portrays this Méséglise and Guermantes setting as the land where he would like to spend the rest of his life, it is not so much a desire for the place in itself but the fact that these places are the scenes of his past life and to live there would be to recapture " Temps Perdu "—the fundamental desire of his entire life and for the unbeliever the only value in life. He must recapture the past and cling to it in memory because there is no " Hope " in God.

He gives further evidence to this interpretation by adding that because there is an element of individuality in places, when he is seized with a desire to see again the Guermantes way it would not be satisfied by being led to the banks of a river in which there were lilies as fair or even fairer than those in the Vivonne. What he wants to see again is Guermantes as he knew it:

. . . avec la ferme qui est peu éloignée des deux suivantes serrées l'une contre l'autre, à l'entrée de l'allée des chênes; ce sont ces prairies où, quand le soleil les rend réfléchissantes comme une mare, se dessinent les feuilles des pommiers, c'est ce paysage dont parfois la nuit dans mes rêves, l'individualité m'étreint avec une puissance presque fantastique et que je ne peux plus retrouver au réveil.[86]

This element of individuality which he gives a landscape does not indicate a differentiation of the place as such from other places but rather its individuality in the part it has played in his life.

The memory of these places is capable of giving Proust a certain joy because for him spiritual reality offers a satisfaction that material life is incapable of rendering.[87] These scenes are real yet inaccessible, true without being actual, and ideal without being abstract.[88] Proustian spirituality suggests Bergson's theory that: ". . . la vraie spiritualité se trouve . . . dans ces souvenirs sensibles d'un passé qui subsiste tel quel et qui constitue notre personnalité." [89]

In later life Proust often wished to see a person without realizing that it was simply because the person recalled to him some element

---

[86] *Ibid.*, p. 266.

[87] Cf. *TR. II.*, pp. 26, 36.

[88] Fiser, *op. cit.*, p. 147.

[89] J. de Tonquédec, *Sur la Philosophie Bergsonienne* (Paris: Beauchesne, 1936), p. 128.

of these landscapes. By their persistence in his impressions they
give to them a foundation, depth and dimension lacking from the
rest. Thus Proust's artistic representation of a " Délos Fleurie "
shows us the picturesque setting of his childhood days and at the
same time enables us to penetrate and to know better " les gisements
profonds de son sol mental " whose echoes of intense emotions
vibrate throughout the entire work. It is always to the " côté de
Méséglises et côté de Guermantes " that his thoughts return transported " comme dans un rêve—dont l'image était née du parfum
d'une tasse de thé—le parfum de Combray, tout chargé de
souvenirs . . ." [90]

" Le Bois de Boulogne "

In the midst of all this scenery reconstructed from his past, one
of Proust's most pretentious landscapes is his phantasmagorical
representation of the Bois de Boulogne. It is during the transformation scene of autumn that he recaptures the complexity of
the Bois and makes it, in the zoological and mythological sense of
the word, " un jardin." [91] The impression of its artificiality comes
not from the point of view that it is artificially created but as we
will observe later because in his mind it existed for a purpose
alien to the life of its individual elements, i. e. its purpose was to
frame the pageant of beautiful women who passed beneath its
trees.[92]

He pictures first its autumn magnificence as viewed from a
distance and later he gives a precise description of objects near at
hand. One may note in the following passage how his attention
to the picturesque aspects of the scene reveals the artistic effects
of nature which he portrays as an unfinished painting:

C'était l'heure et c'était la saison où le Bois semble peut-être le plus
multiple, non seulement parce qu'il est plus subdivisé, mais encore parce
qu'il l'est autrement. Même dans les parties découvertes où l'on embrasse
un grand espace, çà et là, en face des sombres masses lointaines des arbres
qui n'avaient pas de feuilles ou qui avaient encore leurs feuilles de l'été,
un double rang de marronniers oranges semblait, comme dans un tableau
à peine commencé, avoir seul encore été peint par le décorateur qui n'aurait

---

[90] Larcher, *op. cit.*, p. 119.   [91] *S. II.*, p. 292.   [92] *Ibid.*, p. 295.

pas mis de couleur sur le reste, et tendait son allée en pleine lumière pour la promenade épisodique de personnages qui ne seraient ajoutés que plus tard.[93]

The double row of orange chestnuts—the only spot of color against the dark mass of trees—readily suggests a picture just begun upon which the artist has not yet added the rest of its color. There is an element of anticipation in this comparison—anticipation for the multi-colors which the season guarantees but which have not yet manifested themselves.

As the perspective of his impression changes, it is the graceful movement of a single tree which animates the scene and is captured in an onomatopoetic scherzando (étêté et têtu) : " Plus loin, là où toutes leurs feuilles vertes couvraient les arbres, un seul, petit, trapu, étêté et têtu, secouait au vent une vilaine chevelure rouge." [94]

The turning of autumn leaves impresses him as a natural process analogous to their blossoming in the spring and he expresses this act of change in appropriate metaphorical terms : " Ailleurs encore c'était le premier éveil de ce mois de mai des feuilles, et celles d'un empelopsis merveilleux et *souriant*, comme une épine rose de l'hiver, depuis le matin même étaient tout en fleur." [95]

Next a temporary artificial aspect of the Bois gives the impression of a nursery garden :

Et le Bois avait l'aspect provisoire et factice d'une pépinière ou d'un parc, où soit dans un intérêt botanique, soit pour la préparation d'une fête, on vient d'installer, au milieu des arbres de sorte commune qui n'ont pas encore été déplantés, deux ou trois espèces précieuses aux feuillages fantastiques et qui semblent autour d'eux réserver du vide, donner de l'air, faire de la clarté.[96]

Here again Proust's concern with social class distinction creeps into his botanical observations as he carefully discriminates between the trees " de sorte *commune* " and those of " espèces *précieuses*." [97]

The ever returning gleam of sunlight illuminates and transfigures

[93] *Ibid.*, pp. 292-293.
[94] *Ibid.*, p. 293.
[95] *Ibid.*, pp. 293-294.
[96] *Ibid.*, p. 294.
[97] Cf. *supra*, p. 137, for a similar example.

9

nature under the magic of his pen. All the richness of late summer is depicted in his glowing representation of the transient illumination of the trees:

Ainsi c'était la saison où le Bois de Boulogne trahit le plus d'essences diverses et juxtapose le plus de parties distinctes en un assemblable composite. Et c'était aussi l'heure. Dans les endroits où les arbres gardaient encore leurs feuilles, ils semblaient subir une altération de leur matière à partir du point où ils étaient touchés par la lumière du soleil, presque horizontale le matin comme elle le redeviendrait quelques heures plus tard au moment où dans le crépuscule commençant, elle s'allume comme une lampe, projette à distance sur le feuillage un reflet artificiel et chaud, et fait flamber les suprêmes feuilles d'un arbre qui reste le candélabre incombustible et terne de son faîte incendié.[98]

The leaves appear to have undergone an alteration of their substance at a point where they were touched by the sun's light which would flame up like a lamp, project a warm glow and set ablaze the top leaves of a tree which would remain unchanged beneath its flaming crest. The blaze of the sun on the top boughs is that which awakens the impression of a candelabrum and by its contrast accents the more permanent " incombustible et terne " qualities of the trees. Here again Proust betrays the tendency to see nature through civilization. This dazzling image of an incombustible candelabrum lends an element of phantasy to the scene and is reminiscent of Chateaubriand who occasionally received similar impressions.

Proust has created the illusion of vibrating sunlight enveloping the scene, and enchanted by what Chateaubriand terms " les accidents de lumière " he varies the excellencies of the picture:

Ici, elle épaississait comme des briques, et, comme une jaune maçonnerie persane à dessins bleus, cimentait grossièrement contre le ciel les feuilles des marronniers, là au contraire les détachait de lui, vers qui elles crispaient leurs doigts d'or. A mi-hauteur d'un arbre habillé de vigne vierge, elle greffait et faisait épanouir, impossible à discerner nettement dans l'éblouissement, un immense bouquet comme de fleurs rouges, peut-être une variété d'oeillet.[99]

His delightful comparison of the intense sunlight in a blue sky to a piece of yellow Persian masonry patterned in blue displays his sensitiveness to the interpenetration of atmospheric elements. Here

[98] *S. II.*, p. 294.   [99] *Ibid.*

sun and sky become one. Furthermore, the intensity of light in one
spot patterns leaves against the sky and in another obliterates them
from it. It is interesting that the writer not only portrays the
multiple refulgence of sunlight but also notes its function as an
accessory to vegetation, thus giving it a dual purpose. Indirectly
the sun lends color to the landscape by the " fleurs rouges " which
it has brought to blossom.

The picture varies with the time of day and the visual synthesis
the spectator brings to bear upon the scene. We have observed that
in a general way the quality of light is always for Proust an important factor in the landscape because of its effect on color and
form. The dependence of these elements on light is brought out
even more fully in the following description :

J'allais vers l'allée des Acacias. Je traversais des futaies où la lumière
du matin qui leur imposait des divisions nouvelles, émondait les arbres,
mariait ensemble les tiges diverses et composait des bouquets. Elle attirait
adroitement à elle deux arbres; s'aidant du ciseau puissant du rayon et de
l'ombre, elle retranchait à chacun une moitié de son tronc et de ses
branches, et, tressant ensemble les deux moitiés qui restaient, en faisait
soit un seul pilier d'ombre, que délimitait l'ensoleillement d'alentour, soit
un seul fantôme de clarté dont un réseau d'ombre noire cernait le factice et
tremblant contour. Quand un rayon de soleil dorait les plus hautes
branches, elles semblaient, trempées d'une humidité étincelante, émerger
seules de l'atmosphère liquide et couleur d'émeraude où la futaie tout
entière était plongée comme sous le mer.[100]

These unusual contours created by the variations of light and
shadow are evidence of a keen and poetic observation and a desire
to give precision and individuality to the picture. His representation of a single pillar of shade, defined by the surrounding light,
and a single luminous phantom whose artificial, quivering contour
is encompassed in a network of inky shadows, reveals the wealth of
harmony as well as contrast in his impression. The geometric sym-
metry achieved by this " sharp chisel " of light is also striking.
Even the liquid green color of the atmosphere is dependent upon
the variations of a ray of sunlight.[101]

[100] *Ibid.*, p. 295.
[101] Cf. *S. I.*, pp. 257-259, for Proust's description of " un rayon de soleil
sur le balcon."

In the next passage our writer borrows an element from the field
of painting to describe globes of mistletoe as they appear on the
trees and though the analogy is a bit far-fetched it is acceptable:

Car les arbres continuaient à vivre de leur vie propre et quand ils n'avaient
plus de feuilles, elle brillait mieux sur le fourreau de velours vert qui
enveloppait leurs troncs ou dans l'émail blanc des sphères de gui qui étaient
semées au faîte des peupliers, rondes comme le soleil et la lune dans la
Création de Michel-Ange.[102]

In this medley of picturesque impressions Proust discloses a
psychological nuance in his identification of the Bois with the
beautiful women it enframes:

On sentait que le Mois n'était pas qu'un bois, qu'il répondait à une
destination étrangère à la vie de ses arbres, l'exaltation que j'éprouvais
n'était pas causée que par l'admiration de l'automne, mais par un désir.
Grande source d'une joie que l'âme ressent d'abord sans en reconnaître la
cause, sans comprendre que rien au dehors ne la motive. Ainsi regardais-je
les arbres avec une tendresse insatisfaite qui les dépassait et se portait à
mon insu vers ce chef-d'oeuvre des belles promeneuses qu'ils enferment
chaque jour pendant quelques heures.[103]

Here he does not picture the women as products of the landscape
that surrounds them, rather he represents the Bois as a purely
conventional framework for this masterpiece, so to speak, of beautiful women. The uniqueness of the erotical element here lies in the
fact that contrary to other similar impressions, he indicates no
apparent organic link between the landscape and the people it
frames. Marcel was enchanted by the beauty of this autumn scene
but he gives us to understand that his intuitive longing for the
lovely women who were a part of it increases the intensity of his
joy and the value of everything he sees.[104]

As the spectator continues to contemplate the now deserted Bois,
his impressions, as they evoke memories of the past, are transposed
into the domain of sentiment:

Mais forcés depuis tant d'années par une sorte de greffe à vivre en commun
avec la femme, ils m'évoquaient la dryade, la belle mondaine rapide et

---

[102] *S. II.*, p. 296.

[103] *Ibid.*, p. 295.

[104] Cf. *S. I.*, p. 224. Cf. also *infra*, pp. 191-216, for additional examples of
this " eroticism " of nature.

colorée qu'au passage ils couvrent de leurs branches et obligent à ressentir comme eux la puissance de la saison; ils me rappelaient le temps heureux de ma croyante jeunesse, quand je venais avidement aux lieux où des chefs-d'oeuvre d'élégance féminine se réaliseraient pour quelques instants entre les feuillages inconscients en complices.[105]

The fact that these trees had shared the life of feminine humanity for so many years offered ample opportunity for Proust to indulge in his liking for fusing the social and botanical, as for example, he paints " la belle mondaine rapide et colorée." He further conveys the idea that the beauty for which the Bois made him long now existed only within himself, i. e. in the past, and he rebuilds in his imagination this idea of perfection which he had known and which he now longs to see renewed:

L'idée de perfection que je portais en moi, je l'avais prêtée alors à la hauteur d'une victoria, à la maigreur de ces chevaux furieux et légers comme des guêpes, les yeux injectés de sang comme les cruels chevaux de Diomède, et que maintenant, pris d'un désir de revoir ce que j'avais aimé, aussi ardent que celui qui me poussait bien des années auparavant dans ces mêmes chemins, je voulais avoir de nouveau sous les yeux au moment où l'énorme cocher de Mme Swann, surveillé par un petit groom gros comme le point et aussi enfantin que saint George, essayait de maîtriser leurs ailes d'acier qui se débattaient effarouchées et palpitantes. Helas! il n'y avait plus que des automobiles conduites par des mécaniciens moustachus qu'accompagnaient de grands valets de pied. Je voulais tenir sous les yeux de mon corps pour savoir s'ils étaient aussi charmants que les voyaient les yeux de ma mémoire, de petits chapeaux de femmes si bas qu'ils semblaient une simple couronne. Tous maintenant étaient immenses, couverts de fruits et de fleurs et d'oiseaux variés. Au lieu des belles robes dans lesquelles Mme Swann avait l'air d'une reine, des tuniques gréco-saxonnes relevaient avec les plis des Tanagra, et quelquefois dans le style du Directoire, des chiffons liberty semés de fleurs comme un papier peint.[106]

But the narrator had no faith in all these new elements of the spectacle. They passed before him without reality and without the beauty which in the old days his eyes would have endeavored to extract from them and frame. They were merely women in whose elegance he had no belief but his perspicacity leads him to the realization that:

[105] *S. II*, pp. 296.
[106] *Ibid.*, pp. 296-297.

. . . quand disparaît une croyance, il lui survit . . . un attachement
fétichiste aux anciennes qu'elle avait animées, comme si c'était en elles et
non en nous que le divin résidait et si notre incrédulité actuelle avait une
cause contingente, la mort des Dieux.[107]

In his expression of incredulity for these new things Proust recon-
stitutes the atmosphere of another epoch, that which, as previously
mentioned, François Fosca calls " la couleur temporelle." This
contrast of scenes dated 1890 and 1910 makes his characters better
representations of their times and makes of Proust " le peintre de
moeurs." [108]   The following picture of Mme. Swann walking in
the Bois de Boulogne is dated 1890-95:

Ma consolation c'est de penser aux femmes que j'ai connues, aujourd'hui
qu'il n'y a plus d'élégance. Mais comment des gens qui contemplent ces
horribles créatures sous leurs chapeaux couverts d'une volière ou d'un
potager, pourraient ils même sentir ce qu'il y avait de charmant à voir Mme
Swann coiffée d'une simple capote mauve ou d'un petit chapeau que dépassait une seule fleur d'iris toute droite. Aurais-je même pu leur faire comprendre l'émotion que j'éprouvais par les matins d'hiver à rencontrer Mme
Swann à pied, en paletot de loutre, coiffée d'un simple béret que dépassaient
deux couteaux de plumes de perdrix, mais autour de laquelle la tiédeur
factice de son appartement était évoquée, rien que par le bouquet de
violettes qui s'écrasait à son corsage et dont le fleurissement vivant et bleu
en face du ciel gris, de l'air glacé, des arbres aux branches nues, avait le
même charme de ne prendre la saison et le temps que comme un cadre, et
de vivre dans une atmosphère humaine, dans l'atmosphère de cette
femme . . .[109]

Still contemplating, lamenting and questioning the deserted paths
of the Bois, nature itself helps him to understand how paradoxical
it is to seek in reality the pictures that one has stored in one's
memory, which must inevitably lose the charm that comes to them
from memory itself and from their not being apprehended by the
senses:

Le soleil s'était caché. La nature recommençait à régner sur le Bois d'où
s'était envolée l'idée qu'il était le Jardin élyséen de la Femme; au-dessus
du moulin factice le vrai ciel était gris; le vent ridait le Grand Lac de
petites vaguelettes, comme un lac; de gros oiseaux parcouraient rapidement

[107] *Ibid.*, pp. 297-298.
[108] Fosca, *op. cit.*, p. 240. Cf. also *supra*, p. 100.
[109] *S. II.*, p. 298.

le Bois, comme un bois, et poussant de cris aigus se posaient l'un après l'autre sur les grands chênes qui sous leur couronne druidique et avec une majesté dodonéenne semblaient proclamer le vide inhumain de la forêt désaffectée, et m'aidaient à mieux comprendre la contradiction que c'est de chercher dans la réalité les tableaux de la mémoire, auxquels manquerait toujours le charme qui leur vient de la mémoire même et de n'être pas perçus par les sens.[110]

The reality that he had known no longer existed. It sufficed that Mme. Swann did not appear in the same attire and at the same moment for the whole avenue to be altered. This unceasing process of evolution witnessed in the Bois as elsewhere in life Proust describes with philosophical overtones and melancholy undertones:

Les lieux que nous avons connus n'appartiennent pas qu'au monde de l'espace où nous les situons pour plus de facilité. Ils n'étaient qu'une mince tranche au milieu d'impressions contiguës qui formaient notre vie d'alors; le souvenir d'une certaine image n'est que le regret d'un certain instant; et les maisons, les routes, les avenues, sont fugitives, hélas, comme les années.[111]

Seascapes

We have examined Proust's pictorial representation of the open country, churches, flowers, trees and woods which he loved so dearly as a child but the young Proust was also a lover of coastal towns and thus a great deal of space in his novel has been devoted to the description of ocean scenery. Enchanted by the magnificence of the sea its infinite expanse, mists, and variegated colors—Proust has revealed the charm of Balbec in a succession of exquisite sea pictures. In these word paintings saturated with poetry it is interesting to observe how the writer as a descriptive artist makes use of the same pictorial technique with which he has endowed his painter Elstir. The narrator himself states, in connection with his impressions of the sea, that his eyes have been "instruits par Elstir" to retain precisely those elements that previously he had deliberately rejected and that now he would gaze for hours at what in former years he had been incapable of seeing.[112] For example, compare the following terrestrial conception of the sea to Elstir's painting of the "Port de Carquethuit": [113]

[110] *Ibid.*, p. 300.
[111] *Ibid.*, pp. 300-301.
[112] *SG. II.(1).*, p. 215.
[113] Cf. *supra*, pp. 83-87.

Les jours, assez rares, de vrai beau temps, la chaleur avait tracé sur les eaux, comme à travers champs, une route poussièreuse et blanche derrière laquelle la fine pointe d'un bateau de pêche dépassait comme un clocher villageois. Un remorqueur dont on ne voyait que la cheminée fumant au loin comme une usine écartée, tandis que seul à l'horizon en carré blanc et bombé, peint sans doute par une voile mais qui semblait compact et comme calcaire, faisait penser à l'angle ensoleillé de quelque bâtiment isolé, hôpital ou école. Et les nuages et le vent, les jours où il s'en ajoutait au soleil, parachevaient sinon l'erreur du jugement, du moins l'illusion du premier regard, la suggestion qu'il éveille dans l'imagination. Car l'alternance d'espaces de couleurs nettement tranchées comme celles qui résultent dans la campagne, de la contiguïté de cultures différentes, les inégalités âpres, jaunes, et comme boueuses de la surface marine, les levées, les talus qui dérobaient à la vue une barque où une équipe d'agiles matelots semblait moissonner, tout cela par les jours orageux faisait de l'océan quelque chose d'aussi varié, d'aussi consistant, d'aussi populeux, d'aussi civilisé que la terre carrossable sur laquelle j'allais autrefois et ne devais pas tarder à faire des promenades.[114]

From this picture it is evident that both Elstir and Proust himself experienced the same kind of optical illusions. Chernowitz points out that " this experience of nature in terms of visual illusions, Proust transposed from Impressionist painting, which treats the ocean as though it were a landscape." [115]

But the sea from one day to another was rarely the same and so we must observe how Proust was charmed by its multiple changes. Often one may find that his seascapes are characterized by the same grandeur of handling—the steady gradual increase of power that we feel in the gathering waves themselves. For example, in the following picture though the multiple effects of light and atmosphere are the predominating elements of the scene, in a thoroughly interesting way Proust's optical kinetic imagery communicates the impression of unrest which is one of the chief fascinations of ocean scenery:

. . . quelle joie, . . . de voir dans la fenêtre . . . la mer nue, sans ombrages et pourtant à l'ombre sur une moitié de son étendue que délimitait une ligne mince et mobile, et de suivre des yeux les flots qui s'élançaient l'un après l'autre comme des sauteurs sur un tremplin. A tous moments, . . . je retournais près de la fenêtre jeter encore un regard sur ce vaste cirque

---

[114] *SG. II.(1).*, pp. 215-216, also quoted by Chernowitz, *op. cit.*, p. 144.
[115] *Ibid.*

éblouissant et montagneux et sur les sommets neigeux de ses vagues en pierre d'émeraude çà et là polie et translucide, lesquelles avec une placide violence et un froncement léonin, laissaient s'accomplir et dévaler l'écoulement de leurs pentes auxquelles le soleil ajoutait un sourire sans visage.[116]

In this poetic picture movement humanizes the scene while light illuminates and transfigures nature under the spell of his pen. The beautiful effects portrayed here are due to broad masses of light and shade in the sky affecting differently the different parts of the sea beneath them, all of which presents a charming diversity of light, color and tone.

Light creates the impression of " la mer nue, sans ombrages " and serves to portray its gleaming expanse. On the other hand the thin and fluctuant line which sets off the shadowed part of the sea emphasizes the restlessness of an ocean setting. Although the quality of this picture appears dependent on the quality of light, it is movement perceived by the sense of vision that gives it vitality.

It is interesting that Proust's pictorial method here has been precisely analyzed by Chernowitz in his explanation of Impressionism. For instance, Chernowitz states that " Impressionism is an art of movement, first in point of the subject matter itself, which is caught in the act of moving and further with regard to the movement of light and atmosphere arrested on a canvas as perceived at a given instant." [117] In this connection, note that Proust records first the kinetic aspect of the sea—the waves leaping one behind the other—whose movement he makes visible through a comparison to divers on a springboard. Next the movement of light lends contourless form and color to the view. It is as a vast amphitheatre that the sea appears under the dazzling rays of the sun while movement gives it a terrestrial (" montagneux ") appearance. The snowy crests of its emerald waves seem painted " d'après nature " and " en pierre " gives its inner form a complexity which is also receptive to the effects of light, as disclosed in the phrase " çà et là polie et translucide." Note in the latter adjective his attention to the degree of transparency of an object under light. Usually, the steeper the waves the more vivid their color. Here, the

[116] *JF. II.*, p. 100, partly quoted by Chernowitz, *op. cit.*, p. 143.
[117] *Ibid.*, p. 145 .

painter's use of " émeraude " brings out the special richness and depth of their green.

The abstract substantive, " une placide violence," a form of expression which Proust uses to emphasize the sensory quality of an experience,[118] simultaneously pictures opposite impressions, both perceived by the sense of vision but one revealed by light and the other by movement—a synesthetical approach of the delicacy of Paul Valéry's *M. Teste*. This impetuosity of the sea is stressed by " un froncement léonin " to which the play of light adds a tone of placidity. Proust's representation of these waves illuminated by the smiling sun as they go forward and melt into nothing suggests the sublimation of one element of nature to the other. Also, in a curious way he gives the impression that due to an interpenetration of atmospheric elements, the natural force which gives power and violence to the motion of the sea at the same time is receptive to the pleasing effects of sunlight. But far beyond the painter's impressionism there is already digested here a symbolism in the sense of Dante's *Un riso dell'Universo*.

It is interesting to note how in one sentence Proust reveals the harmonious relation of form, color and light, each assuming its importance in his descriptive analysis—" ce vaste cirque (form) éblouissant (light) et montagneux (form), neigeux (color) et ses vagues en pierre d'émeraude (color)"—and the ensemble of which receives an added lustre and transparency from the ever increasing luminosity. Here he represents a landscape whose almost wild beauty exhibits something similar to the music of the spheres, or harmony of the world. And still the primary impression is pictorial.

We have already seen how Proust views nature through the eyes of the master painters. In the following passage note that he pictures his impression of " ces collines de la mer " in terms of the Tuscan primitives:

. . . ici ces collines de la mer qui avant de revenir vers nous dansant, peuvent reculer si loin que souvent ce n'était qu'après une longue plaine sablonneuse que j'apercevais à une grande distance leurs premières ondulations, dans un lointain transparent, vaporeux et bleuâtre comme ces glaciers qu'on voit au fond des tableaux des primitifs toscans.[119]

---

[118] *Ibid.*, p. 159.   [119] *JF. II.*, p. 101.

Again our hero's own terrestrial perception of the sea reveals an organic relation to Elstir's poetic vision and sensibility. In this connection it should be remarked that Proust's metaphorical creations of the sea in urban terms, like Elstir's, are not the result of an artificial symbolism but rather natural optical illusions; [120] i. e. he actually sees the elements of landscape that he expresses. His kinetic imagery again vivifies the picture—the waves " dansant " toward him—and the infinite and misty expanse of this ocean setting has the unique power of producing the impression of aesthetic remoteness. It is the effect of the sun transcribed in distant perspective that creates the opaque bluish illusion.[121]

In the next passage intrigued by nature in its ever changing flux the narrator represents the same scene according to a movement of light which has altered its perspective as well as its color and form:

D'autres fois, c'était tout près de moi que le soleil riait sur ces flots d'un vert aussi tendre que celui que conserve aux prairies alpestres (dans les montagnes où le soleil s'étale çà et là comme un géant qui en descendrait gaiement, par bonds inégaux, les pentes), moins l'humidité du sol que la liquide mobilité de la lumière.[122]

This likening of the green of the waves to that of Alpine pastures is certainly apropos of its other terrestrial details and at the same time distinguishes it from the deep emerald of a previous impression. He continues to explain that this effect is caused less by the moisture of the soil than by the liquid mobility of their light. Note that in addition to describing the multiple effects of sunlight he gives it an inward complexity in the substantive, " liquide mobilité." Here we are confronted with a baroque interchange of planes which characterizes also the poetry of Caldéron and Paul Valéry.

An interesting aspect of Proust's style which may be noted here is his use of the parenthetical insertion to complete the impression or motif, as for instance the line " dans les montagnes ou le soleil s'étale çà et là comme un géant qui en descendrait gaiement, par bonds inégaux, les pentes." This insertion makes more exact his

---

[120] Cf. *supra*, p. 83-87. Cf. also Chernowitz, *op. cit.*, p. 112.
[121] *Ibid.*, p. 57.
[122] *JF. II.*, p. 101.

illusion of landscape elements in the sea and adds still greater diversity to the effects of sunlight passing over the scene. Let us note that as usual it is an impression that Proust seeks to convey and not the description of physical facts. It has been said that Proust enjoyed making these parenthetical insertions just " as might some informal eyewitness who was conveying his impressions of the moment directly, hastily, spontaneously, without taking the trouble to organize them into logical rationally constructed sentences." From this follows his spontaneous word order.[123]

And thus it is light above all, that according to the direction from which is comes and along which our eyes follow it, shifts and fixes the undulations of the sea. Differences of lighting, i. e. illusory distance created by the effect of light on a scene, modifies no less the orientation of a place, then would a distance in space actually traversed. The sensations of distance, illusory or real, inspire in him similar yearnings. The following passage serves to illustrate how this variegated refulgence of light constructs before his sight new goals which it inspires him to attain:

Quand le matin le soleil venait de derrière l'hôtel, découvrant devant moi les grèves illuminées jusqu'aux premiers contreforts de la mer, il semblait m'en montrer un autre versant et m'engager à poursuivre, sur la route tournante de ses rayons, un voyage immobile et varié à travers les plus beaux sites du paysage accidenté des heures. Et dès ce premier matin le soleil me désignait au loin d'un doigt souriant ces cimes bleues de la mer qui n'ont de nom sur aucune carte géographique, jusqu'à ce qu'étourdi de sa sublime promenade à la surface retentissante et chaotique de leurs crêtes et de leurs avalanches, il vînt se mettre à l'abri du vent dans ma chambre . . .[124]

His reference to the diversified landscape of the hours is a completely impressionistic attitude.

It is interesting that each personification of the sun portrays it as a mediator of joy and cheer. For instance, he constantly pictures it as smiling upon the waters leaping gaily down the chaotic waves and its " doigt souriant " is that which points to adventure.

A little later gazing at the same sea through the dining room

---

[123] Eugen Lerch, *Historische französische Syntax* (Braunschweig, 1930-31, 1934, 3 vols.), III, p. 364, noted by Chernowitz, *op. cit.*, pp. 160-161.
[124] *JF. II.*, p. 102.

window of the Balbec hotel he seeks effects analogous to Baudelaire's
" soleil rayonnant sur la mer " :

Me persuadant que j'étais " assis sur le môle " ou au fond du " boudoir "
dont parle Baudelaire, je me demandais si son " soleil rayonnant sur la
mer " ce n'était pas—bien différent du rayon du soir, simple et superficiel
comme un trait doré et tremblant—celui qui en ce moment brûlait la mer
comme une topaze, la faisait fermenter, devenir blonde et laiteuse comme de
la bière écumante comme du lait, tandis que par moments s'y promenaient
çà et là de grandes ombres bleues, que quelque Dieu semblait s'amuser à
déplacer, en bougeant un miroir dans le ciel.[125]

An even more enchanting picture of the sea at Balbec is one in
which its poetic beauty at a particular moment suggests the splendour of " la nymphe Glaukonomèné." One of the Nereids is called
Glauké because the color of the sea is *glaukos*, blue. Proust seems
to confuse this name with *Glaukopis* (meaning with clear eyes) to
which he adds the participial ending *omenos*. Proust often speaks
of the unique world which is created by a master's own sensibility—
" comme chez Vermeer, il y a création d'une certaine âme, d'une
certaine couleur des étoffes et des lieux " [126]—and in this " tableau
vivant " he creates an " image de celle que nous avons d'habitude
de voir " : [127]

Par quel privilège, un matin plutôt qu'un autre la fenêtre en s'entr'ouvrant
découvrit-elle à mes yeux émerveillés la nymphe Glaukonomèné, dont la
beauté paresseuse et qui respirait mollement, avait la transparence d'une
vaporeuse émeraude à travers laquelle je voyais affluer les éléments
pondérables qui la coloraient? [128]

A rather striking feature of this mythological representation of the
sea is the spectator's consistent reference to the sea as " elle," i. e.
the nymph. Such a cultured and scholarly conception of nature
suggests that what was possible for Greek polytheistic pantheism
may be possible at any time for a poetic soul. Now this allusion
to the sea as a nymph connotes its extaordinary beauty but the
poet's specific reference to the nymph " Glaukonomèné "—in the

[125] *Ibid.*, p. 103.
[126] *P. II.*, p. 238. Cf. Chernowitz, *op. cit.*, pp. 72-73.
[127] *JF. III.*, p. 102.
[128] *JF. II.*, p. 145.

sense of Baudelaire's "correspondances" and Flaubert's "rapport fatal"—renders visible the exact color of his impression. Glaukos is a sea green with a bluish grey tinge. Next his imagery proceeds from the abstract "la beauté paresseuse" to a concrete description of its color as "la transparence d'une vaporeuse émeraude." One should note that in recomposing this impression of transparency he renders not only the external appearance of the ocean but hints at its inward chromatic complexity beneath which he sees the ponderable elements that color it.

In the following passage again the harmonious blending of form, color and movement appears inseparable from the light which bathes it:

Elle faisait jouer le soleil avec un sourire alangui par une brume invisible qui n'était qu'un espace vide réservé autour de sa surface translucide rendue ainsi plus abrégée et plus saisissante comme ces déesses que le sculpteur détache sur le reste du bloc qu'il ne daigne pas dégrossir.[129]

The effect of an invisible haze on light is that which gives a languorous appearance to the ever smiling sun. Furthermore, this impression of a translucent surface, evoked by the contrast of light and shadow and pictured in terms of a sculptor's art, enriches his visual imagery and indicates an intellectual as well as an impressionistic perception of the scene.

Haunted by the theme of "la brise marine" as "invitation au voyage" our hero yearns to escape into the vast spaces of ocean and heaven:

Telle, dans sa couleur unique, elle nous invitait à la promenade sur ces routes grossières et terriennes, d'où, installés dans la calèche de Mme de Villeparisis, nous apercevions tout le jour et sans jamais l'atteindre la fraîcheur de sa molle palpitation.[130]

Here then is a latent echo of Watteau's *Ile de Cythère*.

Proust's views of the sea were so varied by the time of the day and season of the year that he himself often had the impression of looking at a series of paintings. For instance, in broad daylight the impression of sea foam suggested to him the delicate work of Pisanello and Gallé:

[129] *Ibid.*, p. 145.   [130] *Ibid.*

. . . alors, dans le verre glauque et qu'elle boursouflait de ses vagues
rondes, la mer, sertie entre les montants de fer de ma croisée comme dans
les plombs d'un vitrail, effilochait sur toute la profonde bordure rocheuse
de la baie des triangles empennés d'une immobile écume linéamentée avec
la délicatesse d'une plume ou d'un duvet dessinés par Pisanello, et fixés
par cet émail blanc, inaltérable et crémeux qui figure une couche de neige
dans les verreries de Gallé.[131]

And as regularly as the season advanced, the picture in his window
changed, and as the days grew shorter, the geometrical effect of the
sun in a violet sky leaning over the sea, gave the impression of a
holy picture:

Bientôt les jours diminuèrent et au moment où j'entrais dans la chambre,
le ciel violet semblait stigmatisé par la figure raide, géometrique, passagère
et fulgurante du soleil (pareille à la représentation de quelque signe
miraculeux, de quelque apparition mystique), s'inclinait vers la mer
sur la charnière de l'horizon comme un tableau religieux au-dessus du
maître-autel . . .[132]

Still later in the season the glow of the setting sun over the sea
evoked simultaneously several sensory impressions. In addition to
the poetic pleasure received from its scenic beauty the colors of the
red sky were associated in his mind with the sensual pleasure to be
derived from the good food he would soon be ordering at Rivebelle:[133]

Quelques semaines plus tard, quand je remontais, le soleil était déjà couché.
Pareille à celle que je voyais à Combray au-dessus du Calvaire à mes
retours de promenade et quand je m'apprêtais à descendre avant le dîner à
la cuisine, une bande de ciel rouge au-dessus de la mer compacte et coupante
comme de la gelée de viande, puis bientôt sur la mer déjà froide et bleue
comme le poisson appelé mulet, le ciel du même rose qu'un de ces saumons
que nous nous ferions servir tout à l'heure à Rivebelle ravivaient le plaisir
que j'allais avoir à me mettre en habit pour partir dîner.[134]

Surrounded by these pictures of the sea the sight of a ship moving
into the night causes him to experience an escape into the elements:

[131] *JF. III.*, pp. 54-55.
[132] *Ibid.*, p. 55.
[133] Cf. *supra*, p. 71, 141.
[134] *JF. III.*, pp. 55-56, also quoted by Chernowitz, *op. cit.*, p. 146. Cf.
also *JF. III.*, p. 56, for Proust's impression of visible black vapors which
like lofty structures percipitate into the sea.

La vue d'un vaisseau qui s'éloignait comme un voyageur de nuit me donnait cette même impression que j'avais eue en wagon, d'être affranchi des nécessités du sommeil et de la claustration dans une chambre. D'ailleurs je ne me sentais pas emprisonné dans celle où j'étais puisque dans une heure j'allais la quitter pour monter en voiture. Je me jetais sur mon lit; et, comme si j'avais été sur la couchette d'un des bateaux que je voyais assez près de moi et que la nuit on s'étonnerait de voir se déplacer lentement dans l'obscurité, comme des cygnes assombris et silencieux mais qui ne dorment pas, j'étais de tous côtés entouré des images de la mer.[135]

In connection with this melange of mental pictures supplemented by reality the spectator declares that, if beneath his window, the flight of sea-martins and swallows had not brought into touch with the reality the scenes that he had before his eyes, he might have believed that they were no more than a selection, changed every day, of sea pictures, which were shown quite arbitrarily in the place in which he happened to be and without having any necessary connection with that place.[136]

At one time Proust even sketches a series of these views by means of Japanese color prints:

Une fois c'était une exposition d'estampes japonaises: à côté de la mince découpure de soleil rouge et rond comme la lune, un nuage jaune paraissait un lac contre lequel des glaives noirs se profilaient ainsi que les arbres de sa rive, une barre d'un rose tendre que je n'avais jamais revu depuis ma première boîte de couleurs s'enflait comme un fleuve sur les deux rives duquel des bateaux semblaient attendre à sec qu'on vînt les tirer pour les mettre à flot. Et avec le regard dédaigneux, ennuyé et frivole d'un amateur ou d'une femme parcourant, entre deux visites mondaines, une galerie, je me disais: C'est curieux ce coucher de soleil, c'est différent, mais enfin j'en ai déjà vu d'aussi délicats, d'aussi étonnants que celui-ci.' [137]

And yet again it is an impressionist exhibition that meets the eye:

J'avais plus de plaisir les soirs où un navire absorbé et fluidifié par l'horizon tellement de la même couleur que lui, ainsi que dans une toile apparaissait impressionniste, qu'il semblait aussi de la même matière, comme si on n'eût fait que découper son avant, et les cordages en lesquels elle s'était amincie et filigranée dans le bleu vaporeux du ciel.[138]

We have already observed how this mirage effect caused by an

[135] *Ibid.*
[136] *Ibid.*, p. 57.
[137] *Ibid.*, pp. 57-58.
[138] *Ibid.*, p. 58.

infinite expanse and distant perspective was an effect which
interested Elstir.[139]

Still another view suggests " une étude de nuages " as though it
were intended to illustrate the special talent of an artist:

> Un autre jour la mer n'était peinte que dans la partie basse de la fenêtre
> dont tout le reste était rempli de tant de nuages poussés les uns contre les
> autres par bandes horizontales, que les carreaux avaient l'air par une
> préméditation ou une spécialité de l'artiste, de présenter une ' étude de
> nuages,' cependant que les différentes vitrines de la bibliothèque montrant
> des nuages semblables mais dans une autre partie de l'horizon et diverse-
> ment colorés par la lumière, paraissaient offrir comme la répétition, chère
> à certains maîtres contemporains, d'un seul et même effet, pris toujours à
> des heures différentes mais qui maintenant avec l'immobilité de l'art
> pouvaient être tous vus ensemble dans une même pièce, exécutés au pastel
> et mis sous verre.[140]

An examination of these sea pictures reveals the fact that Proust's
narrator like his painter Elstir views nature poetically and therefore subordinates the actual physical facts of a scene to his own
subjective vision. Consequently in the manner of the Impressionist
painters, both " see things not as they are but as they appear during
the split second of a first glance at them." [141] Also, it is noteworthy
that in these descriptions, as in most of his others, Proust uses the
imperfect tense which was the favorite method of literary impressionists for prolonging the pictorial element of a scene and depicting
the action as already and still in progress.[142] It may be concluded
that Proust's optic art reaches its peak in these seascapes. Though
he often dreamt of a tempestuous sea, his pictures are more often
of utter gentleness.[143]

---

[139] Cf. *supra*, p. 90.

[140] *JF. III.*, p. 58. Note also Proust's impression of a " Harmony in Grey
and Pink " by Whistler, *Ibid.*, pp. 58-59. Cf. also Chernowitz, *op. cit.*,
pp. 97, 147-148. In a similar fashion cornflowers in a plowed field create
the effect of an old painting. *JF. II.*, p. 153.

[141] Chernowitz, *op. cit.*, p. 105.

[142] *Ibid.*, p. 59.

[143] Cf. *SG. II.(1).*, p. 188, *SG. II.(2).*, pp. 147-148, and *JF. II.*, p. 148,
for additional sea pictures painted by Proust.

Townscapes

We now know Proust to be the master of an extensive range of
scenes. We have seen that he has every type of landscape at his
command and now in his description of Venice we must observe
how, by a representation of the urban aspects of a scene, he
portrays a sort of "townscape."[144]

Venice, the enchanting city built in the sea, finally becomes the
realization of his magical dreams of color, light and medieval
architecture. However, in spite of the extraordinary radiance that
fills his Venetian scenes there is not the same joy in the world of
loveliness as portrayed in his earlier landscapes. The splendour of
these scenes seem to come from without rather than from within.
They appear to be painted not so much from the subjective vision
but from the observation of objective reality. The writer's pen was
dipped in light but not from the reflection of his soul.

In the following passage Proust, as the transient spectator, aims
at representing the individual urban features of the scene—the
details of the streets, monuments, and churches:

Ma mère m'avait emmené passer quelques semaines à Venise et—comme
il peut y avoir de la beauté aussi bien que dans les choses les plus humbles,
dans les plus précieuses—j'y goûtais des impressions analogues à celles que
j'avais si souvent ressenties autrefois à Combray, mais transposées selon
un mode entièrement différent et plus riche. Quand à dix heures du matin
on venait ouvrir mes volets, je voyais fiamboyer, au lieu du marbre noir
que devenaient en resplendissant les ardoises de Saint-Hilaire, l'Ange d'Or
du campanile de Saint-Marc. Rutilant d'un soleil qui le rendait presque
impossible à fixer, il me faisait avec ses bras grands ouverts, pour quand
je serais une demi-heure plus tard sur la piazzetta, une promesse de joie
plus certaine que celle qu'il put être jadis chargé d'annoncer aux hommes
de bonne volonté. Je ne pouvais apercevoir que lui, tant que j'étais couché,
mais comme le monde n'est qu'un vaste cadran solaire où un seul segment
ensoleillé nous permet de voir l'heure qu'il est, dès le premier matin je
pensai aux boutiques de Combray sur la place de l'Eglise qui le dimanche
étaient sur le point de former quand j'arrivais à la messe, tandis que la
paille du marché sentait fort sous le soleil déjà chaud. Mais dès le second
jour, ce que je vis, . . . ce furent les impressions de ma première sortie du

---

[144] This idea of a "townscape" is a thoroughly modern experience which
springs from the dissertation of Elizabeth Küchler, *Das Stadterlebnis bei
Verhaeren* (Hamburg, 1930).

matin à Venise, à Venise où la vie quotidienne n'était pas moins réelle qu'à
Combray, où comme à Combray le dimanche matin on avait bien le plaisir
de descendre dans une rue en fête, mais où cette rue était toute en une eau
de saphir, rafraîchie de souffles tièdes, et d'une couleur si résistante, que
mes yeux fatigués pouvaient pour se détendre et sans craindre qu'elle
fléchît y appuyer leurs regards. Comme à Combray les bonnes gens de la
rue de l'Oiseau, dans cette nouvelle ville aussi, les habitants sortaient bien
des maisons alignées l'une à côté de l'autre dans la grande rue, mais ce
rôle de maisons projetant un peu d'ombre à leurs pieds était à Venise
confié à des palais de porphyre et de jaspe, au-dessus de la porte cintrée
desquels la tête d'un Dieu barbu (en dépassant l'alignement, comme le
marteau d'une porte à Combray) avait pour résultat de rendre plus foncé
par son reflet, non le brun du sol, mais le bleu splendide de l'eau. Sur la
piazza l'ombre qu'eussent développée à Combray la toile du magasin de
nouveautés et l'enseigne du coiffeur, c'étaient les petites fleurs bleues que
sème à ses pieds sur le désert du dallage ensoleillé le relief d'une façade
Renaissance, non pas que quand le soleil tapait fort, on ne fût obligé, à
Venise comme à Combray, de baisser au bord du canal, des stores, mais ils
étaient tendus entre les quadrilobes et les rinceaux de fenêtres gothiques.[145]

In the manner of a mystic Proust reconstructs his impression of
Venice upon things known, adding that the unknown are superior
in kind and only vaguely related to the known ones. Since according to Proust's literary methods it is mainly through such comparisons that the reality of a scene is to be expressed, he seeks
analogy in the life of Combray for each feature of his impression.
This device may have been used to emphasize the extraordinary
splendour and richness of the city as versus the simple life of a
small provincial town. However, ever since Montaigne and Du
Bellay the French method of infiltrating a foreign country has
been to permeate it with the experience of " la douce France."

Proust finds that the " campanile de Saint-Marc " dominates the
city of Venice in the same fashion that " le clocher de Saint-
Hilaire " rules over Combray and " la piazetta " reminds him of
the " Place d'Eglise." Also he observes that in Venice, life can
have an aspect as " quotidienne " as in Combray. The inhabitants
in the same way emerge from houses lined side by side along the
principal street, but the fancy element intrudes upon his impression
and the houses of Venice appear as palaces of porphyry and jasper.

[145] *AD. II.*, p. 110.

The streets are festive but paved with " une eau de saphir " thus making the reality of the town appear unreal. Attentive even to the analogical effects of chiaroscuro he notes that on the piazza the shadow that would have been cast at Combray by the shop awnings here turned into tiny blue flowers scattered by the silhouette of a Renaissance façade.

It is interesting that in his analogical representation of the scene he is attentive to the comparative effects of light, atmosphere and color as well as the individual objective features of the place. In a sort of explosion of splendour this city, on the first morning of his visit, appears immediately enveloped in sunlight. The light of Venice has been a source of inspiration to artists through the ages and Proust also hastens to arrest its radiant effects upon his canvas. The " Campanile de Saint-Marc " is perceived in its dazzling glitter " rutilant d'un soleil qui le rendait presque impossible à fixer " and the vibrating effect of the sun causes him to think of the world as a vast sun-dial where a single segment of light allows one to see what time it is. This is the first time that an impressionist becomes a metaphysician. Proust's voice is sometimes like the voice of Paul Claudel. Similarly from his window at Combray it was the reflection of the sun on the steeple of Saint Hilaire that often told him the time of the day.[146]

His impression of the steeple of St. Mark is transcribed in kinetic imagery reminiscent of his descriptions of the trees of Balbec [147] and the steeples of Martinville.[148] Even in this alien atmosphere a church spire is perceived as an amiable being, alive and promising happiness to his devoted gaze.

Proust's special attention to the architectural details of Venice discloses an interest in more than the sheer pictorial value of a scene. The church spire, the town square and the ornate houses with arched doors, Renaissance façades and Gothic windows are all brought into intimate relation, while the effects of light and shadow enhance their more solid masses and give value and balance to the picture. But his impression acquires real depth by his con-

[146] *S. I.*, p. 97.
[147] Cf. also *JF. II.*, p. 161. Cf. *supra*, pp. 40-46.
[148] Cf. *S. I.*, p. 258. Cf. *supra*, pp. 34-40.

sciousness of the many centuries during which the buildings have grown in their majestic beauty. This effect of the strong lines of architecture enveloped in the glory of the sun, as splendorous as when those buildings first rose into the air, is an artistic motif à la Renoir. However, the main object of this entire passage is to portray the resemblance between Venice and Combray, and his picture is characterized by an urban quality hitherto not represented by Proust.[149]

In the next passage it is the mysterious charm of the canals of Venice that captivates the narrator's attention. His eye still keyed to the effects of sunlight, he continues:

Ma gondole suivait les petits canaux; comme la main mystérieuse d'un génie qui m'aurait conduit dans les détours de cette ville d'Orient, ils semblaient au fur et à mesure que j'avançais, me pratiquer un chemin creusé en plein coeur d'un quartier qu'ils divisaient en écartant à peine d'un mince sillon arbitrairement tracé les hautes maisons aux petites fenêtres mauresques; et, comme si le guide magique avait tenu une bougie entre ses doigts et m'eût éclairé au passage, ils faisaient briller devant eux un rayon de soleil à qui ils frayaient sa route.[150]

This personification of the gondola as " la main mystérieuse d'un génie " is a typically Proustian device and it at once converts the half " civilized " scene into an Oriental civilization of the *Mille et Une Nuits*.[151]

Proust writes that it has been the mistake of some very great artists, by a quite natural reaction from the artificial Venice of bad painters, to attach themselves exclusively to the Venice which they have found more realistic, to some humble " campo " or some tiny deserted " rio." However, it was this Venice that he so often explored because it was easier to find there women of the industrial class, match-makers, pearl stringers and innumerable other scenes which he found interesting subjects for artistic expression.[152] In the following passage he sketches one of those more realistic and humble parts of Venice. He is especially intrigued by the equivocal

[149] Cf. Feuillerat, *op. cit.*, pp. 219-220.

[150] *AD. II.*, p. 115.

[151] Cf. *Ibid.*, p. 143, for a similar passage devoted to this mysterious charm of Venetian canals.

[152] *Ibid.*, p. 115.

impression of Venice as "une ville inondée"—by the effect of churches and houses sunk into a languid sea:

> On sentait qu'entre les pauvres demeures que le petit canal venait de séparer et qui eussent sans cela formé un tout compact, aucune place n'avait été réservée. De sorte que le Campanile de l'église ou les treilles de jardins surplombaient à pic le rio comme dans une ville inondée. Mais pour les églises comme pour les jardins, grâce à la même transposition que dans le Grand Canal, la mer se prêtait si bien à faire la fonction de voie de communication, de rue grande ou petite que de chaque côté du canaletto les églises montaient de l'eau en ce vieux quartier populeux, devenues des paroisses humbles et fréquentées, portant sur elles le cachet de leur nécessité, de la fréquentation de nombreuses petites gens, que les jardins traversés par la percée du canal laissaient traîner dans l'eau leurs feuilles ou leurs fruits étonnés et que sur le rebord de la maison dont le grès grossièrement fendu était encore rugueux comme s'il venait d'être brusquement scié, des gamins surpris et gardant leur équilibre laissaient pendre leurs jambes bien d'aplomb, à la façon de matelots assis sur un pont mobile dont les deux moitiés viennent de s'écarter et ont permis à la mer de passer entre elles.[153]

His transformation of the little boys on the doorsteps, dangling their legs in the water, into sailors seated upon a swing bridge, is especially picturesque. But his primary interest is still in the architectural features of the city:

> Parfois, apparaissait un monument plus beau qui se trouvait là, comme une surprise dans une boîte que nous viendrions d'ouvrir, un petit temple d'ivoire avec ses ordres corinthiens et sa statue allégorique au fronton un peu dépaysé parmi les choses usuelles au milieu desquelles il traînait, et le péristyle que lui réservait le canal gardait l'air d'un quai de débarquement pour maraîchers.[154]

In the next passage his impression of the palaces as a chain of pink marble cliffs recalls Elstir's picture of the Balbec church.[155] In this view of Venice the historical buildings lose significance as architectural monuments and become an intergral part of the landscape:

---

[153] *Ibid.*, p. 116.

[154] *Ibid.*, pp. 116-117.

[155] Cf. *JF. III.*, p. 187. This idea of the persistence of architectural conceptions of nature in different countries is an old idea with Proust, cf. Feuillerat, *op. cit.*, p. 219. Cf. also *supra*, pp. 91-92.

Le soleil était encore haut dans le ciel quand j'allais retrouver ma mère sur la Piazetta. Nous remontions le grand canal en gondole, nous regardions la file des palais, entre lesquels nous passions, refléter la lumière et l'heure sur leurs flancs rosés et changer avec elles, moins à la façon d'habitations privées et de monuments célèbres que comme une chaîne de falaises de marbre au pied de laquelle on va se promener le soir en barque pour voir se coucher le soleil. Telles, les demeures disposées des deux côtés de chenal faisaient penser à des sites de la nature, mais d'une nature qui aurait créé ses oeuvres avec une imagination humaine.[156]

Out of the darkness of history these buildings seem to emerge like rocks from the sea. The mansions along the banks of the canal make one think of objects of nature but since these objects have been so stifled by cultural elements they appear to have been created by human imagination. In this manner Proust makes us feel how intimately the work of man is attached to the earth which sustains it. At the same time his obsession with society problems comes to the fore and he pictures the fashionable and luxurious aspects of this already urban scene:

Mais en même temps (à cause du caractère des impressions toujours urbaines que Venise donne presque en pleine mer, sur ces flots où le flux et le reflux se font sentir deux fois par jour, et qui tour à tour recouvrent à marée haute et découvrent à marée basse les magnifiques escaliers extérieurs des palais), comme nous l'eussions fait à Paris sur les boulevards, dans les Champs-Elysées, au Bois, dans toute large avenue à la mode, parmi la lumière poudroyante de soir, nous croisions les femmes les plus élégantes, presque toutes étrangères, et qui mollement appuyées sur les coussins de leur équipage flottant, prenaient la file, s'arrêtaient devant un palais où elles avaient une amie à aller voir, faisaient demander si elle était là; et, tandis qu'en attendant la réponse elles préparaient à tout hasard leur carte pour la laisser, comme elles eussent fait à la porte de l'hôtel de Guermantes, elles cherchaient dans leur guide de quelle époque, de quel style était le palais, non sans être secouées comme au sommet d'une vague bleue par le remous de l'eau étincelante et cabrée, qui s'effarait d'être resserrée entre la gondole dansante et le marbre retentissant. Et ainsi les promenades, même rien que pour aller faire des visites ou des courses, étaient triples et uniques dans cette Venise où les simples allées et venues mondaines prennent en même temps la forme et le charme d'une visite à un musée et d'une bordée en mer.[157]

The character of Proust's Venetian townscapes remains predomi-

[156] *AD. II.*, p. 117.   [157] *Ibid.*, pp. 117-118.

nantly urban and betrays his enjoyment of the fact that man can
entirely outdo nature.[158]

Nocturnal Skyscapes

In the later part of *A la recherche du temps perdue* which was
conceived during World War I, one may observe that skyscapes,
nocturnal scenes and especially the pageantry of Paris air-raids,
became for Proust interesting subjects for artistic expression.
Though these scenes are not as rich in detail or lyric enthusiasm as
his early landscapes, they contain certain dramatic overtones which
make his descriptions impressive and interesting from a more than
pictorial point of view.

The beauty of airplanes going up into the night was for Proust
a spectacle of great aesthetic delight. In the following passages one
may observe how, from dusk, he follows the gradual metamorphosis
of light in the sky and records the various impressions produced
by planes shooting into its multiply illuminated magnificence:

> Avant l'heure où les thés d'après-midi finissaient, à la tombée du jour,
> dans le ciel encore clair, on voyait de loin de petites taches brunes qu'on
> eût pu prendre, dans le soir bleu, pour des moucherons, ou pour des oiseaux.
> Ainsi quand on voit de très loin une montagne, on pourrait croire que c'est
> un nuage. Mais on est ému parce qu'on sait que ce nuage est immense,
> à l'état solide, et résistant. Ainsi étais-je ému parce que la tache brune
> dans le ciel d'été n'était ni un moucheron, ni un oiseau, mais un aéroplane
> monté par des hommes qui veillaient sur Paris.[159]

It is at dusk that the planes create the illusion—due to the distance from which they are perceived—of gnats or birds against a sky
still blue with the light of day. However, the spectator's knowledge
that these brown spots in the summer sky are neither gnats nor
birds but planes piloted by men watching over Paris reestablishes
that distinction which his first impression overlooked and gives to
the scene an immediate stamp of friendliness.[160]

As darkness envelopes the scene these same planes give the

---

[158] The impression conveyed here does not exactly coincide with some of
Proust's previously elaborated ideas concerning the beauty of unadorned
landscapes, cf. *S. II.*, p. 240. Cf. also *P. I.*, pp. 158-163 and 186-187.

[159] *TR. I.*, p. 60.

[160] Cf. *supra*, p. 82.

appearance of luminous firebrands and human stars disappearing into the night. The poet, attentive to the gradations of light and dark, portrays the even deeper blackness of night due to the extinction of street lights and his thoughts expand from the greatness of the nocturnal sky to the *grandeur militaire*:

Les aéroplanes que j'avais vu quelques heures plus tôt faire comme des insectes des taches brunes sur le soir bleu passaient maintenant dans la nuit qu'approfondissait encore l'extinction partielle des réverbères comme de lumineux brûlots. La plus grande impression de beauté que nous faisaient éprouver ces étoiles humaines et filantes était peut-être surtout de faire regarder le ciel vers lequel on lève peu les yeux d'habitude dans ce Paris dont en 1914, j'avais vu la beauté presque sans défense, attendre la menace de l'ennemi qui se rapprochait. Il y avait certes maintenant comme alors la splendeur antique inchangée d'une lune cruellement, mystérieusement sereine, qui versait aux monuments encore intacts l'inutile beauté de sa lumière, mais comme en 1914, et plus qu'en 1914 il y avait aussi autre chose, des lumières différentes et des feux intermittents, que soit de ces aéroplanes, soit des projecteurs de la Tour Eiffel on savait dirigés par une volonté intelligente, par une vigilance amie qui donnait ce même genre d'émotion, inspirait cette même sorte de reconnaissance et de calme que j'avais éprouvés dans la chambre de Saint-Loup, dans la cellule de ce cloître militaire où s'exerçaient, avant qu'ils consommassent un jour, sans une hésitation, en pleine jeunesse, leur sacrifice, tant de coeurs fervents et disciplinés.[161]

As Proust receives the strongest and most abiding impressions not from the present but from the past, in nature as well as in life, the real beauty of this night scene for him is its re-staging of an impression of the past.[162] It is reminiscent of a Parisian sky whose beauty he had seen in 1914 while awaiting the approaching enemy. Furthermore, the great significance of this celestial drama is its power to attract the attention of generally insensitive Parisians. Even in a minimized degree the recapturing of a past impression is a source of keen delight for the narrator.

In this display of military splendour the poet perceives a harmonious blending of the powers of man and nature. His metamorphic representation of planes in the night as " étoiles humaines " accentuates their luminosity and indicates the pre-eminence of a human effort. It is this human intervention which gives to the scene its

[161] *TR. I.*, p. 145.   [162] Cf. *TR. II.*, p. 53.

amicable aspect. The ancient glory of a moon pouring the useless beauty of its light over the historic building is mingled with beams of light directed by intelligent will power from the planes or from the Eiffel Tower. This changeless but useless beauty of moonlight by its antithesis accents the "vigilance amie" of the intelligently directed flashes.

It is of even greater importance to the narrator that this dramatic exhibition which recalls past visual impressions also inspires feelings of gratitude and peace of mind ("reconnaissance et calme") —emotions which he finds analogous to those experienced at Doncières where so many fervent hearts were being trained for the day when they should make the supreme sacrifice. Thus this blending of the old and new within the narrow limits of a night scene is interfused with vital passion—it not only recalls past impressions but evokes past emotions.

Another scene, in which airplanes shoot up like flaming rockets to join the stars, and searchlight beams give the impression of wandering milky ways, displays again the collaboration of human activity and natural phenomena:

Après le raid de l'avant-veille . . . Des aéroplanes montaient encore comme des fusées rejoindre les étoiles et des projecteurs promenaient lentement dans le ciel sectionné, comme une pâle poussière d'astres, d'errantes voies lactées. Cependant les aéroplanes venaient s'insérer áu milieu des constellations et on aurait pu se croire dans une autre hémisphère en effet, en voyant ces "étoiles nouvelles." [163]

Here the virtuosity of the poet's pen communicates the impression of a magical suffusion wherein these "étoiles nouvelles" ascend to blend themselves with all the natural glories of the empyrean. It is striking that Proust's "miniature" air-raid impressions of World War I anticipated those real ones of World War II.

Proust even discerns an aesthetic beauty in the roar of the planes whose sirens suggest to him a sort of Wagnerianism:

Et ces sirènes était-ce assez wagnérien, ce qui du reste était bien naturel pour saluer l'arrivée des Allemands, ça faisait très hymme national, très Wacht am Rhein avec le Kronprinz et les princesses dans la loge impériale;

---

[163] *TR. I.*, p. 145.

c'était à se demander si c'était bien des aviateurs et pas plutôt des
Walkyries qui montaient.[164]

He takes great pleasure in this comparison of aviators to Walkyries
which he explains with purely musical reasoning: [165] " Dame, c'est
que la musique des sirènes était d'une *Chevauchée*. Il faut décidé-
ment l'arrivée des Allemands pour qu'on puisse entendre du Wagner
à Paris," [166] and he adds why, from certain points of view, the
comparison is not false:

La ville semblait une masse informe et noire qui tout d'un coup passait
des profondeurs de la nuit dans la lumière et dans le ciel où un à un les
aviateurs s'élevaient à l'appel déchirant des sirènes, cependant que d'un
mouvement plus lent, mais plus insidieux, plus alarmant, car ce regard
faisait penser à l'objet invisible encore et peut-être déjà proche qu'il cherchait, les projecteurs se remuaient sans cesse, flairaient l'ennemi, le
cernaient dans leurs lumières jusqu'au moment où les avions aiguillés
bondiraient en chasse pour le saisir. Et escadrille après escadrille chaque
aviateur s'élançait ainsi de la ville transporté maintenant dans le ciel,
pareil à une Walkyrie.[167]

One may easily visualize these planes which follow beams of light
to seize the enemy as those mythological Walkyries who rode
through the air on horses striking sparks from their spears, in
pursuit of the fallen heroes who were to be conducted to Walhalla.
Proust's reference to the sound of the sirens as Wagnerian indicates
his propensity for discovering music in the most unorganized noises
of life.[168]

Another night scene in which Proust paints shades of light and
color in the sky one might find reminiscent of Bernardin de Saint-
Pierre who displayed a passion for the variegated celestial hues.

This time the picture of an evening sky reveals nature as independent of human intervention [169] by the fact that its color is

[164] *Ibid.*, p. 87.
[165] Cf. A. Coeuroy, " Music in the Work of Marcel Proust," *Music
Quarterly*, XII (January 1926), pp. 213-251, cf. also *infra*, pp. 238-241 on
Proust's audible universe.
[166] *TR. I.*, p. 87.
[167] *Ibid.*, p. 88.
[168] Cf. Coeuroy, *op. cit.*, p. 135.
[169] Cf. *S. I.*, pp. 197-198, for an elaboration of this idea in Proust's

independent of the lamps which are lighted an hour earlier in the summer. The spectator apparently thinks that because the city is already illuminated for night the heavens should be dark; and thus he reasons that the daylight which still remains over a large part of the bluish sky is due to " le changement d'heure "—what we think of as daylight saving time—a purely human function to which the functions of nature are oblivious: [170]

Les lumières assez peu nombreuses (à cause des gothas) étaient allumées un peu trop tôt, car le changement d'heure avait été fait un peu trop tôt quand la nuit venait encore assez vite mais stabilisé pour toute la belle saison (comme les calorifères sont allumés et éteints à partir d'une certaine date) et au-dessus de la ville nocturnément éclairée dans toute une partie du ciel—du ciel ignorant de l'heure d'été et de l'heure d'hiver et qui ne daignait pas savoir que 8 h. ½ était devenu 9 h. ½—dans toute une partie du ciel bleuâtre il continuait à faire un peu jour.[171]

The idea of determining light according to " le changement d'heure " seems to be an almost ultra-modern perception of things.

This time under the narrator's transmuting vision the sky dominated by the towers of the Trocadéro, upon first glance, gives the illusion of an immense turquoise sea and the clouds appear as a line of black rocks or fishermen's nets hung side by side. But as he prolongs his gaze at this spectacle of beauty he is overcome by a sort of intoxication during which his vision undergoes alteration; and he no longer perceives a far flung sea but a vertical gradation of blue glaciers. A strange visionary sensation evoked by the mere contemplation of beauty seems to be the only explanation for this decided transformation of impression which took place without any apparent alteration of the physical aspects of the scene:

Dans toute la partie de la ville que dominent les tours du Trocadéro, le ciel avait l'air d'une immense mer nuancée de turquoise qui se retire, laissant déjà émerger toute une ligne légère de rochers noirs, peut-être

description of the artificial lake in Swann's Park. Cf. also *supra*, pp. 116-118.

[170] In a traditionally French manner Proust was always seeking the marks of civilization in a landscape and as we have already remarked the result of his inquiries are not always consistent, see e. g. *S. I.*, pp. 197-198 and *AD. II.*, p. 117.

[171] *TR. I.*, pp. 93-94.

même de simple filets, de pêcheurs alignés les uns auprès les autres, et qui étaient de petits nuages. Mer en ce moment couleur turqoise et qui emporte avec elle sans qu'ils s'en aperçoivent, les hommes entraînés dans l'immense révolution de la terre, de la terre sur laquelle ils sont assez fous pour continuer leurs révolutions à eux, et leurs vaines guerres comme celle qui ensanglantait en ce moment la France. Du reste, à force de regarder le ciel paresseux et trop beau qui ne trouvait pas digne de lui de changer son horaire et au-dessus de la ville allumée prolongeait mollement, en ces tons bleuâtres sa journée qui s'attardait, le vertige prenait: ce n'était plus une mer étendue, mais une gradation verticale de bleus glaciers.[172]

As Proust's landscape sketches are so often permeated with his social, cultural and philosophical preoccupations, likewise this scene is pervaded by his indignation at war. Proust's visualization thus never lacks originality even in his less lyrical passages:

. . . le ciel avait l'air d'une . . . Mer en ce moment couleur turquoise et qui emporte avec elle sans qu'ils s'en aperçoivent, les hommes entraînés dans l'immense révolution de la terre, de la terre sur laquelle ils sont assez fous pour continuer leurs révolutions à eux, et leurs vaines guerres comme celle qui ensanglantait en ce moment la France.[173]

On this same evening as the turquoise leaves the sky, the spectator stumbles bewilderingly along unlighted streets until he reaches the boulevard where suddenly he is overcome by an impression of the Orient which he had recently experienced—in another sense a vision of the Paris of 1815 replaced that of the " Paris du Directoire " :

Comme en 1815 c'était le défilé le plus disparate des uniforms des troupes alliées; et parmi elles des Africains en jupeculotte rouge, des Hindous enturbannés de blanc suffisaient pour que de ce Paris où je me promenais, je fisse toute une imaginaire cité exotique, dans un Orient à la fois minutieusement exact en ce qui concernait les costumes et la couleur des visages arbitrairement chimérique en ce qui concernait le décor, comme de la ville où il vivait Carpaccio fît une Jérusalem ou une Constantinople en y assemblant une foule dont la merveilleuse bigarrure n'était pas plus colorée que celle-ci.[174]

This exotic city of the imagination is conceived in the manner of Carpaccio, i. e. by the gathering of a crowd whose costumes and

---

[172] *Ibid.*, p. 94.   [173] *Ibid.*   [174] *Ibid.*, p. 95.

complexions are sufficiently colorful to create an Oriental impression. It is notable that again Proust recreates the " couleur temporelle " of another epoch.[175] This time it is the Paris of 1815,
occupied by Africans in baggy red trousers and white-turbaned
Hindus, that he makes relive in the present.

Proust shows himself to be a master at grasping the characteristic
atmosphere of any landscape that he wishes to represent. Note in
this connection his representation of " L'obélisque de Louqsor ":

> Bien qu'il fût plus de neuf heures, c'était lui encore qui sur la place de la
> Concorde donnait à l'obélisque de Louqsor un air de nougat rose. Puis il
> en modifia la teinte et le changea en une matière métallique de sorte que
> l'obélisque ne devint pas seulement plus précieux, mais sembla aminci et
> presque flexible. On s'imaginait qu'on aurait pu tordre, qu'on avait peut-
> être déjà légèrement faussé ce bijou. La lune était maintenant dans le
> ciel comme un quartier d'orange pelé délicatement quoique un peu entamé.
> Mais elle devait plus tard être faite de l'or le plus résistant. Blottie toute
> seule derrière elle, une pauvre petite étoile allait servir d'unique compagne
> à la lune solitaire, tandis que celle-ci, tout en protégeant son amie, mais
> plus hardie et allant de l'avant, brandirait comme une arme irrésistible,
> comme un symbole oriental, son ample et merveilleux croissant d'or.[176]

The following nocturnal scene in which Proust renders poetically
the effects of moonlight over the jade green of a city snow is another
illustration of his use of chiaroscuro: [177]

> Celui-ci donnait de ces effets que les villes ne connaissent pas, même en
> plein hiver; ses rayons s'étalaient sur la neige qu'aucun travailleur ne
> déblayait plus, boulevard Haussmann, comme ils eussent fait sur un
> glacier des Alpes. Les silhouettes des arbres se reflétaient nettes et pures
> sur cette neige d'or bleuté, avec la délicatesse qu'elles ont dans certaines
> peintures japonaises ou dans certains fonds de Raphaël; elles étaient allon-
> gées à terre au pied de l'arbre lui-même, comme on les voit souvent dans la
> nature au soleil couchant quand celui-ci inonde et rend réfléchissantes les
> prairies où des arbres s'élèvent à intervalles réguliers. Mais par un
> raffinement d'une délicatesse délicieuse la prairie sur laquelle se dévelop-
> paient ces ombres d'arbres légères comme des âmes, était une prairie
> paradisiaque, non pas verte mais d'un blanc si éclatant à cause de clair de

---

[175] Fosca, *op. cit.*

[176] *SG. II.(1).*, p. 7.   Cf. Polanscak *op. cit.*, p. 40.

[177] Although this scene is not a skyscape as such, its splendour comes
from the sky and, therefore, it merits attention in this part of our study.

lune qui rayonnait sur la neige de jade, qu'on aurait dit que cette prairie était tissue seulement avec des pétales de poiriers en fleurs. Et sur les places, les divinités des fontaines publiques tenant en main un jet de glace avaient l'air de statues d'une matière double pour l'exécution desquelles l'artiste avait voulu marier exclusivement le bronze au cristal.[178]

The dazzling flood of moonlight over the snow-covered city is that which first strikes the eye of the sensitive observer, but it is the contrasting effect of the delicate but sharply cut silhouettes cast by the trees [179] on this moonlit snow which enchants his imagination and awakens the impression of certain Japanese paintings, or backgrounds done by Raphaël. We have observed numerous times that Proust in describing a scene never hesitates to use comparisons drawn from the world of art. His luminarist's vision does not perceive the snow as conventionally white but first as " d'or bleuté " and later, under the more intense white of moonlight, as " la neige de jade." The portrayal of this impression reveals Proust's superb craftsmanship in dealing with complementary colors.

His metaphoric transformation of the shadows into souls is an exquisitely refined psychological nuance and as the writer describes the impression evoked likewise one may describe the linguistic achievement here as " un raffinement d'une délicatesse délicieuse." Furthermore, his representation of the field over which the shadows are cast as " une prairie paradisiaque " carries the spiritual tone introduced by " des âmes " and creates an atmosphere of serenity. In the same sentence he makes an interesting distinction between " verte " and " jade " and the dazzling white of moonlight contains a sensorial quality which suggests the velvety lustre of petals of blossoming pear trees. Finally, the contrasting effect of light and shadow on the statues of the public fountains makes for a balanced picture.

It is evident from this series of picturesque memories that Proust was master of almost every type of landscape. The grandeur of the sea and sky set free the lyric impulses of his soul just as did spring flowers, country lanes and autumn woods. His landscapes, painted

---

[178] *TR. I.*, p. 62.
[179] Cf. *S. I.*, p. 211, for Proust's description of the shadows cast by apple trees. Cf. *supra*, pp. 119-120.

according to his own unique vision of the world and impregnated with his own past memories, most often exhibit the gentle, sublime, luxuriant and cheerful aspects of nature. He represents a world already known to him (which made it all the more real) but forgotten for some time (which restored all its novelty).[180] Proust's fusion of souvenir, impression, observation and emotion in these landscapes results in an exquisite pictorial expressionism. But his stylistic methods are highly complicated and in order that the reader does not miss his unique pictorial quality, it seems desirable to take out of these landscapes and list, in conclusion, first his most striking patterns of direct conveyance, and secondly, his patterns of poetic transformation both of which take one into a realm of dreams. No one in French literature before Proust ever achieved such a highly poetic grasping of things in nature as displayed in the following magic strokes of his literary brush:

PATTERNS OF DIRECT CONVEYANCE

les dos laineux de maisons

S. I., p. 74.

des rues **coiffées de pignons**

S. I., p. 74.

un flot de promeneurs noircissant les rues

S. I., p. 132.

les larges **pétales de satin blanc** des pommiers

S. I., p. 211.

des guêpes passant la journée **à herboriser**

S. I., p. 238.

une violette **laissant fléchir sa tige sous le poids de la goutte d'odeur**

S. I., p. 240.

un sentier **se tapissant du feuillage bleu d'un noisetier**

S. I., p. 240.

quelque fragments de tours **bossuant la prairie**

S. I., pp. 240-241.

des roses mousseuses **en guirlandes dénouées**

S. I., p. 244.

leur mousse **embaumée de lilas**

S. I., p. 196.

rougissants boutons de pommiers

S. I., p. 211.

---

[180] *G. II.*, p. 36.

le soleil **jaunissait la bordure d'une nuée**

S. I., p. 216.

le glaïeul, **laissant fléchir ses glaives avec un abandon royal**

S. I., p. 197.

les fleur de lis **en lambeaux**

S. I., p. 197.

les pommiers **en toilette de bal**

SG. II.(1)., p. 211.

les boutons d'or gardant **un poétique éclat d'orient**

S. I., p. 241.

les fleurs montaient **le blanc et rose proprets de la julienne, lavés comme de la porcelaine avec un soin domestique**

S. I., p. 244.

ses vagues **en pierre d'émeraude**

JF. II., p. 100.

la beauté paresseuse de la mer

JF. II., p. 145.

les sirènes **assez wagneriennes**

TR. I., 94.

Patterns of Poetic Transformation

le cristal successif des heures silencieuses

S. I., p. 130.

les panaches de plumes mauves des lilas

S. I., p. 196.

des giroflées ouvrant **leur bourse fraîche**

S. I., p. 203.

le village **qui sculpte sur le ciel** le relief de ses arrêtes blanches

S. I., p. 216.

le peuplier **qui adresse à l'orage des supplications déseperées**

S. I., p. 220.

une fleur de nymphéa **rougissant comme une fraise**

S. I., p. 243.

un long rayon de lune s'élargissant et se fendillant de toutes les rides de l'eau

S. I., p. 193.

les petits coeurs verts et frais de leurs feuilles

S. I., p. 196.

les boucles étoilées de leur tête odorante

S. I., p. 196.

des pensées qui étaient venues poser **comme des papillons** leurs ailes bleuâtres et glacées

S. I., p. 244.

le vent qui était **le génie particulier de Combray**

S. I., p. 210.

les gouttes d'eau **comme des oiseaux migrateurs**

S. I., p. 217.

une sorte **de règne végétal de l'atmosphère**

S. I., p. 189.

les bouquets célestes des nuages

S. I., p. 189.

un seul arbre, **étêté et têtu, secouait au vent une vilaine chevelure rouge**

S. II., p. 293.

le Bois était **le Jardin elyséen de la Femme**

S. II., p. 300.

un arbre qui reste **le candélabre incombustible et terne**

S. II., p. 294.

les ombres d'arbres **légères commes des âmes**

TR. I., p. 62.

la molle palpitation de la mer

JF. II., p. 145.

les flots qui s'élançaient **comme des sauteurs sur un tremplin**

JF. II., p. 100.

le mer **comme un vaste cirque éblouissant et montagneux**

JF. II., p. 100.

la mer blonde et laiteuse **comme de la bière écumante du lait**

JF. II., p. 145.

une bande de ciel rouge au-dessus de la mer **comme de la gelée de viande**

JF. III., p. 55.

la fine pointe d'un bateau de pêche dépassait **comme un clocher villageois**

SG. II.(1)., pp. 215-216.

un remorqueur fumant au loin **comme une usine ecartée**

SG. II.(1)., p. 215.

le ciel avait l'air **d'une immense mer nuance de turquoise**

TR. I., p. 94.

un nuage jaune paraissait **un lac contre lequel des glaives noirs se profilaient**

JF. III., p. 57.

les aéroplanes montaient **comme étoiles nouvelles**

TR. I., p. 145.

les projecteurs promenaient dans le ciel **comme une pâle poussière d'astres, d'errantes voies lactées**

TR. I., p. 145.

la main mystérieuse dé sa gondole

AD. II., p. 115.

CHAPTER V

THE EROTIC LANDSCAPE

In addition to the psychological, the "painted" and the "pictorial" landscapes there are still other scenes in *A la recherche du temps perdu* which are important for the reason that they disclose the writer's erotical interest in nature. As with many of the modern French writers—Valéry Larbaud, Paul Morand, Montherlant and the prototype of them all, Pierre Loti—there is in Proust a profound relation between the sentiment of love and the sentiment of nature which in a psychoanalytical way manifests itself in the combined expression of his desire for women and curiosity for countries. In the beginning of *Du Coté de chez Swann* the young boy reveals that his dreams of love were always impregnated with the beauties of nature:

> . . . le rêve d'une femme qui m'aurait aimé était toujours présent à ma pensée . . . ce rêve fut imprégné de la fraîcheur des eaux courantes; et quelle que fût la femme que j'évoquais, des grappes de fleurs violettes et rougeâtres s'élevaient aussitôt de chaque côté d'elle comme des couleurs complémentaires.[1]

Furthermore, he always imagines the women he desires in the setting of whatever places he longs to visit. And he tells us that if in his secret longings it was she who attracted him to them, it was not by the simple association of ideas but because his dreams of travel and love were moments in a single undeviating outrush of all the forces of his life.[2] After this function of framing, which as we will observe was not always imaginary, he portrays the loved one as " la divinité protectrice et locale "[3] of her milieu.

Landscape Frames
" Gilberte "

The first manifestation of Proust's landscape framing occurs when, before he had ever seen Gilberte, after learning that she

---

[1] *S. I.*, p. 127.　　　[2] *Ibid.*, p. 124.　　　[3] *TR. II.*, p. 181.

went about to look at old towns he imagines her standing before a cathedral in the Ile de France:

. . . quand je pensais à elle, je la voyais devant le porche d'une cathédrale, m'expliquant la signification des statues, et, avec un sourire qui disait du bien de moi, me présentant comme son ami, à Bergotte. Et toujours le charme de toutes les idées que faisaient naître en moi les cathédrales, le charme des coteaux de l'Ile-de-France et des plaines de la Normandie faisait refluer ses reflets sur l'image que je me formais de Mlle Swann: c'était être tout prêt à l'aimer.[4]

But it was in Swann's park, already pictured as the scene of the birth of his love for a flower,[5] that his love for this young girl was born. It was over a hedge covered with pink hawthorn blossoms that Gilberte first appeared to Marcel literally " framed " by flowers and her apparition Larcher finds comparable to Beatrice's appearance to Dante in the *Vita Nouva*: [6]

La haie laissait voir à l'intérieur du parc une allée bordée de jasmins, de pensées et de verveines entre lesquelles des giroflées ouvraient leur bourse fraîche, du rose odorant et passé d'un cuir ancien de Cordoue, tandis que sur le gravier un long tuyau d'arrosage peint en vert, déroulant ses circuits, dressait aux points où il était percé au-dessus des fleurs, dont il imbibait les parfums, l'éventail vertical et prismatique de ses gouttelettes multi-colores. Tout à coup, je m'arrêtai, je ne pus plus bouger, comme il arrive quand une vision ne s'adresse pas seulement à nos regards, mais requiert des perceptions plus profondes et dispose de notre être tout entier. Une fillette d'un blond roux qui avait l'air de rentrer de promenade et tenait à la main une bêche de jardinage, nous regardait, levant son visage semé de taches roses. Ses yeux brillaient et comme je ne savais pas alors, ni ne l'ai appris depuis, réduire en ses elements objectifs une impression forte, comme je n'avais pas, ainsi qu'on dit, assez " d'esprit d'observation " pour dégager la notion de leur couleur, pendant longtemps, chaque fois que je repensai à elle, le souvenir de leur éclat se présentait aussitôt à moi comme celui d'un vif azur, puisqu'elle était blonde: de sorte que, peut-être si elle n'avait pas eu des yeux aussi noirs,—ce qui frappait tant la première fois qu'on la voyait—, je n'aurais pas été, comme je le fus, plus particu-lièrement amoureux, en elle, de ses yeux bleus.

Le la regardais, d'abord de ce regard qui n'est pas que le porte-parole des yeux, mais à la fenêtre duquel se penchent tous les sens, anxieux et pétrifiés,

---

[4] *S. I.*, p. 147.

[5] Cf. *Ibid.*, pp. 163-164, 200 and *supra*, p. 60.

[6] Cf. Larcher, *op. cit.*, p. 75.

le regard qui voudrait toucher, capturer, emmener le corps qu'il regarde
et l'âme avec lui: puis . . . d'un second regard, inconsciemment supplicateur,
qui tâchait de la forcer à faire attention à moi, à me connaître![7]

A mysterious beauty is born of the mere name Gilberte as its sound
comes to him through an archway throbbing with the fragrance of
these hawthorn blossoms:

> Ainsi passa près de moi ce nom de Gilberte, donné comme un talisman
> qui me permettait peut-être de retrouver un jour celle dont il venait de
> faire une personne et qui, l'instant d'avant, n'était qu'une image incertaine.
> Ainsi passa-t-il, proféré au-dessus des jasmins et des giroflées, aigre et
> frais comme les gouttes de l'arrosoir vert; imprégnant, irisant la zone d'air
> pur qu'il avait traversée—et qu'il isolait,—du mystère de la vie de celle
> qu'il désignait pour les êtres heureux qui vivaient, qui voyageaient avec
> elle; déployant sous l'épinier rose, à hauteur de mon épaule, la quintessence
> de leur familiarité, pour moi si douloureuse, avec elle, avec l'inconnu de sa
> vie où je n'entrerais pas.[8]

And when he finally comes to know Gilberte, he pictures the
Champs-Elysées as their trysting place:

> . . . nous nous acheminions vers les Champs-Élysées par les rues décorées
> de lumière, encombrées par la foule, et où les balcons, descellés par le
> soleil et vaporeux, flottaient devant les maisons comme des nuages d'or.
> Helas! aux Champs-Elysées je ne trouvais pas Gilberte, elle n'était pas
> encore arrivée. Immobile sur la pelouse nourrie par le soleil invisible
> qui çà et là faisait flamboyer la pointe d'un brin d'herbe, et sur laquelle
> les pigeons qui s'y étaient posés avaient l'air de sculptures antiques que
> la pioche du jardinier a ramenées à la surface d'un sol auguste, je restais
> les yeux fixés sur l'horizon, je m'attendais à tout moment à voir apparaître
> l'image de Gilberte suivant son institutrice, derrière la statue qui semblait
> tendre l'enfant qu'elle portait et qui ruisselait de rayons, à la bénédiction
> du soleil.[9]

Thus the shadow of Gilberte lay not only before a church on the
Ile de France where he had first pictured her but also along the
Méséglise way and in the Champs-Elysées. He reflects:

[7] *S. I.*, pp. 203-204.
[8] *Ibid.*, p. 205. Cf. *infra*, pp. 218-238, for the evocative power of sound
in Proust's work.
[9] *S. II.*, p. 269.

. . . cette même Gilberte qui même avant que je l'eusse jamais vue m'apparaissait devant une église, dans un paysage de l'Ile de France, et qui ensuite évoquant non plus mes rêves mais mes souvenirs, était toujours devant la haie d'épines roses, dans le raidillon que je prenais du côté de Méséglise.[10]

"Madame Swann"

The young boy was also beguiled by the special beauty of Gilberte's mother and after seeing her walk in the Bois nearly every day he pictures the Allée des Acacias as the setting of her feminine elegance:

. . . comme j'avais appris que Mme Swann se promenait presque chaque jaur dans l'allée " des Acacias," autour du grand Lac et dans l'allée de la " Reine Marguerite," je dirigeais Françoise du côté du Bois de Boulogne. Il était pour moi comme ces jardins zoologiques où l'on voit rassemblés des flores diverses et des paysages opposés . . . lui, le Bois, complexe aussi réunissant des petits mondes divers et clos,—faisant succéder quelque ferme plantée d'arbres rouges, de chênes d'Amérique, comme une exploitation agricole dans la Virginie, à une sapinière au bord du lac, ou à une futaie d'où surgit tout à coup dans sa souple fourrure, avec les beaux yeux d'une bête, quelque promeneuse rapide,—il était le Jardin des femmes . . . bien avant d'arriver à l'allée des Acacias, leur parfum qui, irradiant alentour, faisant sentir de loin l'approche et la singularité d'une puissante et molle individualité végétale; puis, quand je me rapprochais, le faîte aperçu de leur frondaison légère et mièvre, d'une élégance facile, d'une coupe coquette et d'un mince tissu, sur laquelle des centaines de fleurs s'étaient abattues comme des colonies ailées et vibratiles de parasites précieux . . . Mais c'est Mme Swann que je voulais voir, et j'attendais qu'elle passât, ému comme si ç'avait été Gilberte, dont les parents, imprégnés comme tout ce qui l'entourait, de son charme, excitaient en moi autant d'amour qu'elle, même un trouble plus douloureux . . .[11]

"Les jeunes filles en fleurs"

Another time it is with a botanist's satisfaction that Proust pictures a group of young girls as a hedge of roses outlined against the sea:

. . . qu'il n'était pas possible de trouver réunies des espèces plus rares que celles de ces jeunes fleurs qui interrompaient en ce moment devant moi

[10] *JF. I.*, p. 152.
[11] *S. II.*, pp. 286-288. Cf. *Ibid.*, pp. 297-300, for other pictures of Mme Swann in the Bois de Boulogne.

la ligne du flot de leur haie légère, pareille à un bosquet de roses de Pennsylvanie, ornement d'un jardin sur la falaise, entre lesquelles tient tout le trajet de l'océan parcouru par quelque steamer, si lent à glisser sur le trait horizontal et bleu qui va d'une tige à l'autre, qu'un papillon paresseux, attardé au fond de la corolle que la coque du navire a depuis longtemps dépassée, peut pour s'envoler en étant sûr d'arriver avant le vaisseau, attendre que rien qu'une seule parcelle azurée sépare encore la proue de celui-ci de la première pétale de la fleur vers laquelle il navigue.[12]

Their rich decorative whole appears submitted to all the vibrations of atmosphere:

. . . à la foi dorées et roses, cuites par le soleil et par le vent . . . plus près de la mer, sur une ligne parallèle . . . tiges de roses dont le principal charme était de se détacher sur la mer . . .[13]

Albertine, the rarest and most beautiful of these young girls, wins the intense devotion of our hero and he first imagines her as a mysterious being painted upon a background of sea and having no real existence.[14]   But her image in this colorful setting soon detaches itself and as he discerns its solidity and color, he sees that she has none of that amorous facility which he supposed to be stamped upon her.[15]   However, even after finding her commonplace she remains still a picture in his mind and he sees her again and again:

. . . silhouettée sur l'écran que lui fait, au fond, la mer, et séparée de moi par un espace transparent et azur, le temps écoulé depuis lors, première image, toute mince dans mon souvenir, désirée, poursuivie, puis oubliée, puis retrouvée, d'un visage que j'ai souvent depuis projeté dans le passé pour pouvoir me dire d'une jeune fille qui était dans ma chambre: " c'est elle! "[16]

Albertine becomes inseparable from the natural beauty of Balbec. At times she is no more than a flower by the sea upon which his eyes are daily invited to gaze but a flower that can think and in

---

[12] *JF. III.*, p. 48.
[13] *Ibid.*, pp. 156, 245, cf. also p. 192.
[14] *G. II.*, p. 50.
[15] *G. II.*, p. 51, cf. also *JF. III.*, p. 153.
[16] *JF. III.*, p. 91.

whose mind he is so childishly anxious to occupy a prominent place.[17]   She becomes a rose living with the roses similar to the dead young girl in Malherbe's famous *Consolation à M. Du Périer* and he feels a passionate longing for her such as he had previously felt for a particular flower.

Having become a part of the landscape herself, her kisses, cheeks, eyes, and even her breathing are expressed in terms of landscape.[18] When he first kisses her, it is " toute la plage de Balbec " [19] and her cheeks often appear pale but flushed with a stream of blood which gives them the dazzling clearness of a wintry morning [20] or "une transparence violette . . . comme il arrive quelque-fois pour la mer." [21]

On any given day the appearance of Albertine, like that of the sea, is dependent on those clouds which change the color of everything by concentration, mobility, dissemination and flight.[22]   He even finds her gaze " comme ces ciels voyageurs des jours d'orage qui approchent d'une nuée moins rapide, la côtoient, la touchent, la dépassent " [23] and in the evening her image rises from his heart and begins to shine as a moon among clouds.[24]   She becomes such an intimate part of this Balbec where he first fell in love with her that her very breathing suggests soft breezes from the sea and her sleep is to him " tout un paysage "—an undiscovered country.[25] The following passage illustrates how he relished her sleep with a soothing love, just as he would remain for hours listening to the unfurling of the waves:

. . . son sommeil mettait à mes côtés quelque chose d'aussi calme, d'aussi sensuellement délicieux que ces nuits de pleine lune dans la baie de Balbec devenue douce comme un lac, où les branches bougent à peine, où, étendu sur le sable, l'on écouterait sans fin se briser le reflux . . . je goûtais son sommeil d'un amour désintéressé, apaisant, comme je restais des heures à écouter le déferlement du flot . . . Quelquefois on eût dit que la mer

---

[17] *AD. I.*, p. 136.

[18] *G. II.*, p. 51.

[19] *Ibid.*

[20] *JF. III.*, p. 229.

[21] *Ibid.*, p. 248.   Cf. *G. II.*, p. 52, for Albertine's facial features described again in landscape terms.

[22] *JF. III.*, p. 250.

[23] *Ibid.*, p. 127.

[24] *Ibid.*, p. 220.

[25] *P. I.*, p. 93.

devenait grosse, que la tempête se faisait sentir jusque dans la baie et je me mettais comme elle à écouter le grondement de son souffle qui ronflait.[26]

It was not only the sea at the close of day that came to life for him in Albertine but sometimes the drowsy murmur of the sea upon the shore on moonlit nights.[27]   This lack of distinction between the charms of love and the charms of nature inevitably results in confused impressions.   Consequently when Albertine is posed by his imagination before a horizon of the sea he is not sure whether it is a desire for Balbec or for herself that overcomes him, but he rather believes that his desire for her is itself a lazy, incomplete method of possessing Balbec, as if to possess a thing materially were equivalent to possessing it spiritually.[28]   Likewise when, even without knowing it, he thinks of the other girls, they are for him " les ondulations montueuses et bleues de la mer " [29]—a group passing in outline against the waves.   And it is the sea he hopes to find when he goes in search of them.[30]

Proust finally felt that he should give a different name to each of these Albertines who appeared before him, never the same, called by him for the sake of convenience " la mer "—those seas that succeeded one another on the beach.[31]   Even after he saw nothing more in Albertine than an ordinary woman, an intrigue between her and some person whom she had loved at Balbec would still suffice to reincorporate in her the beach and the unrolling of the tide.[32]

Proust's description of these girls in floral terms is his poetic interpretation of the oneness of the earth and its human fauna, and their delineation here is characterized by a highly refined and spiritualized sensualism which we will find elaborated in his other

[26] *Ibid.*

[27] *Ibid.*, pp. 91-92.

[28] *G. II.*, p. 41.

[29] *JF. III.*, p. 95.

[30] *Ibid.*   In this connection Proust writes: " L'amour le plus exclusif pour une personne est toujours l'amour d'autre chose." *Ibid.* Cf. *Ibid.*, p. 230 for an example of when landscape becomes secondary to the person it frames.

[31] *Ibid.*, p. 250.

[32] *G. II.*, p. 42.   He even had the illusion of recovering Balbec through Albertine after her death. Cf. *AD. I.*, p. 126.

erotical landscapes. They remain always in his memory as the inseparable charm and characteristic flowers of Balbec.[33]

Ferré points out that Proust's eroticized landscapes appear " comme des circonstances accessoires de l'amour " [34] i. e. his observation is superseded by symbolism. Proust never represents a landscape simply to create atmosphere for love. There is always a more profound significance attached to his amalgamation of women and nature.

Landscape " Divinities "

The peasant girl of Méséglise

We have already noted that it was along the Méséglise way, after experiencing a sense of joy at the sight of a particular landscape, that our young narrator first discovered that his feelings for the phenomena of nature were stimulated by the desire to see rise up before his eyes a peasant girl whom he might clasp in his arms.[35] At the moment of this desire he found additional enjoyment in everything that was in his mind—the village of Roussainville, the trees of its woods and the steeple of its church. Furthermore, if this desire for a woman added for him something more exalting than the charms of nature, they in their turn enlarged what he might, in the woman's charm, have found too much restricted.[36] His imagination drawing strength from contact with his sensuality, his sensuality expanding through all the realms of his imagination, his desires became unbounded. It seemed to him that the beauty of the trees was hers also, and that her kiss would set free to him the soul of the landscape from whch she would emerge because she seemed to be not any one example of the general type of " woman " but " un produit nécessaire et naturel de ce sol." [37] In a similar fashion Renaissance poets like Ronsard must have rediscovered the dryades and naiades.

---

[33] *SG. II.(1).*, p. 210. Cf. *JF. III.*, pp. 168, 170, 174-175, 247 for other examples of feminine pulchritude described in landscape terms.

[34] Ferré, *op. cit.*, p. 51.

[35] *S. I.*, p.226.

[36] *Ibid.*

[37] *Ibid.*

It is again evident that Proust makes no distinction between the earth and its inhabitants. He admits that his desire for a peasant girl from Méséglise or Roussainville is one with his desire for Méséglise or Roussainville, and that to wander among the woods of Roussainville without her to embrace was to see those woods and yet know nothing of their secret treasure—their hidden beauty:

Cette fille que je ne voyais que criblée de feuillages, elle était elle-même pour moi comme une plante locale d'une espèce plus élevée seulement que les autres et dont la structure permet d'approcher de plus près qu'en elles la saveur profonde de pays . . .[38]

But it was in vain that he held the whole landscape within his field of vision draining it with an intense gaze which sought to extract from it a woman. He writes:

. . . je la drainais de mes regards qui eussent voulu en ramener une femme . . . Je fixais indéfiniment le tronc d'un arbre lointain, de derrière lequel elle allait surgir et venir à moi; l'horizon scruté restait désert, la nuit tombait, c'était sans espoir que mon attention s'attachait, comme pour aspirer les créatures qu'ils pouvaient recéler, à ce sol stérile, à cette terre épuisée; et ce n'était plus d'allégresse c'était de rage que je frappais les arbres du bois de Roussainville d'entre lesquels ne sortait pas plus d'êtres vivants que s'ils eussent été des arbres peints sur la toile d'un panorama, quand, ne pouvant me résigner à rentrer à la maison avant d'avoir serré dans mes bras la femme que j'avais tant désirée, j'étais pourtant obligé de reprendre le chemin de Combray en m'avouant à moi-même qu'était de moins probable le hasard qui l'eût mise sur mon chemin.[39]

Here also Rimbaud could have spoken but the typical Hamlet-Proust now wonders if she had appeared whether he would have dared to speak to her. For he no longer thinks of those dreams which came to him during his walks as being shared by others, or having any existence apart from himself. They seem now purely subjective, illusory creatures of his temperament. They are in no way connected now with nature, with the world of real things and mean no more to him than a purely conventional framework.[40]

In connection with this erotic approach to nature Ferré suggests that for Proust love becomes an element of geographical information.[41] Such an analysis is questionable. An examination of any

[38] *Ibid.*, p. 227.
[39] *Ibid.*, pp. 228-229.
[40] *Ibid.*, p. 229.
[41] Ferré, *op. cit.*, p. 29.

of the above passages will reveal the fact that it is not by love but through sensuality that he seeks geographical information.[42] Even in the event of Albertine, it was never really love that stimulated his geographical curiosity but merely the quest to satisfy a sensual desire whereby he felt that at the same time he could penetrate an unknown world. As a matter of fact it would be sufficient to say that for Proust the possession of a woman—a native of a region— was the means of penetrating and knowing a country.

"La duchesse de Guermantes"

However, physical possession of a woman was not the only means of acquiring geographical knowledge, for the young boy felt that he might penetrate all the secrets of the mysterious background of the Guermantes property simply by coming in contact for a moment, in Paris, with Madame de Guermantes, the princess paramount of the place. He imagined that her face and her speech must possess the local charm of the forest groves and streams, and the same secular peculiarities that the old customs recorded in her archives.[43] But later when he finally sees her he is surprised that the likeness of those woods is not discernible on the face of the Duchess, about which there was nothing suggestive of vegetation.[44] However, he did perceive in her eyes as in a picture:

. . . le ciel bleu d'une après-midi de France, largement découvert, baigné de lumière même quand elle ne brillait pas; et une voix qu'on eût cru aux premiers sons enroués, presque canaille, où traînait comme sur les marches de l'église de Combray ou la pâtisserie de la place, l'or paresseux et gras d'un soleil de province.[45]

Though in his eyes Madame de Guermantes retained nothing of her native soil, when she described her life as a child he discerned in her speech a territorial, semi-peasant quality which unrolled before his eyes a political and physical map of the whole history of France.[46]

[42] It seems to be a question here of Ferré's use of the word " l'amour " differing from Proust's interpretation which usually involved sex rather than sentiment.
[43] *G. I.*, p. 13.   [44] *Ibid.*, p. 183.   [45] *Ibid.*, p. 183-184.   [46] *Ibid.*, p. 45-46.

It is significant that in this rather voluptuous conception of nature Proust reduces the human being to an element of vegetation. Such an attitude is not surprising or original; it was characteristic of the tradition of France. Curtius writes that " cette union de toutes les valeurs vitales avec le sol natal est si caractéristique de la tradition spirituelle française." [47]   He may be thinking of Du Bellay, Ronsard, Barrès and Péguy. As noted in the introduction the French conception of civilization was so closely connected with the relation of the French people to the soil of France that men were considered products of a " sol déterminé " just as the trees and flowers.[48]   Thus the human being appeared to Proust rooted in the soil, transforming all its forces into branches and flowers and submitting itself to all the vibrations of the atmosphere.[49]   Just as he makes no distinction between the earth and its creatures likewise he does not distinguish between the pleasure evoked from a particular landscape and that of its " plante locale."

Furthermore, Curtius seems to believe that this assimilation of the human to the vegetable—which can be found in Claudel and is exaggerated by Giono—symbolizes a passive attitude toward life. He explains that the vegetable kingdom lacks both the mobility which characterizes the animal and the will which characterizes man. Antagonism of our values, good and bad, begins only above vegetables. Animals present certain forms that we judge noble or vulgar but in the vegetable kingdom similar distinctions do not exist at all, and it is significant that they become possible only in biological zones. Vegetable existence is pure, ignorant of the conflict of values. It is the domain of the instinct and of submission to natural laws from which there is no escape. From this analysis Curtius concludes that Proust's transposition of the human to the vegetable, which was at first the expression of a particular artistic vision, prolongs itself into the sphere of science.[50]

An illustration of this point may be found in Proust's description of his two young friends, Mlle Marie Gineste and Mme Céleste Albaret who, born at the foot of the high mountains in the center of France, seemed to embody the features of that region:

[47] Curtius, *Marcel Proust*, p. 109.   [49] *Ibid.*, p. 110.
[48] *Ibid.*   [50] *Ibid.*, pp. 110-112.

Marie Gineste était plus régulièrement rapide et saccadée, Céleste Albaret plus molle et languissante étalée comme un lac, mais avec de terribles retours de bouillonnement où sa fureur rappelait le danger des crues et des tourbillons liquides qui entraînent tout, saccagent tout . . . leur figure avait . . . gardé l'humidité de la glaise malléable de leurs rivières . . .[51]

Céleste, patterned by the natural laws of her native region, even preserved the rhythm of its streams:

On prétend que le liquide salé qu'est notre sang n'est que la survivance intérieure de l'élement marin primitif. Je crois de même que Céleste non seulement dans ses fureurs mais aussi dans ses heures de dépression gardait le rythme des ruisseaux de son pays. Quand elle était épuisée c'était à leur manière; elle était vraiment à sec. Rien n'aurait pu alors la revivifier. Puis tout d'un coup la circulation reprenait dans son grand corps magnifique et léger. L'eau coulait dans la transparence opaline de sa peau bleuâtre. Elle souriait au soleil et devenait plus bleue encore. Dans ces moments-là elle était vraiment céleste.[52]

" La belle fille à l'aube "

Another time on his way to Balbec by train Marcel sees the peculiar charm of a landscape in the peasant girl who brings milk to the train:

Le paysage devint accidenté, abrupt, le train s'arrêta à une petite gare entre deux montagnes. On ne voyait au fond de la gorge, au bord du torrent, qu'une maison de garde enfoncée dans l'eau qui coulait au ras des fenêtres. Si un être peut être le produit d'un sol dont on goûte en lui le charme particulier, plus encore que la paysanne que j'avais tant désiré voir apparaître quand j'errais seul du côté de Méséglise dans les bois de Roussainville, ce devait être la grande fille que je vis sortir de cette maison et, sur le sentier qu'illuminait obliquement le soleil levant venir vers la gare en portant une jarre de lait.[53]

In this picture, as in La Fontaine's *Perrette* and Wordsworth's *Solitary Highland Girl* the milkmaid is exalted and, even more than the peasant girl whom he so desperately desired along the Méséglise way, appears to be the product of a soil, the charm of which she exhibits. As the phenomena of nature integrate, as a flower is affected by the light which bathes it, so this human flower appears purpled with the glow of morning, her face rosier than the

---

[51] *SG. II.(2).*, pp. 77, 81.   [52] *Ibid.*, pp. 82-83.   [53] *JF. II.*, p. 77.

sky. Furthermore, the artist emphasizes her geographic link to the landscape by picturing the valley as cut off from the rest of the world.

At the sight of the young girl Marcel again experiences a sense of happiness. He feels in her presence the desire to live which is reborn in him whenever he becomes conscious anew of beauty.[54] He realizes, however, that it is not merely a girl as such that inspires him but that as an element of the unknown and unattainable, she excites his imagination and thus evokes a pleasant sensation. Here again one may discern Proust's integration of sensuality and imagination. He writes that the " caractère d'une chose nouvelle," different from anything we have known, is the element proper to beauty and pleasure and, therefore, because this " belle fille " is foreign to the models of beauty that his imagination had sketched— as a symbol of surprise, as a fairy element—she gives him a certain happiness. But it was a happiness that could be realized only by staying there and living by her side.[55] Knowledge of the impossibility of living with her is probably what stimulated in him this feeling of an expected happiness—the typical fairy element where fulfillment would precisely destroy bliss.

However, he explains that a temporary cessation of habit played a great part in this sensation. As a rule, he says, it is with our being reduced to a minimum that we live, most of our faculties lie dormant because they can rely upon habit which knows what there is to be done and has no need of their services. But on this morning of travel, the interruption of the routine of his existence made their presence indispensable. His habits, which were sedentary, played him false and all his faculties came hurrying to take their place, from the basest to the most exalting, from breath, appetite and the circulation of his blood to receptivity and imaginaton.[56] Again the impression is confused: " Je ne sais si, en me faisant croire que cette fille n'était pas pareille aux autres femmes, le charme sauvage de ces lieux ajoutait au sien, mais elle le leur rendait." [57] Life for him would have been exquisite if only he were free to spend hours with her, to go with her to the stream, to the cow, to the train, to feel that he was known to her and had his place in her thoughts.

[54] *Ibid.*   [55] *Ibid.*, p. 78.   [56] *Ibid.*, p. 79.   [57] *Ibid.*

He feels that she could initiate him into the delights of country life, but the dream guide was a dream fairy; thus he cannot be sure if his exaltation was produced by this girl or was on the other hand responsible for the pleasure that he found in the sight of her, in the sense of her presence. In either event she was so closely associated with it that he felt his desire to see her again was not so much a physical desire as a mental desire not to allow this state of enthusiasm to perish utterly and not to be separated forever from the person who, although quite unconsciously, had participated in it. It was not only because this state was a pleasant one that he wanted to retain it but principally because it gave another tonality to all that he saw. It introduced him to an unknown and infinitely more interesting universe.[58] The rugged charm of this milkmaid was part of a life other than the life that he knew and, therefore, the key to his interest in the landscape.

" Madame de Stermaria "

The complex sensibility of Proust's erotic landscape pictures manifests itself most completely in the expression of his desire to seek in Madame de Stermaria a savour of the poetic life led on the Ile de Bretagne. As he pictures her in her romantic Breton setting, his dreams of travel and love again emanate from a single outburst of his imagination:

Et, un mois où elle serait restée seule sans ses parents dans son château romanesque peut-être aurions-nous pu nous promener seuls le soir tous deux dans le crépuscule où luiraient plus doucement au-dessus de l'eau assombrie les fleurs roses des bruyères, sous les chênes battus par le clapotement des vagues. Ensemble nous aurions parcouru cette île empreinte pour moi de tant de charme parce qu'elle avait enfermé la vie habituelle de Mlle de Stermaria et qu'elle reposait dans la mémoire de ses yeux.[59]

Mme de Stermaria, unlike the peasant girl desired along Méséglise, is not merely the figment of his ecstatic imagination but a person known to him and of whose setting he has some knowledge though it is generally enhanced in his dream world. In each of the writer's erotic nature experiences there is always an element of the unknown which stimulates his imagination—in some cases it is the person

[58] *Ibid.*, p. 80.   [59] *Ibid.*, p. 124.

desired and in others the setting of a person already known, but whose soil has many unexplored corners. This feature reminds us of Valéry Larbaud's " monologues interieurs."

The special charm of Bretagne for him is due to the fact that it incloses the everyday life of Madame and therefore he longs to possess her in those regions which enveloped her in so many memories. He curiously describes her native environment as a veil which nature interposes between woman and her pursuers in order that, tricked by the illusion of possessing her more completely, they may be forced to occupy first the scenes among which she lives, and which are of more service to their imagination than sensual pleasures can be, yet would not without that pleasure have had the power to attract them.[60] Here Proust seems to discover a kind of " law " almost unknown to the average human sensibility but evidenced in nature. It is the procedure of Bergson's philosophy to make the experience mysterious.

But when he realizes the impossibility of visiting her in Bretagne, because she evokes for him " une Bretagne idéale," he invites her to dine in the Bois de Boulogne with the secret hope of possessing there the joy of an " Ile de Bretagne sur *la Carte du Tendre*." Such a hope would automatically perish if he dined on the island without her or even with her somewhere else. He says that the attitudes in which one pictures a pleasure exist previously to the type of woman required to give that pleasure.[61] This statement is especially evident in his impression of the Bois previous to his desire for Madame. He writes, for instance, that in the past, long before there was a question of Mme de Stermaria, the island in the Bois had seemed to him especially designed for pleasure.[62] He probably thought of an " Ile de Cythère."

The following pictures of the shores of the lake and the Bois appear to serve a double purpose. A mood of " tristesse " is introduced to render more striking the pleasure which he hopes to experience there, and the landscape itself is the basis for his comparison of the Bois de Boulogne to the Ile de Bretagne. The loneliness that he had previously experienced there, by contrast, projects a melancholy atmosphere into this landscape " faite pour le plaisir."

[60] *Ibid.*   [61] *G. II.*, p. 70.   [62] *Ibid.*

12

The very beauty of the Bois would naturally evoke sadness when one is lonely or when a desire there is not realized:

. . . déjà bien avant . . . quand il ne s'agissait pas encore de Mme de Stermaria, l'île du Bois m'avait semblé faite pour le plaisir parce que je m'étais trouvé aller y goûter la tristesse de n'en avoir aucun à y abriter. C'est aux bords du lac qui conduisent à cette île et le long desquels, dans les dernières semaines de l'été vont se promener les Parisiennes qui ne sont pas encore parties, que ne sachant plus où la retrouver, et si même elle n'a pas déjà quitté Paris, on erre avec l'espoir de voir passer la jeune fille dont on est tombé amoureux dans le dernier bal de l'année, qu'on ne pourra plus retrouver dans aucune soirée avaint le printemps suivant . . . on scrute cet horizon où, . . . nos yeux passant sans transition du parc cultivé aux hauteurs naturelles de Meudon et du mont Valérien, ne savent pas où mettre une frontière et font entrer la vraie campagne dans l'oeuvre du jardinage dont ils projettent bien au delà d'elle-même l'agrément arti- ficiel; ainsi ces oiseaux rares élevés en liberté dans un jardin botanique et qui chaque jour au gré de leurs promenades ailées, vont poser jusque dans les bois limitrophes une note exotique . . . on parcourt anxieusement ce royaume romanesque des rencontres incertaines et des mélancolies amou- reuses, et on ne serait pas plus surpris qu'il fût situé hors de l'univers géographique que si à Versailles, au haut de la terrasse, observatoire autour duquel les nuages s'accumulent contre le ciel bleu dans le style de Van der Meulen, après s'être ainsi élevé en dehors de la nature, on apprenait que, là où elle recommence, au bout du grand canal, les villages qu'on ne peut distinguer, à l'horizon éblouissant comme la mer, s'appellent Fleurus ou Nimègue.[63]

He pictures these shores of the lake as the romantic world of chance encounters and lovers' melancholy, for there during the last weeks of summer the ladies of Paris take the air and one goes there hoping to see the girl with whom one fell in love at the last ball of the season. This time his zoological mind likens these ladies promenad- ing along the shores to rare birds which in their flight lend an exotic note to the surrounding woods. And, just as it is almost impossible for one to discern Dutch towns at the end of the Ver- sailles Gardens, because looking at them one transfigures them into the landscapes of a Dutch painter, likewise, as he scans the horizon of the Bois it is impossible for him to distinguish the boundary of its cultivated garden and the natural heights of Meudon and the Mont Valérien.

[63] *Ibid.*

Later when the narrator learns that Madame de Stermaria will not dine with him he is overcome with grief and he pictures the loneliness of dining on the island alone. His portrayal of the Bois at such a time displays harmony between the setting and the " état d'âme " of the narrator:

> Et le dernier équipage passé, quand on sent avec douleur qu'elle ne viendra plus, on va dîner dans l'île; au-dessus des peupliers tremblants qui rappellent sans fin les mystères du soir plus qu'ils n'y répondent un nuage rose met une dernière couleur de vie dans le ciel apaisé. Quelques gouttes de pluie tombent sans bruit sur l'eau antique, mais dans sa divine enfance restée toujours couleur du temps et qui oublie à tout moment les images des nuages et des fleurs. Et après que les géraniums ont inutilement en intensifiant l'éclairage de leurs couleurs lutté contre le crépuscule assombri, une brume vient envelopper l'île qui s'endort; on se promène dans l'humide obscurité le long de l'eau où tout au plus le passage silencieux d'un cygne vous étonne . . . Alors on voudrait d'autant plus avoir avec soi une amoureuse qu'on se sent seul et qu'on peut se croire loin.[64]

Proust h sketched this scene to objectify the pain of being alone on an island created by nature for pleasure. The sentiment of " douleur " is intensified by his objective portrayal of nature—the shivering poplars, the mysteries of evening, and the last touch of life in the tranquil sky, all accentuate his need of a loving companion. This is not mere romanticism because it is a general situation which stands the test of time. It is not the setting alone, rather the absence of a loved one that is the source of his sadness and the key to his discovery of that sombre tone in nature which is intimately related to his dejected feelings. In other words, his impression of his surroundings is conditioned by his emotions and, likewise, his surroundings intensify and blend with his feelings. His impression of the geraniums striving to resist the gathering darkness and the mist rising to envelop the island symbolizes the young man seeking his loved one in vain and thus overcome with sorrow. As one's spirit is overcome with sadness, so the island is enveloped in a mist. The moist dimness along the water's edge further emphasizes the shivering loneliness. And so by the use of climate and " un paysage d'âme " Proust represents the Bois de Boulogne seen " à travers un spleen " as the habitat of a disillusioned lover.

[64] *Ibid.*, p. 71.

We must not lose sight of the fact that his ultimate interest in the Bois in connection with Mme de Stermaria was its climatic resemblance to the Ile de Bretagne. Proust has a fantastic power of linking one country with another, and his process of transformation glides from the psychological to the geographical as the marine and misty atmosphere of the Bois de Boulogne identifies it in his imagination with the Ile de Bretagne.[65] The more identical the atmosphere of these two places, the more completely would he have been able to possess Madame and the more perfect would have been his realization of Bretagne. For this reason he had wanted desperately to bring her to the island during the cold season when the mist was the greatest. But he laments that even if the weather had not by itself rendered grey and maritime the scenes in which his imagination was living, the hope of possessing her would have been quite enough to raise a curtain of mist in his monotonously nostalgic imagination. Furthermore, the mist in Paris made him think incessantly of the native place of this young woman and since it was probable that it was invading the Bois, especially the shores of the lake, he thought it would make the " île des Cygnes " something like the Ile de Bretagne whose foggy atmosphere had always enwrapped in his mind like a garment " la pâle silhouette de Mme de Stermaria." [66] But he finally realized that his secret hope of possessing that Bretagne by such means would have been impossible:

On poursuit la réalité. Mais, à force de la laisser échapper, on finit par remarquer qu'à travers toutes ces vaines tentatives où on a trouvé le néant, quelque chose de solide subsiste, c'est ce qu'on cherchait. On commence à dégager, à connaître ce qu'on aime, on tâche à se la procurer, fût-ce au prix d'un artifice. Alors, à defaut de la croyance disparue, le costume signifie la suppléance à celle-ci par le moyen d'une illusion volontaire.[67]

In this event the reality pursued was Bretagne and as his desire to go there was unfulfilled he hoped to procure it by the strategy of a symbolic possession of Mme de Stermaria in the Bois. But he recognized that to envelop her in a similar atmosphere was only " une illusion volontaire " and that within half an hour of home he would not have found himself in Bretagne. To walk with her in the dusk of the island by the water's edge was only a matter of

[65] *Ibid.*, p. 72.   [66] *Ibid.*   [67] *Ibid.*

clothing her in her native costume.[68] If she had come, he no doubt
would have been disappointed at meeting only a woman instead
of the region which she seemed to possess.

Just as he had sought the sea in Albertine and the natural beauty
of Roussainville in a peasant girl he sought Bretagne in Mme de
Stermaria. One may receive the impression in the beginning that
his interest in this island was for its romantic setting, but as we
find that his desires for both Madame and her native land were so
closely allied the romantic idea seems to lose importance. He did
not invite her to dine in the Bois simply because it would present
a pleasant background for his amorous desires but because geo-
graphically and atmospherically it could be identified with Bretagne.
He believed that by transplanting there this " plante locale " of
Bretagne he would learn the romance of a region unknown to him.
When he realized that his dreams of both were to remain unfulfilled,
he appeared more concerned with the impossibility of knowing
Bretagne than with Madame's refusal of his invitation. However,
Proust so greatly eroticizes nature that it is almost impossible to
determine which was the greater loss to him.

It may be concluded from these passages that very often Proust's
interest in the wonders of natural scenery was stimulated by
amorous desires which had in turn been excited by the exotic
elements embodied in the desired one. But the fact that love or
sensuality was the means and not the end by which he aspired to
open the door to unknown worlds seems to minimize its greatness.
However, it should be noted that with Proust's sensuality there was
always crystallization, spiritualization, and transfiguration—a particularly lusty but poetic kind of, what a moral theologian would
call, *delectatio morosa*. It was this poetic-erotic conception of nature
which brought to his attention the reciprocal influence of man and
his habitat and because he made no distinction between the two
he reduced the human being to an element of vegetation.

" Angoisse à Venise "

Proust's mother was certainly his most important " love " and
at this point it seems fitting to cite his picture of Venice which

[68] *Ibid.*

reflects the " angoisse " caused by his mother's departure from the city and consequently displays again an intimate relation between the objective expression of a scene and the sentiment of the narrator :

Le soleil continuait de descendre. Ma mère ne devait pas être loin de la gare. Bientôt, elle serait partie, je resterais seul à Venise, seul avec la tristesse de la savoir peinée par moi et sans sa présence pour me consoler. . . . Les choses m'étaient devenues étrangères. Je n'avais plus assez de calme pour sortir de mon coeur palpitant et introduire en elles quelque stabilité. La ville que j'avais devant moi avait cessé d'être Venise. Sa personnalité, son nom, me semblaient comme des fictions menteuses que je n'avais plus le courage d'inculquer aux pierres. Les palais m'apparaissaient réduits à leurs simples parties, quantités de marbres pareilles à toutes les autres, et l'eau comme une combinaison d'hydrogène et oxygène, éternelle, aveugle, antérieure et extérieure à Venise, ignorante des Doges et de Turner. Et cependant ce lieu quelconque était étrange comme un lieu où on vient d'arriver, qui ne vous connaît pas encore—comme un lieu d'où l'on est parti et qui vous a déjà oublié. . . . J'avais beau raccrocher désespérément ma pensée à la belle coudée caractéristique du Rialto, il m'apparaissait avec la médiocrité de l'évidence comme un pont non seulement inférieur, mais aussi étranger à l'idée que j'avais de lui, qu'un acteur dont, malgré sa perruque blonde et son vêtement noir, nous savons bien qu'en son essence il n'est pas Hamlet. Tels les palais, le canal, le Rialto, se trouvaient dévêtus de l'idée qui faisait leur individualité et dissous en leurs vulgaires éléments matériels. Mais en même temps ce lieu médiocre me semblait lointain . . . je sentais que cet horizon si voisin que j'aurais pu atteindre en une heure, c'était une courbure de la terre tout autre que celle des mers de France, une courbure lointaine qui se trouvait, par l'artifice du voyage, amarrée près de moi . . . et c'était ma détresse que le chant de " sole mio," s'élevant comme une déploration de la Venise que j'avais connue, semblait prendre à témoin . . . J'étais étreint par l'angoisse que me causait, avec la vue du canal devenu tout petit depuis que l'âme de Venise s'en était échappée, de ce Rialto banal qui n'était plus le Rialto, ce chant de désespoir que devenait " sole mio " et qui, ainsi clamé devant les palais inconsistante, achevait de les mettre en miettes et consommait la ruine de Venise. . . .[69]

This experience in Venice is not different in kind from the desperately sad nights he spent as a child when his mother had not kissed him " good night." If there was ever an " Oedipus " bound to his mother, it was Proust.

Much later in life our narrator reflects that there was not a year

[69] *AD. II.*, p. 146-148.

that did not have as its "frontispiece," or inserted in its days, the picture of a woman he had ardently desired. It was a picture often arbitrary, as sometimes he had never seen the woman, as for example the chambermaid of Mme Putbus, Mlle d'Orgeville, or a young lady whose name he had seen in the daily newspaper. He sensed her to be beautiful, lost his heart to her and created for her an imaginary body which dominated with its full height a landscape of the region where he had read in "L'Annuaire des Châteaux" that her family's estate was situated. It was from this publication that he acquired knowledge of Mme de Stermaria's family estate. In the case of the women he had known the setting was at least double:

Chacune s'élevait, à un point différent de ma vie, dressée comme une divinité protectrice et locale, d'abord au milieu d'un de ces paysages rêvés dont la juxtaposition quadrillait ma vie et où je m'étais attaché à l'imaginer ensuite, vue du côté du souvenir, entourée des sites où je l'avais connue et qu'elle me rappelait y restant attachée; car si notre vie est vagabonde, notre mémoire est sédentaire, et nous avons beau nous élancer sans trêve, nos souvenirs, eux, rivés aux lieux dont nous nous avons détaché continuent à y continuer leur vie casanière, comme ces amis momentanés que le voyageur s'était faits dans une ville et qu'il est obligé d'abandonner, quand il la quitte parce que c'est là qu'eux qui ne partent pas, finiront leur journée et leur vie, comme s'il était là encore, au pied de l'église, devant la porte et sous les arbres du cours.[70]

We have seen that the world of dream and memory was the source of a great deal of Proust's landscape material. The above shows how he dreamed of his women in a particular region and the following passage shows how his memory of a woman carried with it the memory of the setting which framed her. Even after Albertine is dead, her memory brings back vivid pictures of the roads they traveled together:

La fraîcheur du soir se levait, c'était le coucher du soleil, dans ma mémoire au bout d'une route que nous prenions ensemble pour rentrer, j'apercevais, plus loin que le dernier village, comme une station distante, inaccessible pour le soir même où nous nous arrêterions à Balbec, toujours ensemble. . . . Ce n'était plus assez de fermer les rideaux, je tâchais de boucher les yeux et les oreilles de ma mémoire, pour ne pas voir cette bande orangée du couchant, pour ne pas entendre ces invisibles oiseaux qui

---

[70] *TR. II.*, p. 181.

se répondaient d'un arbre à l'autre de chaque côté de moi qu'embrassait alors si tendrement celle qui maintenant était morte. . . . Que de fois j'avais traversé pour aller chercher Albertine, que de fois j'avais repris au retour avec elle la grande plaine de Cricqueville, tantôt par des temps brumeux où l'inondation du brouillard nous donnait l'illusion d'être entourés d'un lac immense, tantôt par des soirs limpides où le clair de lune, dématérialisant la terre, la faisait paraître à deux pas céleste, comme elle n'est, pendant le jour, que dans les lointaines, enfermait les champs, les bois le firmament auquel il les avait assimilés dans l'agate arborisée d'un seul azur.[71]

[71] *AD. I.,* pp. 103-104. Cf. also *Ibid.,* p. 201.

CHAPTER VI

THE AUDIBLE LANDSCAPE

It now remains to speak of Proust's audible universe. Sound had for him as great an evocative power as any of the other sense stimuli and it follows that the world of sound evoked for him landscapes as delightful as those stemming from the other senses. He was especially interested in the poetry of place-names.

Place-names

Proust's entire world was " enchanté des noms." [1] That which he saw first in a country was " le pouvoir évocateur " of its name:

Je n'eus besoin pour les faire renaître que de prononcer ces noms: Balbec, Venise, Florence, dans l'intérieur desquels avait fini par s'accumuler le désir que m'avaient inspiré les lieux qu'ils désignaient. Même au printemps, trouver dans un livre le nom de Balbec suffisait à réveiller en moi le désir des tempêtes et du gothique normand; même par un jour de tempête le nom de Florence ou de Venise me donnait le désir du soleil, des lys, du palais des Doges et de Sainte-Marie-des-Fleurs. [2]

For Proust, names permanently absorbed the image he formed of places due to the fact that he subordinated its reappearance in him to their own special laws. In consequence of this, names made a place more beautiful but at the same time different from anything that it could be in reality. But he was aware of the fact that by increasing the arbitrary delights of his imagination, they aggravated the disenchantment that was in store for him when he set out upon his travels: [3]

Ils exaltèrent l'idée que je me faisais de certains lieux de la terre, en les faisant plus particuliers, par conséquent plus réels. Je ne me représentais pas alors les villes, les paysages, les monuments, comme des tableaux plus our moins agréables, découpés çà et là dans une même matière, mais chacun d'eux comme un inconnu, essentiellement différent des autres, dont mon âme avait soif et qu'elle aurait profit à connaître. [4]

---

[1] *G. II.*, p. 205.   [3] *Ibid.*, p. 245.
[2] *S. II.*, p. 244.   [4] *Ibid.*

Their character was much more individual still by being designated by names, names that were only for themselves, proper names such as people have.[5] *Known* place-names were necessarily connected with the most renowned treasures of a place, usually an old cathedral or some architectural monument. But Proust creates a progressive myth around an *unknown* place-name as soon as he hears it or sees it written, as is shown, for example, in his image of Balbec:

Certain noms de villes, Vézelay, ou Chartres, Bourges ou Beauvais servent à désigner, par abréviation, leur église principale. Cette acception partielle où nous le prenons si souvent, finit—s'il s'agit de lieux que nous ne connaissons pas encore,—par sculpter le nom tout entier qui dès lors quand nous voudrons y faire entrer l'idée de la ville—de la ville que nous n'avons jamais vue—lui imposera—comme un moule,—les mêmes ciselures, et du même style, en fera une sorte de grande cathédrale. Ce fut pourtant à une station de chemin de fer, au-dessus d'un buffet, en lettres blanches sur un avertisseur bleu, que je lus le nom, presque de style persan, de Balbec.[6]

As a boy he had pictured in the name of Balbec a sea-side place in the midst of those funereal coasts, " fameuses par tant de naufrages qu'enveloppe six mois de l'année le linceul des brumes et l'écume des vagues." [7]   And ever since the day when he learned that its church was a most curious example of Norman Gothic architecture and so exceptional that it was described as Persian in inspiration his dreams of Balbec had been impregnated with pictures of Gothic architecture and stormy seas:

Et ces lieux qui jusque-là ne m'avaient semblé que de la nature immémoriale, restée contemporaine des grands phénomènes géologiques,—et tout aussi en dehors de l'histoire humaine que l'Océan ou la grande Ourse, avec ces sauvages pêcheurs pour qui, pas plus que pour les baleines, il n'y eut de moyen âge—, ç'avait été un grand charme pour moi de les voir tout d'un coup entrés dans la série des siècles, ayant connu l'époque romane, et de savoir que le trèfle gothique était venu nervurer aussi ces rochers sauvages à l'heure voulue, comme ces plantes frêles mais vivaces qui, quand c'est le printemps, étoilent çà et là la neige des pôles. Et si le gothique apportait à ces lieux et à ces hommes une détermination qui leur manquait, eux aussi

---

[5] *Ibid.*

[6] *JF. II.*, pp. 81-82. Cf. *SG. II.(2).*, p. 201, for etymology of Balbec. Cf. also Ferré, *op. cit.*, p. 35.

[7] *S. II.*, p. 241.

lui en conféraient une en retour. J'essayais de me représenter comment
ces pêcheurs avaient vécu, le timide et insoupçonné essai de rapports sociaux
qu'ils avaient tenté là, pendant le moyen âge, ramassés sur un point des
côtes d'Enfer, aux pieds des falaises de la mort; et le gothique me semblait
plus vivant maintenant que, séparé des villes où je l'avais toujours imaginé
jusque-là, je pouvais voir comment, dans un cas particulier, sur des rochers
sauvages, il avait germé et fleuri en un fin clocher.[8]

Words present little pictures of things, clear and normal, but
names present a confused picture, which draws from the brightness
or darkness of their sound, the color in which it is uniformly
painted.[9] But as we shall see in the following passage, Proust's
pictures evoked from names are colored also by his readings and his
historical knowledge. For instance, he pictures Parma through his
literary reminiscences of *La Chartreuse de Parme*, Florence through
the easy ethnology of its name, and Balbec through the historic
and legendary traditions of Normandy:

Le nom de Parme, une des villes où je désirais le plus aller, depuis que
j'avais lu *La Chartreuse*, m'apparaissait, compact, lisse, mauve et doux;
si on me parlait d'une maison quelconque de Parme dans laquelle je serais
reçu, on me causait le plaisir de penser que j'habiterais une demeure lisse,
compacte, mauve et douce, qui n'avait de rapport avec les demeures d'aucune
ville d'Italie puisque je l'imaginais seulement à l'aide de cette syllabe
lourde du nom de Parme, où ne circule aucun air, et de tout ce que je lui
avais fait absorber de douceur stendhalienne et du reflet des violettes. Et
quand je pensais à Florence, c'était comme à une ville miraculeusement
embaumée et semblable à une corolle, parce qu'elle s'appelait la cité des lys
et sa cathédrale, Sainte-Marie-des-Fleurs. Quant à Balbec, c'était un de
ces noms où comme sur une vieille poterie normande qui garde la couleur
de la terre d'où elle fut tirée, on voit se peindre encore la représentation de
quelque usage aboli, de quelque droit féodal, d'un état ancien de lieux d'une
manière désuète de prononcer qui en avait formé les syllabes hétéroclites
et que je ne doutais pas de retrouver jusque chez l'aubergiste qui me ser-
virait du café au lait à mon arrivée, me menant voir la mer déchaînée
devant l'église et auquel je prêtais l'aspect disputeur, solennel et médiéval
d'un personnage de fabliau.[10]

It is atmosphere, climate, and historical as well as psychological
associations which work out the transformation and transfiguration
which seemed to start from the sound of the names. As Mr. Chernowitz points out, " the names of other towns inspire even more

[8] *Ibid.*, p. 241-242.   [9] *Ibid.*, p. 245.   [10] *Ibid.*, p. 246.

complex associations and vie with each other in synaesthetic 'local color.' " [11]   He adds that compared to such descriptions as these, Rimbaud's " Sonnet des voyelles " sounds most elementary : [12]

. . . mais j'avais beau les comparer, . . . entre Bayeux si haute dans sa noble dentelle rougeâtre et dont le faîte était illuminé par le vieil or de sa dernière syllabe; Vitré dont l'accent aigu losangeait de bois noir le vitrage ancien; le doux Lamballe qui, dans son blanc, va du jaune coquille d'oeuf au gris perle; Coutances, cathédrale normande que sa diphtongue finale, grasse et jaunissante couronne par une tour de beurre; Lannion avec le bruit, dans son silence villageois, du coche suivi de la mouche; Questambert, Pontorson, risibles et naïf, plumes blanches et becs jaunes éparpillés sur la route de ces lieux fluviatiles et poétiques; Benodet, nom à peine amarré que semble vouloir entraîner la rivière au milieu de ses algues, Pont-Aven, envolée blanche et rose de l'aile d'une coiffe légère qui se reflète en tremblant dans une eau verdie de canal; Quimperlé, lui, mieux attaché et, depuis le moyen âge, entre les ruisseaux dont il gazouille et s'emperle en une grisaille pareille à celle que dessinent, à travers les toiles d'araignées d'une verrière, les rayons de soleil changés en pointes émoussées d'argent bruni ? [13]

Such pictorial eloquence brings to mind Rousseau's statement in his *Essay on the Origin of Language* that " sounds are never more effective than when they produce the impression of color." [14] Here the poet's pen appears to have been dipped in chromatic complexity and though his voluptuous melting of tone and color is abundant evidence of hyperaesthesia it is also convincing for us healthier readers.   Although his pictures are based on a previous knowledge of the individual characteristics of each town they reveal a delightful sense of genuine spontaneity.   There is an interplay of impressions but the general effect is intellectual.

Most effective is Proust's method of painting with language and word images sounds which for him are loaded with all the poetry of color.   Chernowitz in his study of Proust's power of color discrimination notes how he " distinguishes between an egg-shell white and pearl-gray, between a yellowish tinge and the shade of butter,

---

[11] Chernowitz, *op. cit.*, p. 35.

[12] *Ibid.*

[13] *S. II.*, pp. 246-247.

[14] Babbitt, *op. cit.*, p. 174, quoted from Rousseau's *Essay on the Origin of Language.*

between the grisaille akin to the gray of a spider web and that of a brownish silver." [15] But it is especially interesting that these scarcely noticeable differences in shade are the exact echo of the scarcely noticeable phonetical differences of e. g. the a's in Lamballe, the nasal sound in Coutances, etc.

Proust explains that these images were, however, false for the reason that they were necessarily much simplified. The object to which his imagination aspired, which his senses perceived incompletely and without any immediate pleasure, he had submitted to the protection of names and because he had accumulated there a store of dreams, those names magnetized his desires: [16]

. . . mais les noms ne sont pas très vastes; c'est tout au plus si je pouvais y faire entrer deux ou trois des " curiosités " principales de la ville et elles s'y juxtaposaient sans intermédiaires . . .[17]

but he continues that perhaps the enforced simplicity of these images was one of the reasons for the hold they had over him: [18]

. . . n'ayant pas la place de faire entrer dans le nom de Florence les éléments qui composent d'habitude les villes, je fus contraint à faire sortir une cité surnaturelle de la fécondation, par certains parfums printaniers, de ce que je croyais être, en son essence, le génie de Giotto. Tout au plus— et parce qu'on ne peut pas faire tenir dans un nom beaucoup plus de durée que d'espace—comme certains tableaux de Giotto eux-mêmes qui montrent à deux moments différents de l'action un même personnage, ici couché dans son lit, là s'apprêtant à monter à cheval, le nom de Florence était-il divisé en deux compartiments. Dans l'un, sous un dais architectural, je contemplais une fresque à laquelle était partiellement superposé un rideau de soleil matinal, poudreux, oblique et progressif; dans l'autre (car ne pensant pas aux noms comme à un idéal inaccessible mais comme à une ambiance réelle dans laquelle j'irais me plonger, la vie non vecue encore, la vie intacte et pure que j'y enfermais donnait aux plaisirs les plus matériels, aux scènes les plus simples, cet attrait qu'ils ont dans les oeuvres des primitifs), je traversais rapidement,—pour trouver plus vite le déjeuner qui m'attendait avec des fruits et du vin de Chianti—le Ponte-Vecchio encombré de jonquilles, de narcisses et d'anémones.[19]

That was what he envisioned and not what was about him. During the time in which he examined these visions of Florence, Venice and

---

[15] Chernowitz, *op. cit.*, p. 36.
[16] *S. II.*, p. 247.
[17] *Ibid.*, p, 247-248.
[18] *Ibid.*, p. 248.
[19] *Ibid.*, p. 248-249.

Pisa he never ceased to believe that they corresponded to a reality independent of himself.   Though his senses had not perceived at all what had been elaborated by the spell of his dreams, it was that which inflamed his desire all the more, by seeming to promise that it should be satisfied.[20]   For all that, the motive force of his exaltation was a longing for aesthetic enjoyment, though his intuition had discovered the essence and fragrance of these towns from their names.   The guide books ministered actually more to his desire than books on aesthetics, and more again than guide books the railway time tables which impregnated his imagination: [21]

Certes, quand je me répétais, donnant ainsi tant de valeur à ce que j'allais voir, que Venise était "l'école de Giorgione, la demeure du Titien, le plus complet musée de l'architecture domestique au moyen âge" je me sentais heureux . . . je pensais que déjà le Ponte-Vecchio était jonché à foison de jacinthes et d'anémones et que le soleil du printemps teignait déjà les flots du Grand Canal d'un si sombre azur et de si nobles émeraudes qu'en venant se briser aux pieds des peintures du Titien, ils pouvaient rivaliser de riche coloris avec elles.[22]

In the first sentence he reveals that the evaluation of a place for him is according to its aesthetic possibilities—its status in the world of art.   The fact that the name of Venice is associated in his mind with the names of great artists such as Giorgione and Titian increases its value in his estimation and is bound to influence his vision.   This is similar to the "literary" case of Parma.

Also it is interesting to observe that his dream picture of Venice is partially dependent on the change of season and weather.   It was "à cause du temps" that he imagined the Ponte-Vecchio already heaped with an abundance of hyacinths and anémones and the extraordinary radiance of the scene he perceived through the glories of light.   His remembrance of pictures of the Canaletto might even have colored his dreams.

Proust delights in an opportunity to match the creative power of nature with that of the artist; in fact, he almost fuses the two domains.[23]   Here through the coloring of his own imagination he

[20] *Ibid.*, p. 250.

[21] *Ibid.* Cf. also *JF. II.*, pp. 81-82.

[22] *S. II.*, pp. 250-251.

[23] Proust often speaks of "les beautés des paysages ou du grand art" as interchangeable, cf. *Ibid.*, p. 240.

subtly renders the coloring of the Grand Canal as once seen and always visible through the " tempérament " of Titian. He does not minimize the power of nature by representing it as the rival of a human creation but rather enhances it in a double way—first, through the old painter's richness, and secondly, by his own artistic transfiguration. Again this comparison of the effects of nature to the effects of art is part of his stylistic individuality. From his impression of the sun tinging the waves of the canal with " un si sombre azur et de si nobles émeraudes " we can be sure that Proust's eye saw the greenish reflection of the sun in the glittering water spots of the blue Canale Grande exactly as Titian, himself, once had seen it; and Proust, the artist-traveler, has a secret communion with all those who through the centuries have seen Venice with artistic eyes, and thus possess in their hearts a " Venise retrouvée " and not a " Venise perdue," as does the travelling crowd.

The following passage further illustrates how the reality of a country is for Proust according to the exaltation that he experiences in imagining it. It it is evidence of a certain hyperaesthesia causing a pathological confusion of the sense impressions, all the better for us—in spite of what psychiatrists may say—to whom access into the realm of beauty is forbidden by definition. These visions of Florence and Venice had so intensely excited his desire to visit them and stimulated his longing for a vital aesthetic enjoyment that he actually reaches " le dernier degré de l'allégresse " [24] when he *hears* his father say: " Il doit faire encore froid sur le Grand-Canal, tu ferais bien de mettre à tout hasard dans ta malle ton par-dessus d'hiver et ton gros veston." [25] At these words he was raised to " une sorte d'extase "—a state which he had until then believed impossible: [26]

. . . je me sentis vraiment pénétrer entre ces "rochers d'améthyste pareils à un récif de la mer des Indes "; par une gymnastique suprême et au-dessus de mes forces, me dévêtant comme d'une carapace sans objet de l'air de ma chambre qui m'entourait, je le remplaçai par des parties égales d'air vénitien, cette atmosphère marine, indicible et particulière comme celle des rêves que mon imagination avait enfermée dans le nom de Venise, je sentis s'opérer en moi une miraculeuse désincarnation; elle se doubla aussitôt de

---

[24] *Ibid.*, p. 252.   [25] *Ibid.*, p. 253.   [26] *Ibid.*

la vague envie de vomir qu'on éprouve quand on vient de prendre un gros mal de gorge, . . .[27]

He explains that it was not until this pronouncement of his father's that he reached this supreme happiness, for not until then was the fact revealed to him that contrary to his imaginings it was not the men " majestueux et terribles comme la mer " who would be walking in Venice next week but he, himself, might be the person whom he had seen in a photograph of St. Mark's standing in front of the portico.[28] The sensation caused by the realization that he is actually going to Venice evokes all that his imagination had enclosed in its name, and he experiences a complete transmutation of environment, i. e. he becomes oblivious to his actual surroundings and has the impression of dwelling in his dream world. In other words, he seems to undergo a psychological change of skin analogous to the serpent's physical transformation.

His senses perceived in reverie what his imagination had conceived during his waking hours. It is by the complete interpenetration of sensation and imagination that he arrives at this state of " extase " and in view of his reaction it seems to have been an organic rather than a mechanical combination exactly as is the case with really ecstatic persons, either of the mystical or of the hysterical type. The experience was too great a strain on his nervous system, which in turn caused the physical disturbance. This " gymnastique suprême " by which he indicates a muscular effort is only the external picture of a mental effort to recapture his visions of Venice. The mental effort was so intense that it caused physical strain and fatigue, but it brought his whole being closer to the reality of his fantasy. It was a moment in which he believed that he was touching an eternal and supersensible world. The parallel here with the mystics is complete.

After the original sensation was received the narrator seems to have been devoid of any rational faculties, a state which led him to this illusory world. The " miraculous disincarnation " which he felt at work within him was certainly a nervous reaction but also a kind of " spiritual " union of the senses and intellect, a simpli-

[27] *Ibid.* Compare this experience to the sensation evoked by the taste of the madeleine dipped in tea. Cf. *supra*, pp. 18-22.
[28] *S. II.*, pp. 252-253.

fication of his personality which one may call enthusiasm, enrapture
or even religious frenzy. This state is for him extra-temporal
because in it he reaches the highest degree of happiness. Thus the
phenomenon of art-intoxication is in Proust analogous to mystical
" drunkenness." A neurologist would stress this statement because
as a result of such emotional unrestraint the narrator was put to
bed with a fever, had to abandon all idea of travelling, and was
forced to avoid excitement.[29] And all this was caused by the
auditive elements pronounced by Marcel's father: Venice—Canale
Grande.

Names constantly lent mystery to the projection of his already
enchanted reveries. He confesses that at an age when a name offers
an image of the unknowable, while at the same moment it suggests
also a real place, it forces us to identify one with the other to such
a point that we set out to seek in a city a soul which it does not
embody but which we have no longer the power to eliminate from
the sound of its name.[30] But direct geographical knowledge of
places had an even more deceiving effect. For instance, as soon
as he arrived in Balbec it was as if he had opened a name which
ought to have been kept hermetically closed and where, as he
expelled all the images that had been living in it until then, a
tramway, a café, people walking in the square, etc., came crowding
into the interior of those two syllables which, closing over them, let
them now frame the porch of the Persian church and would never
cease to contain them.[31]

And it is not only to the physical universe—towns and rivers—
that names give an individuality, but there is the social universe
also. Especially interesting are Proust's musings on the name
Guermantes—a name which represented to him the highest peak of
aristocracy. For him every renowned chateau in the province had
its lady or its fairy just as every forest has its spirit and every
stream its nymph:[32]

[29] *Ibid.*, p. 253. In Huysman's *A Rebours*, Des Esseintes—the sensation
seeker—had similar experiences.
[30] *G. I.*, p. 10.
[31] *JF. II.*, pp. 84-85. Cf. *Ibid.*, for his allusions to the phonetic geography
of Quimperlé and Pont-Aven. Cf. *Ibid.*, p. 82, for the disenchantment encountered upon his first visit to Balbec-Plage. Cf. also comments by
Ferré, *op. cit.*, p. 35.
[32] *G. I.*, p. 10.

Parfois, cachée au fond de son nom, la fée se transforme au gré de la vie de notre imagination qui la nourrit; c'est ainsi que l'atmosphère où Mme de Guermantes existait en moi après n'avoir été pendant des années que le reflet d'un verre de lanterne magique et d'un vitrail d'église, commençait à éteindre ses couleurs, quand des rêves tout autres l'imprégnèrent de l'écumeuse humidité des torrents.[33]

But let a sensation from a past year enable our memory to make us hear the name with the particular ring that it had then for our ears, while the name itself has apparently not changed we feel the distance that separates the dreams which at different times its identical syllables have meant to us: [34]

Pour un instant, du ramage réentendu qu'il avait en tel printemps ancien, nous pouvons tirer, comme des petites tubes dont on se sert pour peindre, la nuance juste, oubliée, mystérieuse et fraîche des jours que nous avions cru nous rappeler, quand, comme les mauvais peintres, nous donnions à tout notre passé étendu sur une même toile les tons conventionnels et tous pareils de la mémoire volontaire. Or, au contraire, chacun des moments qui le composèrent, employait, pour une création originale, dans une harmonie unique, les couleurs d'alors que nous ne connaissons plus et qui, par exemple, me ravissent encore tout à coup si, grâce à quelque hasard, le nom de Guermantes ayant repris pour un instant après tant d'années, le son, si différent de celui d'aujourd'hui, qu'il avait pour moi le jour du mariage de Mlle Percipied, il me rend ce mauve si doux, trop brillant, trop neuf, dont se veloutait la cravate gonflée de la jeune duchesse, et comme une pervenche incueillissable et refleurie, ses yeux ensoleillés d'un sourire bleu. Et le nom de Guermantes d'alors est aussi comme un de ces petits ballons dans lesquels on a enfermé de l'oxygène ou un autre gaz: quand j'arrive à le crever, à en faire sortir ce qu'il contient, je respire l'air de Combray de cette année-là, de ce jour-là, mêlé d'une odeur d'aubépines agitée par le vent du coin de la place, précurseur de la pluie, qui tour à tour faisait envoler le soleil, le laissait s'étendre sur le tapis de laine rouge de la sacristie et le revêtir d'une carnation brillante, presque rose, de géranium, et de cette douceur, pour ainsi dire wagnérienne, dans l'allégresse, qui conserve tant de noblesse à la festivité.[35]

Here again the separate sense impressions melt together voluptuously. All the poetry of color is born of murmuring sound but it should be noted that Proust maintains a certain magic by always reintroducing words stemming from other senses, e. g. " doux," " ramage," etc. In other words he actually writes a sort of synaes-

---

[33] *Ibid.*, pp. 10-11.   [34] *Ibid.*, p. 11.   [35] *Ibid.*, pp. 11-12.

thetic rhapsody around a name in which " l'audition colorée " is the dominant note.

If the name Guermantes resumed for a moment the sound it had had for him on the day of Mlle Percepied's marriage, it brought back to him " ce mauve si doux " with which the scarf of the young duchess had glowed. From the echo of its " ramage " in that remote spring he could extract the exact, forgotten " nuance " of the days which he had believed himself to be recalling.

Something similar was extracted from the sound of Roussainville and Martinville which, because he had heard them pronounced by his aunt so often at dinner, retained a certain somber charm in which were blended extracts of the flavor of " preserves," the odor of fire logs, the page of one of Bergotte's books and the color of the stony front of the opposite house.[36]

The name Guermantes, emitting poetic associations, evokes a reaction analogous, though less intense, to the exaltation excited by dreams of Venice.[37] This time the sound of the name strikes such a highly tuned chord of his imagination that he has the impression of breathing the air of the Combray of that day blended with the fragrance of hawthorn blossoms. Here the synaesthetic impressions are complicated by the olfactory senses brought into play.

But he continues that, even apart from rare moments such as these, in which suddenly we feel the original entity resume its form, carve itself out of the syllables now dead, if in the rush of everyday life, names have lost all their color, on the other hand when, in our dreams we seek to return to the past, to suspend the perpetual motion by which we are borne along, gradually we see reappear, side by side but entirely separate from one another, the tints which in the course of our existence have been successively presented to us by a single name.[38] Proust's scission of his psychological experience with the name Guermantes leads to a historical division of sensibilities.

And thus it was that the name Guermantes successively assumed numerous shapes in his mind, the earliest of which were the most beautiful because his musings were forced by reality to establish new

[36] *JF. II.*, p. 86.   [37] Cf. *supra*, p. 226.   [38] *G. I.*, p. 12.

positions.[39]   It is noteworthy to observe how these transpositions took place in his mind:

Et, en même temps que Mme de Guermantes changeait sa demeure, issue elle aussi de ce nom que fécondait d'année en année telle ou telle parole entendue qui modifiait mes rêveries; cette demeure les reflétait dans ses pierres mêmes devenues réfléchissantes comme la surface d'un nuage ou d'un lac. Un donjon sans épaisseur qui n'était qu'une bande de lumière orangée et du haut duquel le seigneur et sa dame décidaient de la vie et de la mort de leurs vassaux avait fait place—tout au bout de ce " côté de Guermantes " où, par tant de beaux après-midi, je suivais avec mes parents le cours de la Vivonne—à cette terre torrentueuse où la duchesse m'apprenait à pêcher la truite et a connaître le nom des fleurs aux grappes violettes et rougeâtres qui décoraient les murs bas des enclos environnants: puis ç'avait été la terre héréditaire, le poétique domaine, où cette race altière de Guermantes, comme une tour jaunissante et fleuronnée qui traverse les âges, s'élevait déjà sur la France, alors que le ciel était encore vide, là où devaient plus tard surgir Notre-Dame de Paris et Notre-Dame de Chartres, alors qu'au sommet de la colline de Laon la nef de la cathédrale ne s'était pas posée comme l'Arche du Déluge au sommet du mont Ararat, emplie de Patriarches et de Justes anxieusement penchés aux fenêtres pour voir si la colère de Dieu s'est apaisée, emportant avec elle les types des végétaux qui multiplieront sur la terre, débordante d'animaux qui s'échappent jusque par les tours où des boeufs se promenant paisiblement sur la toiture, regardent de haut les plaines de Champagne; alors que le voyageur qui quittait Beauvais à la fin du jour ne voyait pas encore le suivre en tournoyant dépliées sur l'écran d'or du couchant, les ailes noires et ramifiées de la cathédrale.[40]

It was this feudal, medieval Guermantes, evoked by a group of beautiful " mutae cum liquida " and the langour of a nasal, like the scene of a novel, or an imaginary landscape, which all of a sudden would become impregnated with heraldic details within a few miles of a railway station. He recalled the names of neighboring localities as if they had been situated at the foot of Parnassus: [41]

Je revoyais les armoiries qui sont peintes aux soubassements des vitraux de Combray, et dont les quartiers s'étaient remplis, siècle par siècle, de toutes les seigneuries que, par mariages ou acquisitions cette illustre maison avait fait voler à elle de tous les coins de l'Allemagne, de l'Italie ou de la France: terres immenses du Nord, cités puissantes du Midi, venues se rejoindre et se composer en Guermantes et, perdant leur matérialité, inscrire

---

[39] *Ibid.*   [40] *Ibid.*, pp. 12-13.   [41] *Ibid.*, p. 13.

allégoriquement leur donjon de sinople ou leur château d'argent dans son champ d'azur. J'avais entendu parler des célèbres tapisseries de Guermantes et je les voyais, médiévales et bleues, un peu grosses, se détacher comme un nuage sur le nom amarante et légendaire, au pied de l'antique forêt où Childebert chassa si souvent, et ce fin fond mystérieux des terres, ce lointain des siècles, il me semblait qu'aussi bien que par un voyage je pénétrerais dans leurs secrets, rien qu'en approchant un instant à Paris Mme de Guermantes, suzeraine du lieu et dame du lac, comme si son visage et ses paroles eussent du posséder le charme local des futaies et des rives, et les mêmes particularités séculaires que le vieux coutumier de ses archives.[42]

But reality forces the alteration of these images of beautiful heraldry and coats-of-arms as later he learns that the castle had borne the name of Guermantes only since the 17th century when the family had acquired it, that their title was not taken from those parts and that the village of Guermantes had received its name from the castle around which it had been built. As for the tapestries, he learned that they were by Boucher, bought in the 19th century by a Guermantes who was a devotee of the fine arts. These revelations introduced into the castle elements foreign to the name of Guermantes which made it impossible for him to extract, solely from the resonance of the syllables, the stone and mortar of its walls: [43]

Alors, au fond de ce nom s'était effacé le château reflété dans son lac, et ce qui m'était apparu, autour de Mme de Guermantes comme sa demeure, ç'avait été son hôtel de Guermantes limpide comme son nom, car aucun élément matériel et opaque n'en venait interrompre et aveugler la transparence. Comme l'église ne signifie pas seulement le temple, mais aussi l'assemblée des fidèles, cet hôtel de Guermantes comprenait toutes les personnes qui partageaient la vie de la duchesse, mais ces personnes que je n'avais jamais vues n'étaient pour moi que des noms célèbres et poétiques, et connaissant uniquement des personnes qui n'étaient elles aussi que des noms, ne faisaient qu'agrandir et protéger le mystère de la duchesse en étendant autour d'elle un vaste halo qui allait tout au plus en se dégradant.[44]

It is rather ironical that later the name of Guermantes had no old mortar between the syllables. Modern linguists since Gilliéron would say that the *rm* and the *nt* were a mirage to Proust and were

[42] *Ibid.*, pp. 13-14.   [43] *Ibid.*, p. 14.   [44] *Ibid.*

gliding sounds which reflected *un hôtel lisse* and not *un château rouilleux.* As a matter of fact we have already noted that he refers to the orange light which glows from the resounding syllable " antes." [45]

The name Guermantes had finally lost all mystery, he had seen perish the last of the dwellings that had issued from its syllables, when one day an old friend of his father's, by speaking of the Duchess, restored to it a personality of its own. The remark was that " elle à la plus grande situation dans le faubourg Saint-Germain, elle à la première maison du faubourg Saint-Germain." [46] This time our hero decided to seek in the " salon " of Mme de Guermantes, different from all those other mansions of which he had dreamed, the mystery of her name which he could not discern in her person.[47] However, in spite of reality the name still retained a great deal of his earliest impressions of her:

. . . elle m'était apparue dans l'éclair d'une métamorphose avec des joues irréductibles, impénétrables à la couleur du nom de Guermantes et des après-midi au bord de la Vivonne, à la place de mon rêve foudroyé, comme un cygne ou un saule en lequel a été changé un Dieu ou une nymphe et qui désormais soumis aux lois de la nature glissera dans l'eau ou sera agité par le vent. Pourtant ces reflets évanouis, à peine les avais-je eu quittés qu'ils s'étaient reformés comme les reflets roses et verts du soleil couché, derrière la rame qui les a brisés, et dans la solitude de ma pensée le nom avait eu vite fait de s'approprier le souvenir du visage.[48]

Later when he frequently saw the Duchess, if he could not integrate in her the name Guermantes, he blamed it on the weakness of his mind to accomplish the whole act that he demanded of it.[49]

The Transposition of Sounds into Scenery

But names were not for Proust the only sounds endowed with poetic images and we shall now observe how his landscapes were diversified by the disposition of his tonal acuity. For Proust every-

---

[45] Cf. *S. I.*, p. 247. Cf. *supra*, p. 142.

[46] *G. I.*, p. 26.

[47] *Ibid.*

[48] *Ibid.* Cf. *G. II.*, p. 112, *SG. II.(2).*, p. 194, for the geographical etymology of other proper names.

[49] *Ibid.*, p. 27.

thing was capable of poetic transposition and the following passages further illustrate how the world of hearing awakened for him as infinite a number of correspondences as had the world of odor, taste, and sight.[50]

In the piano part of a sonata he hears the " mauve agitation des flots " [51] and a single dialogue of music he perceives as " un arc-en-ciel, dont l'éclat faiblit, s'abaisse, puis se relève et avant de s'éteindre, s'exalte un moment comme il n'avait pas encore fait: aux deux couleurs qu'elle avait jusque-là laissé paraître, elle ajouta d'autres cordes diaprées, toutes celles du prisme . . ." [52]

Another time the sonata paints for him a picture of the " Bois de Boulogne tombé en catalépsie " [53] as he hears the piano lament " comme un oiseau abandonné de sa compagnie " and the violin replies " comme d'un arbre voisin." [54]

The sound of church bells translated for him the atmospheric incidents of the day:

D'autres fois encore, aux premières cloches d'un couvent voisin, rares comme les dévotes matinales, blanchissant à peine le ciel sombre de leurs giboulées incertaines que fondait et dispersait le vent tiède, j'avais discerné une de ces journées tempêtueuses, désordonnées et douces, où les toits mouillés d'une ondée intermittente que sèchent un souffle ou un rayon, laissent glisser en roucoulant une goutte de pluie et, en attendant que le vent recommence à tourner, lissent au soleil momentané qui les irise leurs ardoises gorge-de-pigeons; une de ces journées remplies par tant de changements de temps, d'incidents aériens, d'orages, que le paresseux ne croit pas les avoir perdues, parce qu'il s'est intéressé à l'activité qu' à défaut de lui l'atmosphère, agissant en quelque sorte à sa place, a déployée . . .[55]

The golden sound of these chimes contains not only light but " la sensation de la lumière a aussi la saveur fade des confitures . . ." [56] and it was for Proust " comme une traduction pour aveugles . . . une traduction musicale du charme de la pluie ou du charme du soleil." [57]

---

[50] J. Benoist-Méchin, *La Musique et l'immortalité dans l'oeuvre de Marcel Proust* (Paris: Kra, 1926), p. 68.

[51] *S. I.*, p. 300.

[52] *S. II.*, p. 193.

[53] *JF. I.*, p. 147.

[54] *S. II.*, p. 193-194.

[55] *P. I.*, p. 109-110.

[56] *Ibid.*, p. 111.

[57] *Ibid.*, p. 112.

Proust was also fond of describing highly visualized scenes in terms of music. For instance, the imperceptible reflection of light at dusk on the canals of Venice he describes as " l'écho . . . d'une dernière note de lumière indéfiniment tenue sur les canaux comme par l'effet de quelque pédale optique, les reflets des palais déroulés comme à tout jamais en velours plus noir sur le gris crépusculaire des eaux." [58] By the transformation of this ray of light into a note of music, Proust succeeds in conveying the delicacy of his vision.

There are also scenes transposed from the correspondence of sounds. In the following passage the military aspect of Doncières is pictured by its martial music which blends with the ordinary noises of the town:

C'était, moins loin de Balbec que le paysage tout terrien ne l'aurait fait croire, une de ces petites cités aristocratiques et militaires entourées d'une campagne étendue où par les beaux jours, flotte si souvent dans le lointain une sorte de buée sonore intermittente qui—comme un rideau de peupliers par ses sinuosités dessine le cours d'une rivière qu'on ne voit pas—révèle les changements de place d'un régiment à la manoeuvre, que l'atmosphère même des rues, des avenues et des places, a fini par contracter une sorte de perpétuelle vibratilité musicale et guerrière, et que le bruit le plus grossier de chariot ou de tramway s'y prolonge en vagues appels de clairon, ressassés indéfiniment, aux oreilles hallucinées par le silence.[59]

The joyous cries of children at play, bathers and newspaper vendors, blended with the sound of the waves, trace for Proust pictures of the beach from which they come:

C'est qu'un matin de grande chaleur prématurée, les mille cris des enfants qui jouaient, des baigneurs plaisantants, des marchands de journaux m'avaient décrit en traits de feu, en flammèches entrelacées, la plage ardente que les petites vagues venaient une à une arroser de leur fraîcheur; alors avait commencé le concert symphonique mêlé au clapotement de l'eau dans lequel les violons vibraient comme un essaim d'abeilles égaré sur la mer . . . tandis que montant doucement, la mer à chaque déferlement de lame, recouvrait complètement de coulées de cristal la mélodie dont les phrases apparaissaient séparées les unes des autres commes ces anges luthiers qui au faîte de la cathédrale italienne s'élèvent entre les crêtes de porphyre bleu et de jaspe écumant.[60]

There is a double movement here which stems from " grande

---

[58] *G. I.*, p. 130.   [59] *Ibid.*, p. 63.   [60] *SG. II.(1).*, p. 210.

chaleur" and "les mille cris," the collaboration of which is responsible for his total impression. The intense heat of the day
penetrates his reveries and completes "en traits de feu" the vision
awakened by the myriad sounds of a busy seaside resort. As he
pictures the hum of violins mingled with the splash of waves one
may note the ease with which he blends noise and music. But it is
notable that in the last sentence he returns to extravagant visual
imagery to elaborate his auditory impression. The melody, whose
phrases appeared to be separated from one another, was buried by
the sea in layers of crystal just like those angel lutanists which on
the roof of the Italian cathedral rise between the peaks of blue
porphyry and foaming jasper.

In a similar manner, in the morning when he is still half asleep,
the noises which enter his room from the street sketch for him all
the figures which pass along it:

Dehors, des thèmes populaires finement écrits pour des instruments variés,
depuis la corne du raccommodeur de porcelaine, ou la trompette du rem-
pailleur de chaises, jusqu'à la flûte du chevrier qui paraissait dans un beau
jour être un pâtre de Sicile, orchestraient légèrement l'air matinal, en une
"ouverture pour un jour de fête." L'ouïe, ce sens délicieux, nous apporte
la compagnie de la rue dont elle nous retrace toutes les lignes, dessine toutes
les formes qui y passent, nous en montrant la couleur. Les rideaux de fer
du boulanger, du crémier, lesquels s'étaient hier abaissés le soir sur toutes
les possibilités de bonheur féminin, se levaient maintenant comme les
légères poulies d'un navire qui appareille et va filer, traversant la mer
transparente, sur un rêve de jeunes employées. Ce bruit du rideau de fer
qu'on lève eût peut-être été mon seul plaisir dans un quartier différent.[61]

Musical Patterns of the Audible World

Proust's extraordinary acuteness to sound endowed him with an
amazing capacity for discovering harmony in all the scattered roar
and rustle of life. Coeuroy remarks in his article *Music in the
Work of Proust*,[62] that Proust was possessed of so delicate a sense
of hearing that he actually organized this unorganized world of
noises. One may note, for instance, in his sketches of "les cris
de Paris" that a hundred different sounds seemed orchestrated in
the matutinal air. The scarcely modulated declamations of the

[61] *P. I.*, p. 158.　　　　　　　　[62] Coeuroy, *op. cit.*, p. 135.

various peripatetic vendors recalled to him the recitatives of Boris Godounov or the vague melancholy of Maeterlinck transposed into music by Debussy:

> Bien distincts dans ce quartier si tranquille . . . m'arrivaient, chacun avec sa modulation différent, des récitatifs déclamés par ces gens du peuple comme ils le seraient dans la musique, si populaire, de Boris, où une intonation initiale est à peine altérée par l'inflexion d'une note qui se penche sur une autre, musique de la foule qui est plutôt un langage qu'une musique. C'était "ah! le bigorneau, deux sous le bigorneau," qui faisait se précipiter vers les cornets où on vendait ces affreux petits coquillages . . .[63]

The spirit of each vendor frequently introduced variations into the words of all these chants and yet a ritual suspension interposing a silence in the middle of a word, especially when it was repeated a second time, constantly reminded him of some old church:

> Dans sa petite voiture conduite par une ânesse qu'il arrêtait devant chaque maison pour entrer dans les cours, le marchand d'habits, portant un fouet, psalmodiait: "Habits, marchand d'habits, ha . . . bits" avec la même pause entre les deux dernières syllabes d'habits que s'il eût entonné en plain-chant: "Per omnia saecula saeculo . . . rum" ou: 'Requiescat in pa . . . ce ' bien qu'il ne dût pas croire à l'éternité de ses habits et ne les offrît pas non plus comme linceuls pour le suprême repos dans la paix. Et de même, comme les motifs commençaient à s'entrecroiser dès cette heure matinale, une marchande de quatre-saisons, poussant sa voiturette, usait pour sa litanie de la division grégorienne:
>
> > *A la tendresse, à la verduresse*
> > *Artichauts tendres et beaux*
> > *Arti . . . chauts.*
>
> bien qu'elle fût vraisemblablement ignorante de l'antiphonaire et des sept tons qui symbolisent, quatre les sciences du quadrivium et trois celles du trivium.[64]

Another time from his window he listened to the noises and songs of the street and analyzed them into definite musical styles. Note the following passage:

> . . . j'allai me mettre un instant à la fenêtre. Il y eut d'abord un silence, où le sifflet du marchand de tripes et la corne du tramway firent résonner l'air à des octaves différents, comme un accordeur de piano aveugle. Puis

---

[63] *P. I.*, p. 160. Cf. Leo Spitzer, "Etymologie d'un cris de Paris," *Romanic Review*, XXXV (October, 1944), pp. 244-250.

[64] *P. I.*, pp. 161-162.

peu à peu devinrent distincts les motifs entrecroisés auxquels de nouveaux s'ajoutaient. Il y avait aussi un nouveau sifflet, appel d'un marchand dont je n'ai jamais su ce qu'il vendait, sifflet qui, lui, était exactement pareil à celui d'un tramway, et comme il n'était pas emporté par la vitesse on croyait à un seul tramway, non doué de mouvement, ou en panne, immobilisé, criant à petits intervalles comme un animal qui meurt . . . Le ronflement d'un violon était dû parfois au passage d'une automobile, parfois à ce que je n'avais pas mis assez d'eau dans ma bouillotte électrique. Au milieu de la symphonie détonait un " air " démondé: remplaçant la vendeuse de bonbons qui accompagnait d'habitude son air avec une crécelle, le marchand de jouets, au mirliton duquel était attaché un pantin qu'il faisait mouvoir en tous sens, promenait d'autres pantins, et sans souci de le déclamation rituelle de Grégoire le Grand, de la déclamation reformée de Palestrina et de la déclamation lyrique des modernes, entonnait à pleine voix, partisan attardé de la pure mélodie: " Allons les papas, allons les mamans, contentez vos petits enfants, c'est moi qui les fais, c'est moi qui les vends, et c'est moi qui boullotte l'argent. Tra la la la. Tra la la la laire, tra la la la la la la. Allons les petits! " De petits Italiens, coiffés d'un béret, n'essayaient pas de lutter avec cet aria vivace, et c'est sans rien dire qu'ils offraient de petites statuettes. Cependant qu'un petit fifre réduisait le marchand de jouets à s'éloigner et à chanter plus confusément quoique presto: " Allons les papas, allons les mamans." . . .[65]

This transposition of the noises of everyday life into musical patterns was not an attempt on Proust's part to weave a romantic spell but rather an indication that he diversified his own personality and widened his own capacity for enjoying life, intellectually and emotionally, by making the variegated individualities of the arts—especially music and painting—a part of his own life and an inseparable part of his Paris.

Proust's mind was so naturally inclined to music that in the silvery faint bells of an angelus he spontaneously visualizes scenes from " Pélléas et Mélisande " [66] and as already noted he even perceives a Wagnerianism in the roar of German planes over Paris.[67] In the twittering of birds at daybreak he notes the enchantment of a " sublime Siegfried " [68] and it is the " pianissimo " of faint noises that gives the impression of distance to a moonlit " surface of silence." [69]

[65] *Ibid.*, pp. 186-187.
[66] *SG. II.(2).*, p. 45.
[67] *TR. I.*, p. 87.
[68] *Ibid.*, p. 82.
[69] *S. I.*, p. 53.

It may be said in conclusion that for Proust a universe merely audible was as full of variety as any other.   The reality of a country for him, most often, was according to the poetic associations emitted from the sound of its name and, because of his unusual auditive sensibility, sounds possessed for him unlimited aesthetic possibilities and awakened an infinite number of images borrowed from nature. By a sort of reciprocal phenomena, on the other hand, his impressions of the exterior world are often characterized by an orchestral sonority.

CONCLUSION

Proust's whole novel, from the pictorial point of view, is a series of landscapes stemming from his recollection of Combray, "Balbec" Venice, Paris and Doncières. These landscapes provided the background for the unfolding of his "story" and prove by this fact alone their importance. In this study, therefore, an attempt has been made to determine the function of landscape in the work of Marcel Proust and to analyze how he has presented it to the reader through literary art. The first result of our investigation shows that Proust never painted from direct observation, in spite of his many parallels to the impressionist painters. His landscapes are drawn rather from memory, reverie, and imagination.

A whole series of landscapes was revealed to Proust in later life through the identification of past memories with present sensations. We have seen how the individual scenes of these recollections occupied his thoughts as a young boy. For instance, in his memories of Combray, Balbec and Paris he recalled, in addition to impressions left upon him by Illiers, Cabourg and Paris, places seen in paintings, scenes which framed the women he desired, place-names which for him were packed with imaginary pictures of places he longed to visit in the future and sounds which had traced in his imagination scenes of the places from which they came.

These cerebral landscapes, it is true, furnished Proust with both inspiration and subject matter for his great work. However, as far as the genesis of such landscapes was concerned we have to admit that the sight of a real landscape first revealed to him his ability as a creative artist and all the mysterious forces of his soul were aroused either by the apparition of a landscape which caused an unusually profound happiness or the sudden reappearance of a vaguely familiar scene from the past.

Proust's contemplation of these scenes together with the "ghost" landscapes usually revealed the details of his own past life. To recreate these memories into a work of art was for Proust tantamount to forgetting the present and—at least for a moment—

193

attaining immortality. Accordingly, his poetic enthusiasm achieved itself in a page of style in which he intensely felt the enchantment that he had succeeded in transcribing—the throb of one happy moment.

1. The above being true in general, the primary function of landscape for Proust was its power to convert impressions from the past into an intellectual equivalent—a work of art.

2. It is evident from the passages studied that his acquaintance with the Impressionist painters—Monet, Manet, Turner, Pissaro and Whistler—revealed to him new aspects of natural beauty which were incorporated into his work by rearrangement and reflection. It influenced particularly his representation of coastal scenery. A discussion of Elstir's technical excellencies as discerned from his water colors discloses Proust's own method of viewing nature poetically and the reconstruction of his visual experiences.

3. The elaboration of his pictorial memories shows that he looked at the outer world through the human emotions of awe, reverence and love. Certainly, he experienced a landscape through the senses and painted it with artistic exactitude as the background of human life. But as we follow the vernal freshness of his spring songs to the autumnal decay of meditative scenes, we can state that the new truth he has to offer is the uniqueness of his images due to his retrospective penetration into the " deepest layers of his mental soil " which transposed reality into a magic picturesqueness, strange, fascinating and delicate. The result is not only a landscape " vu a tràvers un tempérament " but a challenge to every reader to subscribe to his pictorial view as the best possible and *non varietur* form.

Another striking feature in his portrayal of the exterior world is his eroticizing of nature. Women were painted upon a background of natural scenery. They exalted the charms of nature, and landscape in turn enhanced feminine beauty. These women, as we noticed, became so much a part of their background that Proust was haunted by the idea that he could discover the secret treasures of nature only by means of their physical possession. He stubbornly wanted to experience through the senses the poetry created by his imagination. As with many Frenchmen before him,

Proust absurdly dreamed of women as a means of knowing new worlds and in the course of his reveries the human being was often transposed into biological realms, but never debased to the degree that it is, for instance, in Jules Romains.

4. Proust in his landscape painting displayed, in addition to his unique visual acuity, an unusual sense of hearing. Therefore, his audbile universe, more than any other is an elaboration of the highest delights of his imagination. Names caused him to seek in a place characteristics that he imagined there but which it did not embody. Thus reality often forced the alteration of his musings which caused the disenchantment encountered in the course of his travels.

One sees clearly from his auditive scenes that it was with an unusual tonal sensibility, schooled theoretically in modern aesthetics, that he painted with words the color of sounds, sketched scenery from the correspondence of sounds and extracted harmony from the unorganized noises of the world.

Proust's literary method of presenting a landscape proved to be a highly involved process; he presented an original impression as soon as it was received through the senses, but because landscape was for him not only a spectacle to be seen but something to be explained, he hastened to interpret it by intellectual investigation. Now investigation of the impression spontaneously led to the evocation of past epochs, the recollection of his own past observations and feelings, and analogies in art, music and literature. Thomistic psychology probably would not admit a fundamental difference between *souvenir* and *mémoire* as Proust did under the influence of Bergson. Furthermore, to communicate the impression exactly as he felt it, the scene underwent a poetic transformation by style. In some cases the crystallization of his landscape experiences seemed a veritable " état de trance " where he experienced a sort of personal " transfiguration."

An examination of the first impression usually revealed either objective historic associations or subjective souvenirs from his own past or both. In order not to remain in the abstract we will reiterate a few examples of Proust's impression, souvenir and transformation of landscape. He recalled for instance, the streets of

Combray as a sort of magic world wherein one would meet Golo and Geneviève de Brabant, and the church which epitomized the town appeared in its ancient medieval setting of Gothic splendour. The river scenery along the Vivonne gleamed with emblems of the eternal aristocracy of the Guermantes while the history of the counts of Combray was hidden beneath a field of buttercups. The ducal park of Guermantes was colored by the mystery of the Merovingian age and the very sound of its name suggested the romance and heraldry of its medieval past.

But this is only the first step of wholesale transformation in Proust's interpretation of the outer world. Next his investigation sought to penetrate the landscape by identifying it with particular details of his own past. For instance, he found that his memory of the church of Combray was linked with the activities of his daily life in the provincial town—walks with his grandmother, errands to the local bakery, and even the unpleasant routine of bidding his mother goodnight. The glory of the hawthorn blossom was identified with the religious exercises of May which he attended during his childhood days. Impressions of the Bois evoked the atmosphere of his youth colored by the ladies' fashions of his time. And it is striking that his first actual impression of Venice was reconstructed by means of its comparison to Combray—thus making it his very own Venice. The beauty of a Paris night scene was its restaging of a similar spectacle witnessed by him in 1914. His thoughts of dining with Mme de Stermaria on the Isle de Bois were impregnated with a previous conception of the Bois as a place especially designed for pleasure and lovers' melancholy.

It is also significant that in the representation of these landscapes which are impregnated with souvenirs of his past Proust introduced a kind of comparative " état d'âme," i. e. he indicated the permanence of his devotion to the various elements of a scene by stressing the similarity of past and present sentiments. What he felt after many years at the sight of a Gothic church spire, an old road lined with elm trees, hawthorn blossoms, apple trees, the odor of lilacs, etc. awakened sentimental analogies from the past. The bond established between certain landscapes and his heart brought out the inner spirit of a place and interpreted its eternal character for Proust as no mere outward description could do. Proust's landscape representation, in addition to impression, judgment, historical reminiscences, personal souvenir, comparative sensibility, includes the use of art analogies. He seemed to look at nature through the eyes of the great master painters, and he saw there for instance, Hubert Robert's moonlit ruins, the sun and moon of Michel Angelo's *Création,* Van der Meulen's clouds against a blue sky and the glazed shadows of Leonardo da Vinci. The dome of St. Hilaire was sketched in the manner of Piranesi's views of Rome and there was the exoticism of Carpaccio in a Parisian twilight. The magnificence of the sea appeared to him in the style of the Tuscan masters, Japanese prints, Pisanello and Gallé. His dreams of Florence were impregnated with the genius of Giotto and architectural splendours while the Grand Canal was colored by the temperament of Titian.

Proust's art obsession comes to the fore also without names of masters: the steeples of Martinville created the impression of flowers painted upon the sky, and the spire of St. Hilaire appeared so delicate against the heavens that it gave the impression of being sketched there by the fingernail of an artist. Stone steps along the streets of Combray seemed cut by some sculptor of Gothic images, arched cliffs suggested the form of a cathedral and an imaginary marine landscape created the illusion of an entire Gothic city. All of this is sufficient evidence of Proust's highly cultivated, sophisticated and even "unnatural" conception and representation of natural scenery.

Finally Proust gave eternity to his landscape impressions not only through the transformation of the whole—as we have seen above—into a magic landscape but also through the metaphoric transposition of its single elements. Under the unique strokes of his literary brush his entire outer world was transposed into a kind of living mythology. The steeples of Martinville seen from a distance were represented as legendary young ladies and the trees along the old Balbec road became the vanished friends of his childhood. Hawthorn and apple blossoms were transposed into blushing young girls, some " en robe de fête " and others " en toilette de bal." Lilacs had all the delicacy and grace of " nymphes du Printemps " and when he looked at the sea he even visualized " la nymphe Glaukonomène." The movement of a white moon in an afternoon sky had the dignity of a shy actress wishing to avoid attention. Also a whole scene was often transformed by the "pictorial" metaphor. This device was used most often in his portrayal of coastal scenery as, for instance, the picture of "le Port de Carquethuit," the cliffs of Creuniers and many others.

Even the most inanimate aspects of a scene were vivified by this Proustian procedure. A Gothic spire was represented as a living being endowed with a conscience and "le doigt de Dieu." Airplanes were seen as "étoiles humaines" and in Venice his gondola led him through narrow canals as "la main mystérieuse d'un génie."

Especially striking are Proust's personifications of meteorological phenomena. In a coastal scene the shadows cast by the arched cliffs were transformed into mythological deities (Deésses marines). The smiling sun which was either dancing over the waves of the sea or gilding clouds—siren-like—constantly invited him to adventure. The steady fall of raindrops was pictured as a flock of migrating birds and even the wind over the meadows became to young lovers "le génie particulier de Combray." This is the unique world created by his own sensibility and endowed with all the poetry of his artistic soul.

Personal transmutation, transcending the realm of literature, was the culmination of Proust's experience with landscape. Upon rare occasions when his mind discovered an identity between the past and present, resurrection of a past scene was so complete that his entire being believed itself surrounded by it. What actually happened in such an event was that under the condition of intense joy evoked by the memory of a landscape once known and finally "retrouvé" he made such an effort to fuse himself with it that his present surroundings seemed lost to him. He then contemplated this scene of the past as he would a present scene and converted it into what *was* for him a pseudo-mystical epiphany and *is* for us a work of art. Such has been the Proustian procedure, with the fundamental scenes of Combray, Balbec and Venice.

BIBLIOGRAPHY

I. WORKS BY MARCEL PROUST

A. Books

Portraits de Peintres (Quatre pièces pour piano de Reynaldo Hahn; illustrations de Mme Madeleine Lemaire). Paris: Au Ménestrel, 1896.

Les Plaisirs et les jours (Illustrations de Mme Madeleine Lemaire. Préface d'Anatole France et quatre pièces pour piano de Reynaldo Hahn). Paris: Calmann-Lévy, 1896; new edition, Gallimard (1921), 1924.

A la recherche du temps perdu, Paris, 1913-1927.

Du Côté de chez Swann, Grasset, 1913, 1 vol.; new edition: Gallimard (1919), 1927, 2 vols.

A l'Ombre des jeunes filles en fleurs, Gallimard (1919), 1927, 3 vols.

Le Côté de Guermantes, I, Gallimard (1920), 1928.

Le Côté de Guermantes, II; *Sodome et Gomorrhe*, I, Gallimard (1921), 1927.

Sodome et Gomorrhe, II, Gallimard (1922), 1927, 3 vols.

La Prisonnière, Gallimard (1923), 1927, 2 vols.

Albertine Disparue, Gallimard (1925), 1926, 2 vols.

Le Temps Retrouvé, Gallimard (1927), 1927, 2 vols.

Pastiches et mélanges. Paris: Gallimard (1919), 1927.

Chroniques. Paris: Gallimard, 1927.

B. Articles, Translations and Prefaces

Proust, Marcel. "John Ruskin," *Gazette des Beaux-Arts*, XXIII (1900), 310-318; XXIV, 135-146.

———. "Un professeur de Beauté," *Les Arts de vie*, IV (août, 1905), 67-79.

John Ruskin. *La Bible d'Amiens* (Traduction, Notes et Préface par Marcel Proust). Paris: Mercure de France (1904), 1926.

———. *Sésame et les Lys* (Traduction, Préface et Notes par Marcel Proust). Paris: Mercure de France (1906), 1935.

Jacques-Emile Blanche. *Propos de Peintre*, I, *De David à Degas* (Préface de Marcel Proust). Paris: Emile-Paul, 1919.

Paul Morand. *Tendres Stocks* (Préface de Marcel Proust), Paris: Gallimard, 1921.

C. Correspondence

Barney, Natalie Clifford. *Aventures de l'esprit.* Paris: Emile-Paul, 1929, pp. 59-74.

Bibesco, Marthe Lucie. *Au Bal avec Marcel Proust.* Paris: Gallimard, 1929.

199

Billy, Robert de. *Lettres et conversations.* Paris: Edition des Portiques, 1930.

Clermont-Tonnerre, E. *Robert de Montesquiou et Marcel Proust.* Paris: Flammarion, 1925.

Correspondance générale (vols. 1-5 publiés par Robert Proust et Paul Brach; vol. 6 par Suzy Proust-Mante et Paul Brach). Paris: Plon, 1930-1936, 6 vols.

Daudet, Lucien. *Autour de soixante lettres de Marcel Proust.* Paris: Gallimard, 1929.

Hommage à Marcel Proust. Paris: Gallimard, 1927.

Lettres à la Nouvelle Revue Française. Paris: Gallimard, 1932.

Pierre-Quint, Léon. *Comment travaillait Proust.* Paris: Editions des Cahiers Libres, 1928.

———. [Editor]. "Lettres inédites de Marcel Proust à Paul Brach ...," *La Revue Universelle,* XXXIII (April 1, 1928), 1-13.

———. *Comment parut " Du Côté de chez Swann,"* (Lettres à René Blum, Bernard Grasset et Louis Brun). Paris: Kra, 1926.

Pouquet, Jeanne Maurice. *Le Salon de Mme Armand de Caillavet.* Paris: Hachette, 1926.

Quelques Lettres de Marcel Proust a Jeanne Simone Gaston de Caillavet, Robert de Flers, Bertrand de Fenélon. Paris: Hachette, 1929.

Robert, Louis de. *" Comment debuta Proust,"* Revue de France, Jan. 1 and 15, 1925.

———. *De Loti à Proust.* Paris: Flammarion, 1928.

Unpublished Letters from Marcel Proust to Walter Berry. Paris: The Black Sun Press, 1930.

II. REFERENCES

A. Specific

Abatangel, Louis. *Marcel Proust et la musique.* Paris, 1939.

Abraham, Pierre. *Proust; recherches sur la création intellectuelle.* Paris: Rieder, 1930.

Alden, Douglas. *Marcel Proust and his French Critics.* Los Angeles: Lymanhouse, 1940.

Ames, Van Meter. *Proust and Santayana, The Aesthetic Way of Life.* New York: Willett Clark & Co., 1937.

Bell, Clive. *Marcel Proust.* New York: Harcourt Brace & Co., 1929.

Benoist-Méchin. *La Musique et l'Immortalité dans l'oeuvre de Marcel Proust.* Paris: Kra, 1926.

Blondel, Charles. *La Psychographie de Marcel Proust.* Paris: Vrin, 1932.

Brasillach, Robert. *Portraits.* Paris: Plon, 1935.

Cabeen, D. *A Selected Bibliography of Works on Proust.* New York, 1937.

Cattaui, Georges. *L'Amitié de Proust.* Paris: Librairie Gallimard, 1935.

Celly, Raoul. *Répertoire des thèmes de Marcel Proust.* Paris: Librairie Gallimard, 1935.

Chernowitz, Maurice. *Proust and Painting.* New York: International University Press, 1945.

Cochet, Marie-Anne. *L'Ame proustienne.* Bruxelles: Imprimerie des Etablissements Collignon, 1929.

Coeuroy, André. *Musique et littérature.* Paris: Bloud et Gay, 1923.

Crémieux, Benjamin. *Du Côté de Marcel Proust.* Paris: Lemarget, 1929.

Curtius, Ernst Robert. *Marcel Proust.* Traduit de l'allemand par Armand Pierhal. Paris: Les Editions de la Revue Nouvelle, 1928.

Dandieu, Arnaud. *Marcel Proust; sa révélation psychologique.* Paris: Firmin-Didot, 1930.

Daudet, Charles. *Répertoire des personnages de " A la recherche du temps perdu."* Paris: Librairie Gallimard, 1928.

Dolowitz, Grace Belle. *A Critical Study of the Composition of Proust's Sodome et Gomorrhe.* Bryn Mawr, 1945.

Dreyfus, Robert. *Souvenirs sur Marcel Proust.* Paris: Grasset, 1926.

Duffner, Jean. *L'oeuvre de Marcel Proust* (étude médico-psychologique). Paris, 1931.

Ferré, André. *Géographie de Marcel Proust.* Paris: Sagittaire, 1939.

Feuillerat, Albert. *Comment Marcel Proust a composé son roman.* New Haven: Yale University Press, 1934.

Fiser, Emeric. *L'Esthétique de Marcel Proust.* Préface de Valéry Larbaud. Paris: Rieder, 1933.

Germain, André. *De Proust à Dada.* Paris: Kra, 1924.

Hier, Florence. *La Musique dans l'oeuvre de Marcel Proust.* New York: Publication of the Institute of French Studies, 1932.

Hommage à Marcel Proust. Paris: Gallimard (1923), 1927.

Hudson, Stephen. *Céleste and Other Sketches.* London: The Blackmore Press, 1930.

Kinds, Edmond. *Etude sur Marcel Proust: sensation, souvenir, art.* Paris: Le Rouge et le Noir, 1933.

Larcher, P. L. *Le Parfum de Combray.* Paris: Mercure de France, 1945.

Le Bidois, Robert. " Le Langage parlé des personages de Proust." *Le Français Moderne.* Paris, 1939.

Lemaître, Georges. *Four French Novelists.* London: Oxford University Press, 1938.

Léon, Derrick. *Introduction to Proust.* London: Trubner & Co., 1940.

Lindner, G. D. *Marcel Proust.* Stanford University: Stanford University Press, 1942.

Massis, Henri. *Le Drame de Marcel Proust.* Paris: Grasset, 1937.

Mauriac, François. *Proust.* Paris: Marcelle Lesage, 1926.

Monkhouse, Elizabeth. *La révélation de Marcel Proust.* Paris: Palais-Royal, 1936.

Moore, Margaret. " Les arts plastiques dans l'oeuvre de Proust." Unpublished Master's thesis, Romance Language Department, University of Chicago, 1928.

Polanscak, Anton. *La Peinture du décor et de la nature chez Proust.* Paris: Etudes et Editions, 1941.

Pommier, Jean. *La Mystique de Marcel Proust.* Paris: Droz, 1939.

Pierre-Quint, Léon. *Marcel Proust, sa vie, son oeuvre.* Paris: Kra, (1925) 1928.

Raphael, Pierre. *Introduction à la correspondance de Marcel Proust. Répertoire de la correspondance de Proust.* Paris: Sagittaire, 1938.

Scheikevitch, Marie. *Souvenirs d'un temps disparu.* Paris: Plon, 1935.

Scott-Moncrieff, Charles Kenneth [Editor]. *Marcel Proust, An English Tribute.* New York: T. Seltzer, 1923.

Seillière, Ernest. *Marcel Proust.* Paris: Editions de la nouvelle revue critique, 1931.

Silva Ramos, G. de. "Bibliographie proustienne," in *Letters à la NRF.* Paris: Librairie Gallimard, 1932.

Souday, Paul. *Marcel Proust.* Paris: Kra, 1927.

Souza, Sybil de. *L'Influence de Ruskin sur Proust.* Montpellier, 1932.

————. *La Philosophie de Marcel Proust.* Paris: Reider, 1939.

Spagnoli, John J. *The Social Attitude in Proust.* New York: Institute of French Studies, 1936.

Talvar, Hector. *La Fiche bibliographique française* (No. 17). Paris, 1928.

Tiedtke, Irma. *Symbole und Bilder im Werke Marcel Prousts.* Hamburg: Evert, 1936.

Wegener, Alfons. *Impressionismus und Klassizismus im Werke Marcel Prousts.* Frankfurt: Carolus-Druckerei, 1930.

Wilson, Edmund. *Axel's Castle.* New York: Scribner, 1931.

B. GENERAL

Alonso, Amado and Lida, Raimundo. *El Impresionismo en el lenguaje.* Buenos Aires: Instituto de Filología (Universidad de Buenos Aires), 1936.

Auerbach, Erich. *Mimesis.* Bern: Francke, 1946. (On Proust: 482 ff.)

Babbitt, Irving. *The New Laokoon.* Boston: Houghton, Mifflin Co., 1910.

Barre, A. *Le Symbolisme.* Paris: Jouve, 1911.

Baudelaire, Charles. *Oeuvres complètes de Charles Beaudelaire* (edited by F.-F. Gautier and Y. G. Le Dantec), Paris: Gallimard, 1918-1937, 13 vols.

Bergson, Henri. *Essai sur les données immediates de la conscience.* Paris (1889), Alcan, 1908.

————. *Matière et Mémoire.* Paris: Alcan, 1900.

————. *Le Rire.* Paris: Alcan, 1914.

————. *L'Evolution créatrice.* Paris: Alcan, 1909.

Bernardin de Saint-Pierre. *Oeuvres complètes de Bernardin de Saint-Pierre.* Paris: Aimé Martin, 1818-1820, 12 vols.

Blanche, Jacques-Emile. *Propos de Peintre*. Paris: Emile-Paul, 1919-1928, 3 vols.

Boeniger, Y. *Lamartine et le sentiment de la nature*. Paris, 1934.

Bosanquet, Bernard. *A History of Aesthetics* (1892). New York: Macmillan, 1934.

Bourger, R. *Histoire du paysage en France*. Paris: Laurens, 1908.

Brunetière, Ferdinand. *Le Roman naturaliste*. Paris: Plon, 1912, 2 vols.

Brutsch, C. *Essai sur la poésie de Verhaeren. La campagne—les villes—le jardin*. Paris: E. de Boccard, 1929.

Buchner, M. L. *A Contribution to the Study of the Descriptive Technique of Jean-Jacques Rousseau*. Baltimore: The Johns Hopkins Studies in Romance Literatures and Languages, 1937.

Chaix, Marie Antoinette. *La Correspondance des arts dans la poésie contemporaine*. Paris: Felix Alcan, 1919.

Chandler, Albert Richard and Barnhart, Edward N. *A Bibliography of Psychological and Experimental Aesthetics, 1864-1937*. Berkeley: University of California Press, 1938.

Charlier, Gustav. *Le Sentiment de la nature chez les romantiques français, 1762-1830*. Bruxelles: Hayez, 1912.

Chateaubriand, François-René de. *Oeuvres complètes de Chateaubriand*. Paris: Garnier, 1859-1861, 12 vols.

Cornelia, W. B. *The Classical Sources of the Nature References in Ronsard's Poetry*. New York: Publication of the Institute of French Studies, 1934.

Curtius, Ernst Robert. *The Civilization of France*. Translated by Olive Wyon. London: Allen, 1932.

Dauzat, Albert. *Le Sentiment de la nature et son expression artistique*. Paris: Alcan, 1914.

Dewhurst, Wynford. *Impressionist Painting, its Genesis and Development*. London: G. Newnes, 1904.

Ditchy, J. E. *Le thème de la mer chez les Parnassiens*. Paris: "Les Belles-Lettres," 1927.

Downey, J. E. *Creative Imagination*. New York: Harcourt, Brace, 1929.

Droz, Edouard. *Sur le sentiment de la nature dans la littérature française*. Paris, 1898.

Duret, Théodore. *Les Peintres impressionnistes*. Paris: Librairie Parisienne, 1878.

Fontaine, A. *Les Doctrines d'art en France*. Paris: Laurens, 1909.

Geffroy, G. *Claude Monet, sa vie, son temps, son oeuvre*. Paris: Crès, 1922.

Girard, J. *Essai sur l'évolution du sentiment de la nature au XVIe siècle, de Jean Lemaire à Du Bartas*. Paris, 1932.

Goncourt, Edmond de. *Journal des Goncourt*. Paris: Charpentier, 1887-1896, 9 vols.

Hammond, William A. *A Bibliography of Aesthetics and of the Philosophy of the Fine Arts from 1900 to 1932* (revised and enlarged editions). New York: Longmans, Green and Co., 1934.

Huysmans, J.-K. *A Rebours.* Paris (1884): Charpentier, 1903.

Jan, Eduard von. *Die Landschaft des französischen Menschen.* Weimar: H. Böhlau, 1935.

Küchler, Elizabeth. *Das Stadterlebnis bei Verhaeren.* Diss. Hamburg, 1930.

Kuhn, H. *Michelets Landschaftsschilderungen in "La Mer" und "La Montagne."* Diss. Würzburg, 1933.

Laprade, Victor de. *Histoire du sentiment de la nature.* Paris: Didier, 1867-1883.

———. *Le Sentiment de la nature chez les Modernes.* Paris, 1869.

La Sizeranne, Robert de. *Ruskin et la religion de la beauté.* Paris: Hachette, 1898.

Lecomte, Georges. *L'Art impressionniste,* Paris: Chamerot & Renouard, 1892.

Lemaître, Georges. *From Cubism to Surrealism in French Literature.* Cambridge: Harvard University Press, 1941.

Lerch, Eugen. *Historische französische Syntax.* Braunschweig, 1930-1931, 1934, 3 vols.

Lessing, Gothold Ephraim. *Laokoon.* Translated by Hon. Sir Robert Phillimore, bart. London: Routledge, [n. d.].

Manwaring, Elizabeth Wheeler. *Italian Landscape in Eighteenth Century England.* New York: Oxford University Press, 1925.

Mauclair, Camille. *L'Impressionnisme, son histoire, son esthétique, ses maîtres.* Paris: L'Art ancien et moderne, 1904.

Maury, Paul. *Arts et littérature comparés.* Paris: "Les Belles-Lettres," 1934.

McCann, G. L. *Le sentiment de la nature en France dans la première moitié du dix-septième siècle.* Nemours, 1926.

Michel, E. *Great Masters of Landscape Painting.* Philadelphia: Lippincott, 1910.

Minnaert, M. *Light and Color in the Open Air.* London: G. Bell, 1940.

Montesquiou-Fezensac, Robert de. *Professionnelles Beautés.* Paris: Felix Juven, 1905.

———. *Les Roseaux Pensants.* Paris: Bibliothèque-Charpentier, 1897.

Mornet, Daniel. *Le sentiment de la nature en France de J.-J. Rousseau à Bernardin de Saint-Pierre.* Paris, 1907.

Mustoxidi, T.-M. *Bibliographie générale de l'esthétique française des origines à 1914.* Paris: Champion, 1920.

Pollock, M. *Light and Water.* London: G. Bell, 1903.

Pope, F. R. *Nature in the Work of Lemonnier.* New York: Publication of the Institute of French Studies, 1933.

Rousseau, J.-J. *La Nouvelle Héloise.* Edited by Daniel Mornet. Paris: Hachette, 1925-26.

Ruskin, John. *The Works of John Ruskin.* Edited by E. T. Cook and A.

Wedderburn. London: G. Allen, New York: Longmans, Green, and Co., 1903-1912, 39 vols.

Sagne, J. *Le sentiment de la nature dans l'oeuvre de Stendhal.* Zurich, 1932.

Schilla, A. *Francis Jammes, unter besonderer Berücksichtigung seiner Naturdichtung.* Diss. Königsberg, 1929.

Skard, Sigmund. *The Use of Color in Literature.* Philadelphia: American Philosophical Society, 1946.

Spronck, Maurice. *Les Artistes littéraires; études sur le XIXᵉ siècle.* Paris: Lévy, 1889.

Stendhal (Henri Beyle). *La Chartreuse de Parme.* Edition complète, revue et corrigée. Paris: Garnier, 1925.

Tonquedec, J. de. *Sur la Philosophie Bergsonienne.* Paris: Beauchesne, 1936.

Venturi, Lionello. *History of Art Criticism* (trans. by Charles Mariott), New York: Dutton, 1936.

Walker, T. C. *Chateaubriand's Natural Scenery.* Baltimore: The Johns Hopkins Press, 1946.

Zola, Emile. *L'Oeuvre.* Paris: Charpentier, 1921, 2 vols.

C. ARTICLES

Adelson, D. "Proust's Earlier and Later Styles: A Textual Comparison," *Romanic Review*, XXXIV (April, 1943), 127-38.

Alden, D. W. "Proust et Flaubert Controversy," *Romanic Review*, XXVIII (October, 1937), 230-240.

Aldington, Richard. "The Approach To Marcel Proust," *English Review*, XXX (1920), 488-493.

Bédé, J. A. "Chateaubriand et Marcel Proust," *Modern Language Notes*, XLIX (June, 1934), 353-360.

———. "Marcel Proust—Problèmes récents," *Le Flambeau*, XIX (1936), 311-324, 439-452.

Belvianes, Marcel. "Les cris de Paris. Leurs rapports avec la musique," *Ménéstrel*, LXXXVII (23 janvier, 1925).

Benoist-Méchin, Jacques. "De la musique considérée par rapport aux opérations du language dans l'oeuvre de Marcel Proust," *Intention*, II (janvier, 1923), 12-21.

Bernard, Emile. "Le Symbolisme pictural 1886-1936," *Mercure de France*, CCLXVIII (15 juin, 1936), 514-530.

Bisson, L. A. "Marcel Proust and Mme Lucien Daudet—a source and an explanation of affective memory," *Modern Language Review*, XXXVI (October, 1941), 493-499.

Blanche, Jacques-Emile. "Du Côté de chez Swann," *Echo de Paris*, (16 décembre, 1913).

Boisse, L. "Le paysage et la nature dans l'oeuvre de Gustave Moreau," *Mercure de France*, CXIX (1917), 417-428.

Brach, Paul. " De Balbec à Venise," *Nouvelle revue française*, XX (janvier, 1922), 238-239.

Brasillach, Robert. " Art poétique de Marcel Proust," *Revue française*, XXVII (25 juin, 1931), 43-58.

Burchell, Samuel. " Marcel Proust: An interpretation of his life," *Psychoanalytic Review*, XV (1928), 300-303.

Bussom, T. W. " Proust and Painting," *Romanic Review*, XXXIV (February, 1943), 54-70.

Casa, Illan de. " Marcel Proust et les parfums," *Revue hébdomadaire*, VIII (17 août, 1935), 355-362.

Cassou, Jean. " Proust, poète et mystique," *Nouvelles littéraires* (6 juin, 1931).

Cattaui, Georges. " Meaning and Purpose of Proust," *Saturday Review of Literature*, CLIV (November 12, 1932), 506.

Chazel, P. " L'idéalisme de Marcel Proust," *Foi et vie*, XXVIII (16 novembre, 1925), 1094-1102.

Chernowitz, M. E. " Bergson's Influence on Marcel Proust," *Romanic Review*, XXVII (1936), 45-50.

Coeuroy, A. " Music in the Work of Marcel Proust," *Music Quarterly*, XII (January, 1926), 132-151.

Cowley, M. " Marcel Proust's Unfinished Symphony," *New Republic*, LXXXI (December, 1934), 139.

Crémieux, Benjamin. " La psychologie de Marcel Proust," *Revue de Paris*, V (1924), 838-861.

Curtius, Ernst Robert. " Sur Marcel Proust. Classicisme et esthéticisme," *Revue nouvelle*, IV (décembre, 1927), 7-9.

Fernandez, Ramon. " Note sur l'esthétique de Proust," *Nouvelle revue française*, XXXI (1928), 272-280.

Fosca, François, " La couleur temporelle chez Marcel Proust," *Nouvelle revue française*, XX (janvier, 1922), 240-242.

Geiger, A. " Die Landschaft und der moderne Roman," *Literarisches Echo*, XVI (1914), 1165-1168.

Hogan, J. A. " Marcel Proust's Aesthetic Theory," *Ethics*, XLIX (January, 1939), 187-203.

Huyghe, René. " Affinités électives: Vermeer et Proust," *Amour de l'art*, XVII (1936), 7-15.

Ironside, R. " The Artistic Vision of Proust," *Horizon*, IV (July, 1941), 28-41.

Kolb, Philip. " Inadvertent Repetition of Material in ' A la recherche du temps perdu,' " *Publications of the Modern Language Association*, LI (1936), 249-262.

Laurent, Henri. " Marcel Proust et la musique," *Le Flambeau* (1929), I, 241-256, II, 49-64.

Maurois, André. " Proust et Ruskin," *Essays and Studies*, XVII (1932), 25-32.

Mauriac, François. "L'art de Proust," *Revue hébdomadaire*, II (1921), 373-76.

Messières, René de. "Un document probable sur le premier état de la pensée de Proust: Mystères par Ferdnand Gregh," *Romanic Review*, XXXIII (April, 1942), 113-131.

Mourey, Gabriel. "Marcel Proust, Ruskin, et Walter Pater," *Monde nouveau* (15 août, 15 octobre, 1926), 702-704, 896-909.

Murray, Jessie. "Proust et Ruskin," *Mercure de France*, CLXXXIX (1926), 100-112.

————. "Le symbolisme spatial dans l'oeuvre de Proust," *French Quarterly*, XI (June, 1929), 96-108.

Murray, J. Middleton. "Marcel Proust: A New Sensibility," *Quarterly Review*, CCXXXVIII (July, 1922), 86-100.

Neumeyer, Eva Maria. "The Landscape Garden as a Symbol in Rousseau, Goethe and Flaubert" *Journal of the History of Ideas* VIII (April, 1947), 187-217.

O'Brien, Justin M. "La Mémoire involontaire avant Proust," *Revue de littérature comparée*, XIX (1939), 19-36.

————. "Marcel Proust as a *Moraliste*," *Romanic Review*, XXXIX (February, 1948), 50-69.

Ortega Y Gasset. "Le Temps, la distance et la forme chez Proust," *Nouvelle revue française*, XX (janvier, 1922), 267-279.

Pérès, Jean. "Le rêve de la veille dans certaines parties de l'oeuvre de Marcel Proust," *Revue politique et littéraire*, LXV (3e septembre, 1927), 513-517.

Pierhal, Armand. "Sur la composition wagnérienne de l'oeuvre de Proust," *Bibliothèque universelle et revue de Genève* (juin, 1929), 710-719.

Praviel, A. "Un analyste parisien: Marcel Proust," *Correspondant*, CCXC (10 janvier, 1923), 75-86.

Roditi, E. "Trick perspectives," *Quarterly Review*, XX (October, 1944), 541-555.

Santayana, George. "Proust on essences," *Life and Letters*, II (June, 1929), 455-459.

Spanjer, G. "Die Darstellung der Landschaft in den Dichtungen G. Frenssens," *Niederdeutsche Welt*, XI (1936), 370-373.

Spitzer, Leo. "Zum Stil Marcel Prousts," *Stilstudien*, Munich: M. Hueber, 1928, II, 365-497.

————. "Etymologie d'un cri de Paris," *Romanic Review*, XXXV (October, 1944), 244-250.

Stanford, W. B. "Synaesthetic metaphor," *Comparative Literature Studies*, VI-VII (1942), 26-30.

Ullmann, S. de. "Laws of Language and Laws of Nature," *Modern Language Review*, XXXVIII (1934), 328-338.

Vial, F. "Le symbolisme bergsonien du temps dans l'oeuvre de Marcel Proust," *Publications of the Modern Language Association*, LV (December, 1940), 1191-1212.

Vigneron, Robert. "Genèse de Swann," *Revue d'histoire de la philosophie et d'histoire générale de la civilisation,* XVII (15, janvier, 1937), 67-115.

————. "Marcel Proust et Robert de Montesquiou—Autour de *Professionnelles Beautés,*" *Modern Philology,* XXXIX (1941), 159-195.

————. "Marcel Proust ou l'angoisse créatrice," *Modern Philology,* XLII (May, 1945), 212-230.

————. "Prétentions et defaillances," *Modern Philology* XLIV (November, 1946), 102-128.

Werner, W. L. "Psychology of Proust," *Sewanee Review,* XXXIX (July, 1931), 276-281.

Wilson, Claudine. "Marcel Proust as a Lover of Language," *French Quarterly,* X (June, 1928), 57-70.

Wilson, C. M. "Proust's Color Vision," *French Review,* XVI (1943), 411-415.

Wilson, E. "Personality of Proust," *New Republic,* LXI (February, 1930), 316-321.

Wright, R. "A Sensitive Petronius," *Nineteenth Century,* XCIII (March, 1923), 378-388.

INDEX

Adelson, D., 47, 48.

Aesthetics, of Proust, 29, 34, 51, 58.

Aesthetic experiences, examples of, 14-16, 20, 24, 31, 52, 89, 179-181, 183.

Albertine, inseparable from the natural beauties of Balbec, 155-158, 171.

Ames, Van Meter, 63.

Analogies, art, 39, 44, 52-53, 74, 82, 87, 100, 105, 116-117, 120, 126, 130-133, 147, 179; between nature and living persons, 29, 38, 47-57, 74, 87-88, 92-93, 106-107, 154-158; literary, 105; music, 41, 142-143, 187-188, 191; mythological, 33, 129; psychological, 104-105; sentimental, 42-43, 45-46, 54; with the past, 33. *See also* Metaphoric transformation; Impressions; Illusions.

Art, and immortality, 52, 58; in the Proustian universe, 34; Proust's conception of, 30.

Arbres de Balbec, objective impression emotionalized, 30-36.

Aubépines, a series of impressions, 46-57, 91.

Audible world, musical patterns of, 189-191. *See also* Sounds; Place-names.

Babbitt, Irving, 52, 62, 176.

Balbec, background for Albertine, 155-158; dreams of, 174; disenchantment, 181; evocative power of its name, 174-175; subjective recollection of, 18-21.

Balzac, 51.

Barrès, Maurice, 1, 161.

Baudelaire, 7, 83, 129, 130.

Bellini, G., 100.

Benoist-Méchin, J., 187.

Bergson, H., 16, 34, 115, 165, 195.

Bernardin de Saint-Pierre, 5, 6, 105, 143.

Boileau, 4.

Bornecque, J. H., 67.

Boudin, E., 66.

Bremond, 53.

Buffon, 88.

Bussom, T. W., 60, 61, 67.

Cabourg, 7.

Caldéron, 127.

Cathedral of Lisieux, 10.

Carpaccio, 75, 145.

Cézanne, 23, 61.

Chateaubriand, 2, 5, 6, 118.

Chernowitz, analysis of Proust's seascapes, 66-67, 69; on Elstir's pictorial methods, 61-63, 70-71; on the "equivoques" of Elstir, 63, 64; on Impressionism, 69-70, 71-72, 106, 125; on Proust's aesthetics, 29; on Proust's illusions, 28, 30; on the identity of Elstir, 59-61; on the sound of names, 175; *see also* 11, 26, 45, 51, 104, 133, 176.

Chiaroscuro, 71, 136, 146-147; examples of, 70-71, 73-74.

Claudel, P., 136, 161.

Clermont-Tonnère, 46, 91.

Clochers de Martinville, as source of literary inspiration, 22-30; impressionistic transcription of, 27; poetic transformation of, 29; rendered through spiritualization, 23-30.

Cloudscape, 108.

Coeuroy, A., 143, 189.

Colette, Mme., 97.

Color, acuity, 107, 108, 131, 176; fusion, 105; in Elstir, 75; in sound, 175-177, 182; vision, 108-110, 143, 147; vocabulary, 102, 126-127, 129-130, *See also* Synaethesthesia.

Combray, 36; environment to the apparition of new truths, 113-115; historic, 101; objective impression of, 21, 36-46; pictorial impressions of, 80-85; subjective recollection of, 14-16, 19-21; urban aspects of, 80-85.

Curtius, R. E., 1, 88-89, 161; on the